IMAGES
of America

LINWOOD

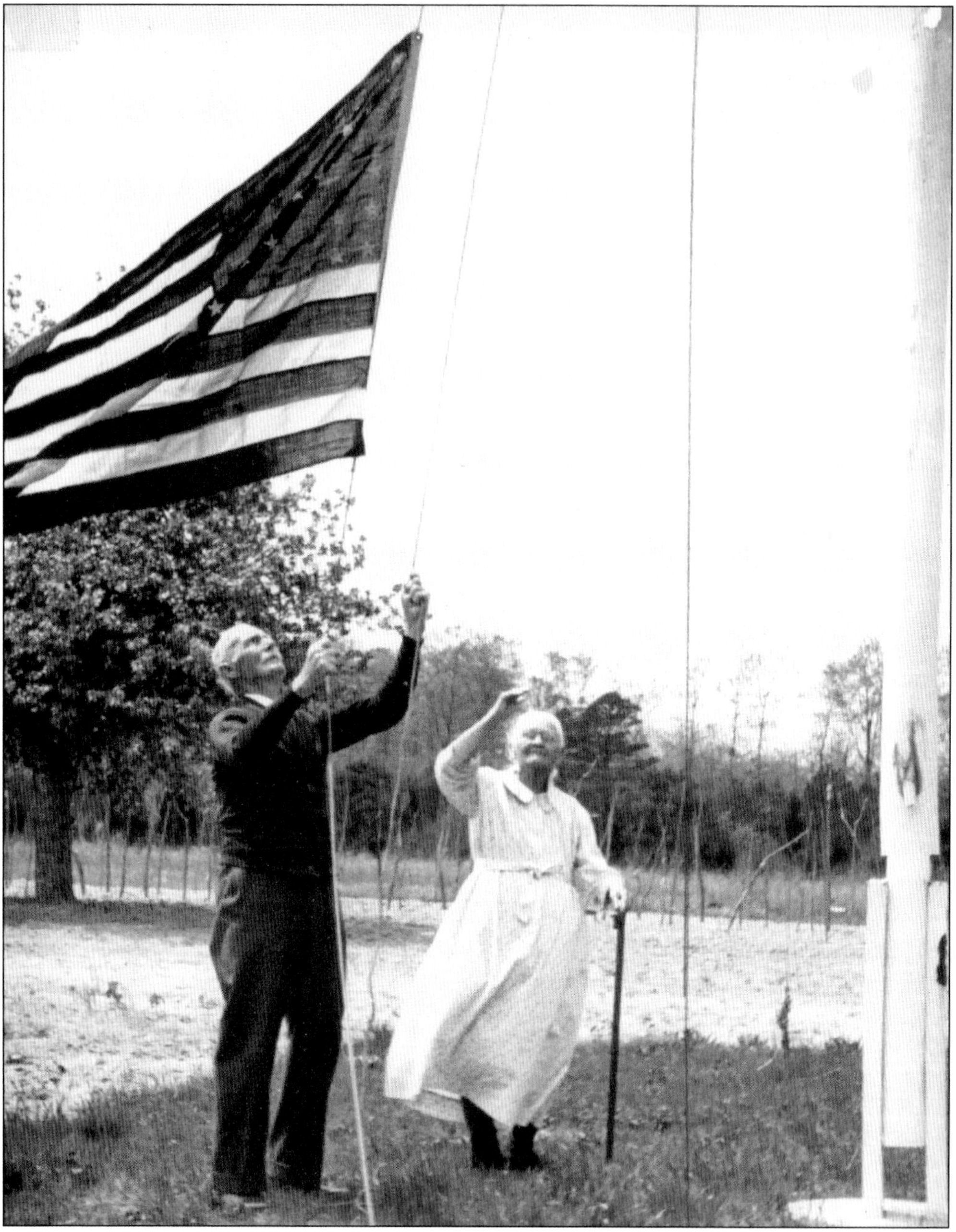

Lewis Somers and Mary Ella Price were descendants of some of the earliest families to settle in this region. Shortly after their marriage in 1879, they moved into the Shore Road home built in 1830 by Lewis's grandfather, Edmond Somers. Mary was a teacher in Bakersville (Northfield) for three years. After a stint at sea in the merchant marines, Lewis was in the Coast Guard at the Great Egg Harbor Life Saving Station in Longport for many years. He later became a postman and was the first rural free delivery mailman along the shore delivering mail by horse and buggy as far as Scullville. Captured in a classic American photograph c. 1939, Lewis and Mary are representative of the continuity of Linwood's history. Some of their descendants still call Linwood home and are active in serving the community.

IMAGES
of America

LINWOOD

Carolyn Adams Patterson

ARCADIA
PUBLISHING

ISBN 978-0-7385-1098-9

Published by Arcadia Publishing
Charleston, South Carolina

Printed in the United States of America

Library of Congress Catalog Card Number: 2002108565

For all general information contact Arcadia Publishing at:
Telephone 843-853-2070
Fax 843-853-0044
E-mail sales@arcadiapublishing.com
For customer service and orders:
Toll-Free 1-888-313-2665

Visit us on the Internet at www.arcadiapublishing.com

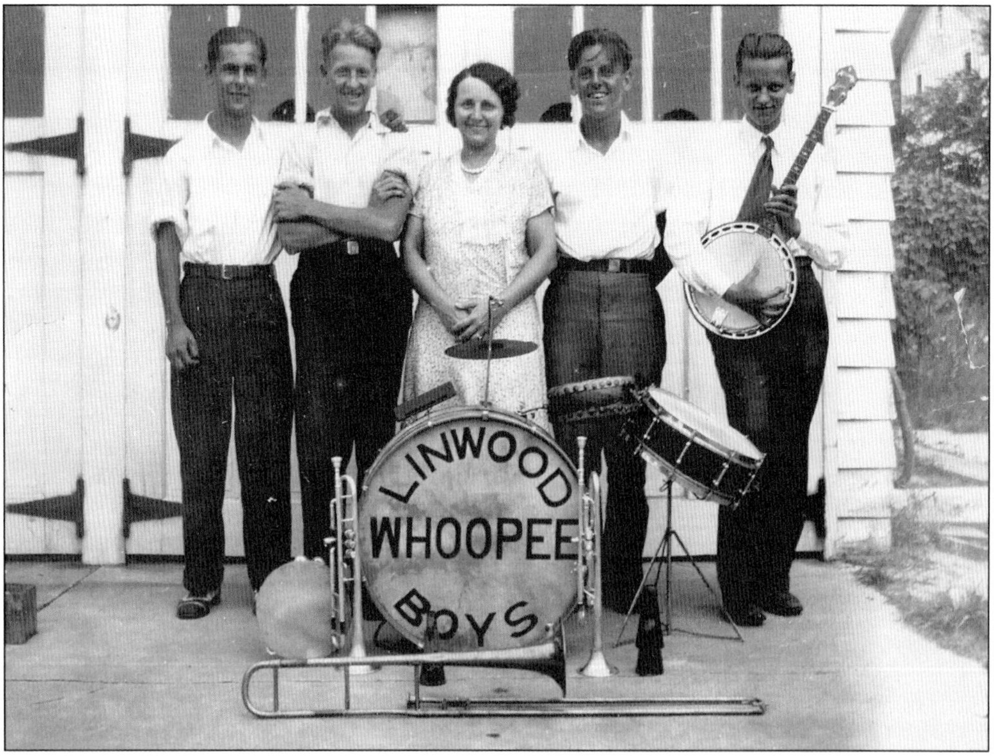

The Linwood Whoopee Boys was a popular musical group around town in 1933. From left to right are Robert Minor, Robert Shewel, Nettie Johnson, Emerson Johnson, and Bryant Johnson.

Contents

ACKNOWLEDGMENTS

Anyone who undertakes a project like this has a great many people lending a hand along the way, and there is not usually enough space to acknowledge all of them. I would like to start with my daughters Karen Warren and Sharon Betz, who urged me to undertake the work with a positive "You can do this, Mom!" My son Bob was an invaluable sounding board for reviewing the style and flow of the text. Support from friends and community resources was outstanding and encouraged me to believe that people are ready for a book on Linwood's history.

The Linwood Historical Society graciously opened its collection of photographs, and the Atlantic County Historical Society gave generous assistance. Unless otherwise noted, all photographs in this book are from the collection of the Linwood Historical Society. Pictures from the Atlantic County Historical Society are identified as from ACHS. Credit is also given to individuals who lent their photographs for use in the book.

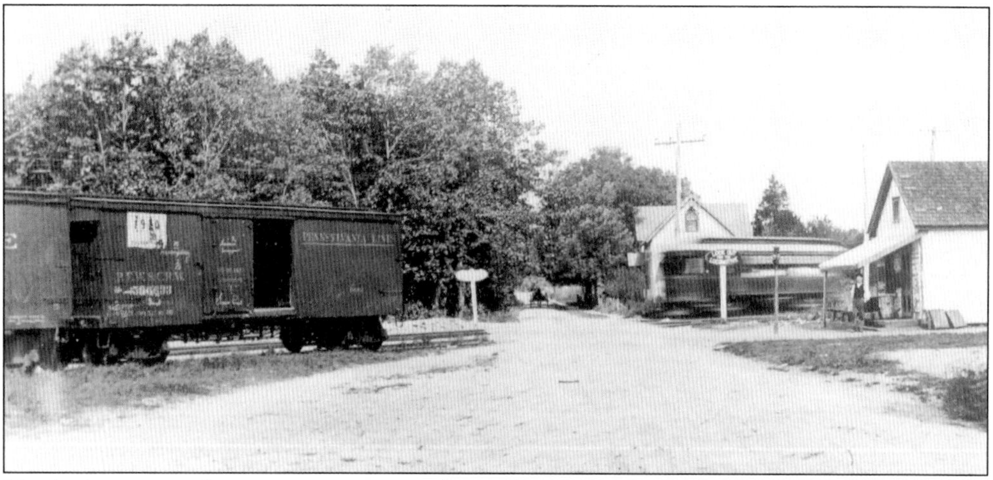

Maple Avenue at the train station was a busy place in 1910. Warren Potter's store is on the right and William Scull's store is beyond the train car. Elsie Wolfbrandt Thompson remembered going to Scullie's on Saturday nights with a large bowl to carry ice cream back to the family. A horse and buggy in the distance appears to be on its way to Bargaintown.

INTRODUCTION

Linwood's history began with the Indians of the Leni Lenape tribes who came during the summers to fish and hunt along the bay and Patconk (Patcong) Creek. Evidence of their visits was uncovered by the plows of the early farmers as well as modern-day bulldozers. Old-timers remembered Indian grave sites uncovered during the construction of the Linwood Country Club. The Sea Shore Road (Shore Road) was laid out in 1716 on part of an old Indian trail that ran from Port Republic to Somers Ferry (Somers Point).

The first European settlers to the area known as Great Egg Harbor were Quakers who migrated from Long Island, New York, in the 1690s. In 1695, Philadelphia merchant Thomas Budd sold huge tracts of land to seven men whose last names are now recognized as the family names of the first families of Linwood and its neighboring towns. Somers, Skull, Conover, Steelman, and Adams were among the leadership, and since they settled here, their surnames were adopted and used as place names throughout the area.

Farming, shipbuilding, shipping, and fishing were the livelihoods that sustained families from the 1700s well into the 20th century. Except for population growth and technological improvements, visitors here in 1730, 1830, and 1930 would have noticed few changes in the lifestyles of the residents. Farms made up the bulk of land use and men still went out every day to work the bay.

The gracious Victorian sea captains' homes along Shore Road are beloved reminders of how important the sea was in Linwood's history. Many of the captains were also prominent community leaders. There were other men, living in less magnificent homes, who ran packet ships carrying goods up and down the East Coast and many others who made their living just gathering the rich bounty of the bay and nearby ocean.

Early in the 1830s, the village was a section of Egg Harbor Township called Leeds Ville, which, according to legend, was named for a store on Shore Road owned by Daniel Leeds. Eventually, the name was shortened to one word—Leedsville. In 1881, citizens petitioned the government to establish a post office for Leedsville. The government required that a new name for the town be selected, and Linwood was chosen. In 1889, Linwood withdrew from Egg Harbor Township to establish the borough of Linwood. The borough incorporated as a city in 1931.

After World War II, changes in Linwood differed little from those taking place elsewhere in the nation. New technologies brought new industries. Low-cost college educations made available through the GI Bill helped prepare veterans to fill positions in the new industries. The

Naval Aviation Facility in Pomona and the Prudential Office Complex in Linwood brought many of the veterans to this area, and they needed homes. Farmland was worth more for housing than for crops. Dairy barns gave way to Gold Coast housing, and the old plantation of John Scull made way for a high school and the new Prudential office. Within a few years, the rural atmosphere was replaced by suburban living.

This publication documents part of Linwood's history with images of its people and places up through mid-20th century. The scope of the work was limited by the photographs that were available at the time and how well they were documented. Readers who wonder why some topics were omitted may be able to fill the gaps from their own collections. The book demonstrates the importance of preserving history through photographs. If people are encouraged to collect and share pictures of their part in Linwood's history, then the book will have achieved one of its main goals. The main goal, of course, was to preserve and share the images of old Linwood. Enjoy your visit.

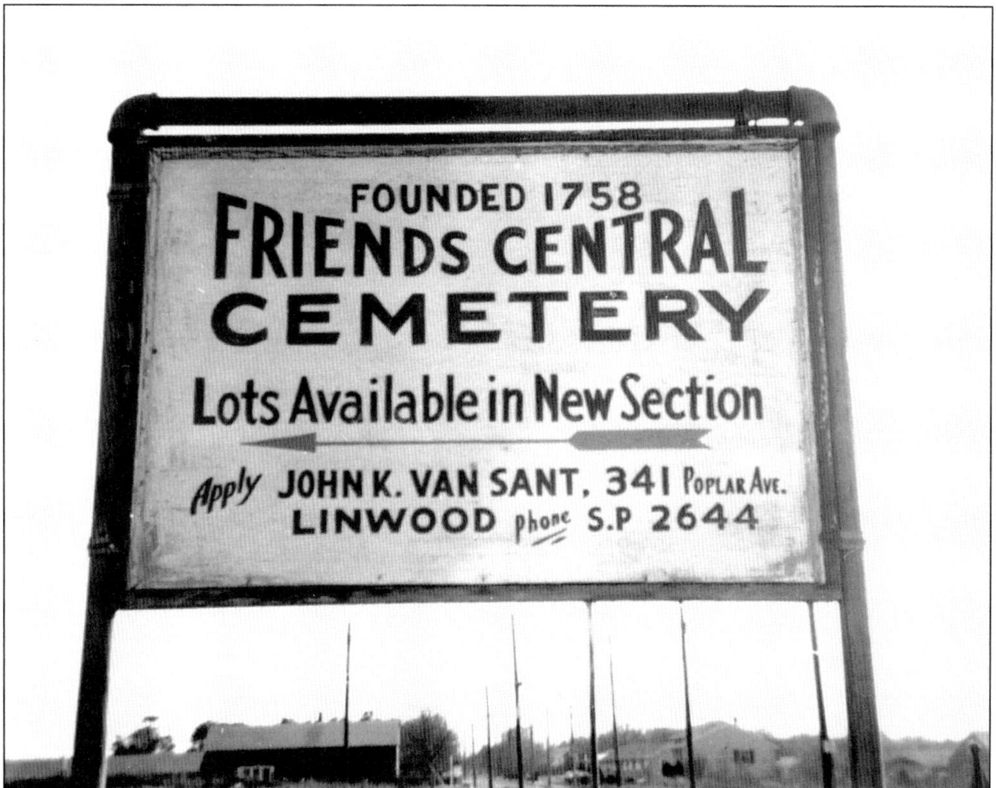

In 1725, Quaker meetings were begun in John Scull's home on the old Sea Shore Road. By the end of the century, the Quaker influence had declined. The Friends Cemetery, established near Scull's house, is the only reminder of the Quaker's presence.

One

LEEDSVILLE

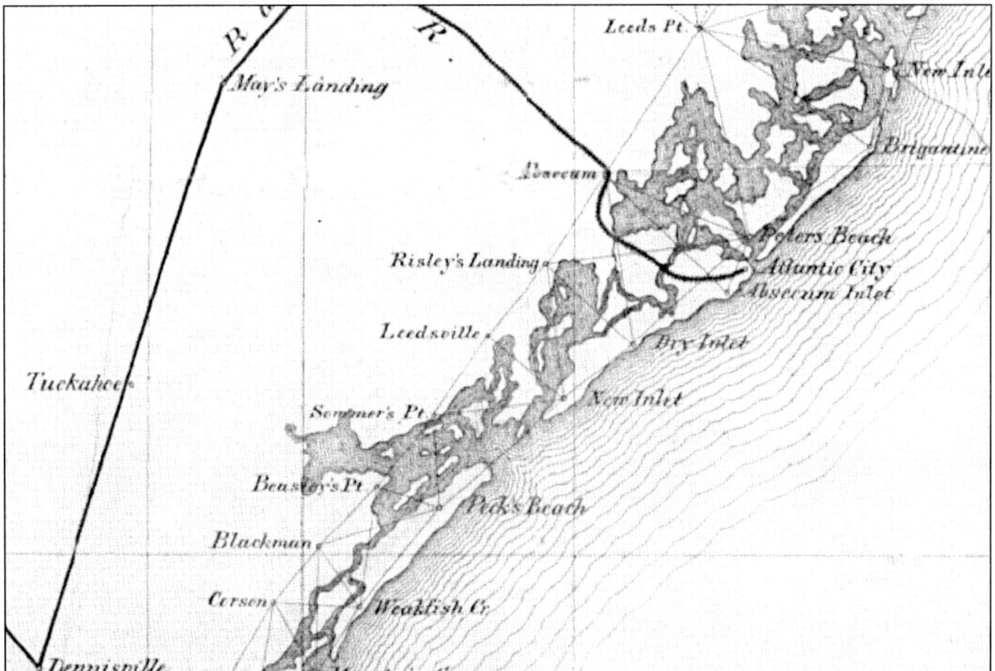

As shown on this 1856 map, Leedsville was midway along the mainland route between Atlantic City and Peck's Beach (Ocean City). Easy access to the Great Egg Harbor inlet through Scull's Bay created a strong maritime presence throughout most of Leedsville's history. By 1856, several sea captains had built homes along Shore Road and were very influential citizens of the community. An 1872 Beers and Comstock map identified close to 20 sea captains as property owners here. They often contributed land for the construction of schools and churches. Photographs of the homes, churches, and schools of Leedsville are featured in this chapter.

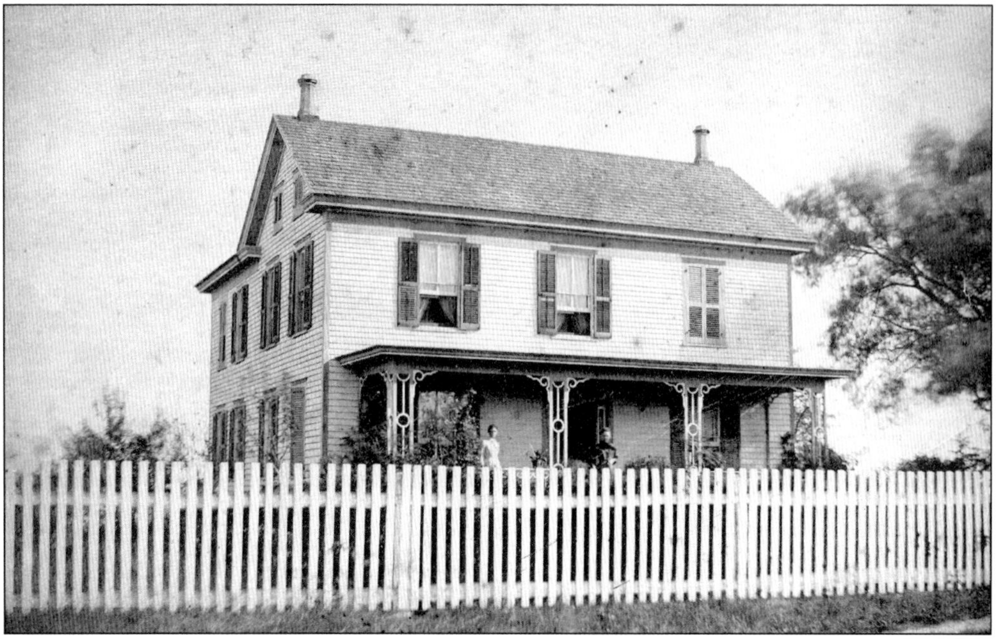

Capt. John Walker Tilton was one of Leedsville's most influential citizens. His letter about the need for a centrally located church for "the seamen of nearby docks and shipyards" resulted in the creation of Central Methodist Episcopal Church. He was also instrumental in the construction of the 1873 Leedsville School. His most famous exploit at sea occurred during the Civil War, when he successfully eluded Confederate privateers on his way to Key West, Florida, with a load of coal. The Tilton home on Shore Road was built by Joseph R. Risley *c.* 1860. Roy Black, owner of Linwood Hardware, demolished the home in the 1930s to build Linco Park, which is pictured below.

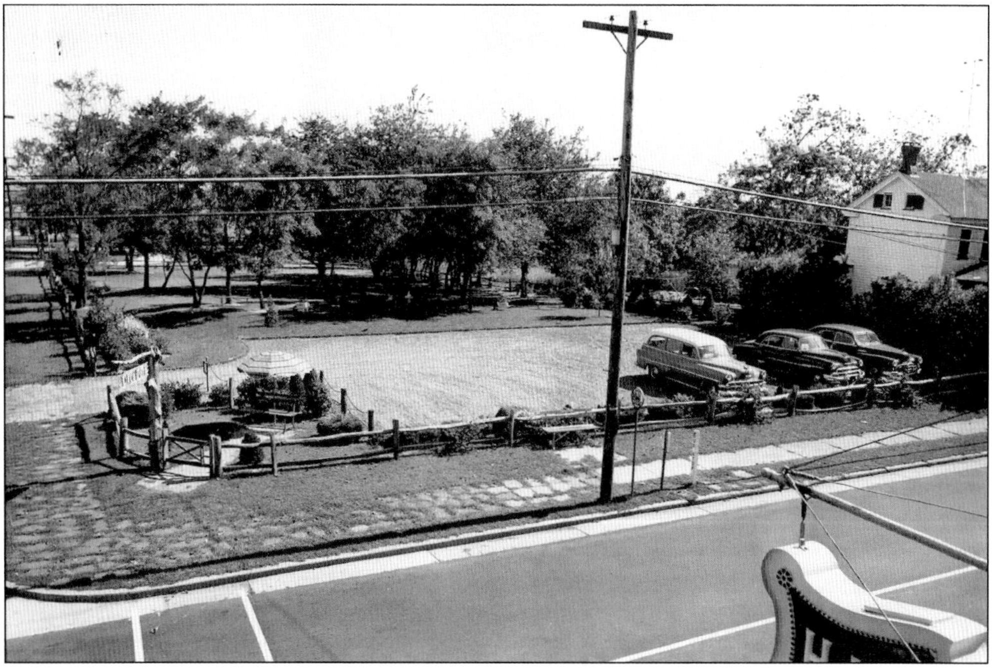

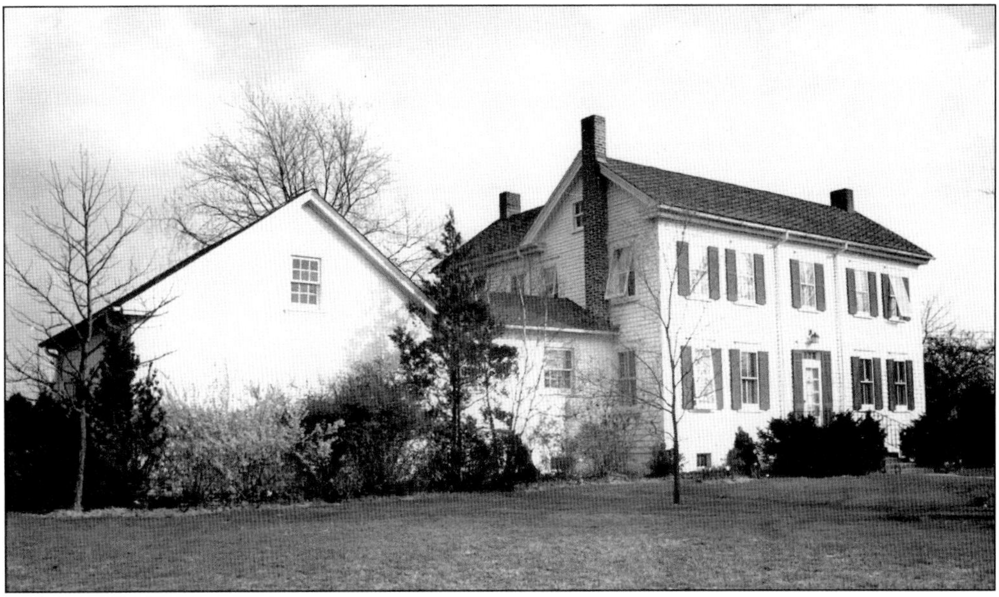

Thomas E. Morris built his home on Shore Road in 1853 on land he purchased the year before from John Somers, who had a shipyard on Scull's Bay. Married to Susan VanSant, Morris was appointed as deputy customs collector by Abraham Lincoln in 1862 and served until 1886. Morris served terms in both the New Jersey State Assembly in 1859 and New Jersey State Senate from 1860 to 1862.

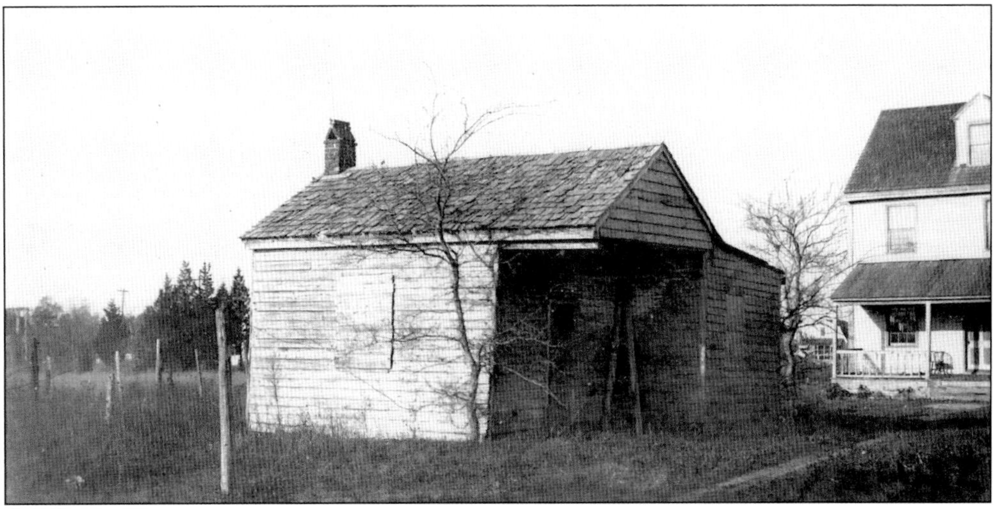

The customs house was originally on Shore Road in Somers Point but it was moved to the Morris property in Leedsville and added to the back of the house. The home on the right was the birthplace of Commandant Richard Somers, hero of Tripoli. (Courtesy of ACHS.)

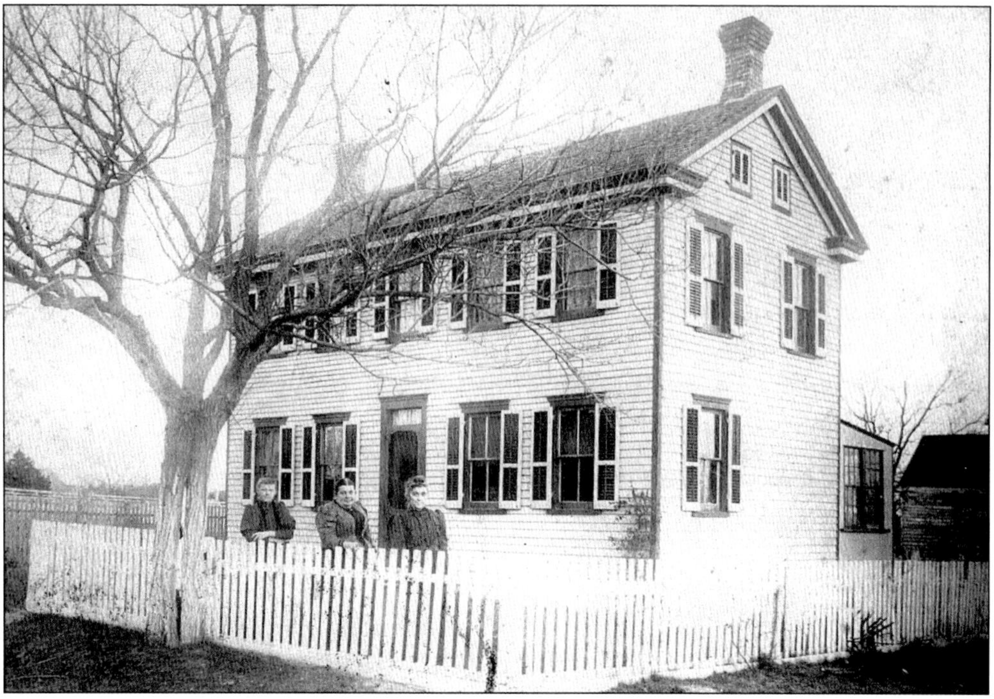

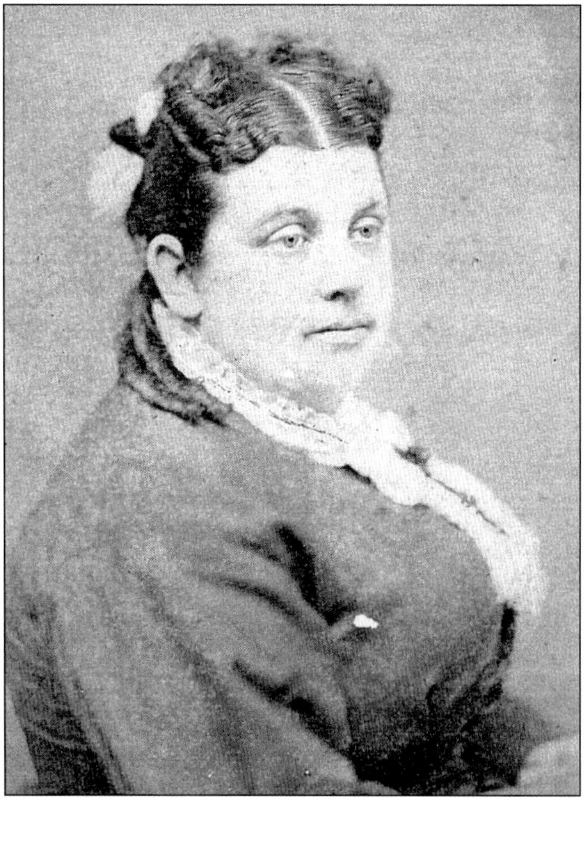

In 1865, Louisa VanSant married Capt. William B. Rose and they built their home on Shore Road next door to her father, John VanSant. Louisa, who died in 1904, was listed as a physician in the 1900 census. Marie Cavileer Gandy remembered that "Lou" Rose had a small store here in 1903. Eleanor Bozzelli acquired the property in 1945 and kept a stable where children could get pony rides. The Antiques Collectors Club owned the home and used it as their headquarters from 1970 to 1994. It has since been converted back to a private residence.

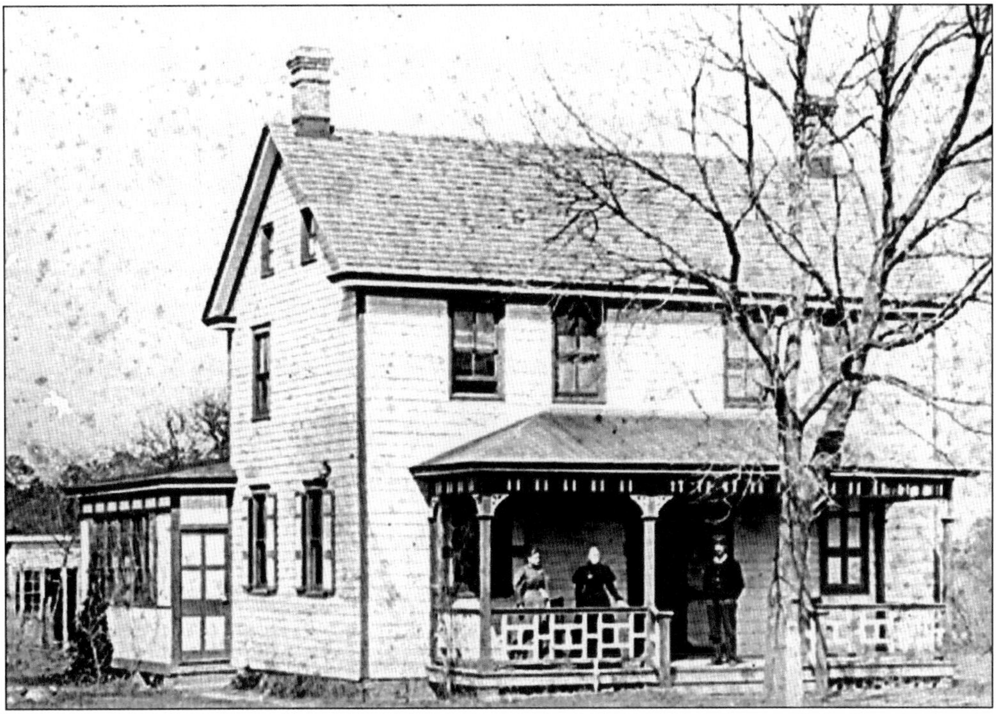

The Edmond Somers home was built in 1830 using ship timber in part of the construction. Although he operated a store in Leedsville, Somers was sometimes referred to as Captain Somers. His grandson Lewis, who inherited the home in 1885, is pictured on the porch. The women are unidentified.

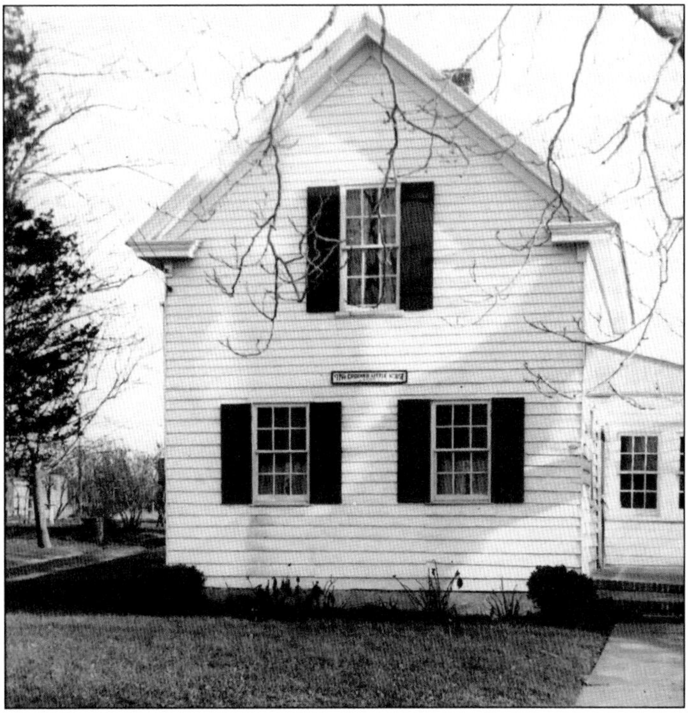

Edmond Somers's store was across the street in this building from 1821 to 1863. His account books contain a detailed record of the barter system used by farmers, baymen, and tradesmen who earned store credit with the goods and services that they provided to Somers. The store was also the Somers Point post office for many years, serving customers who lived from Somers Point to part of Bakersville (Northfield). The house, known as the "crooked little house," was torn down.

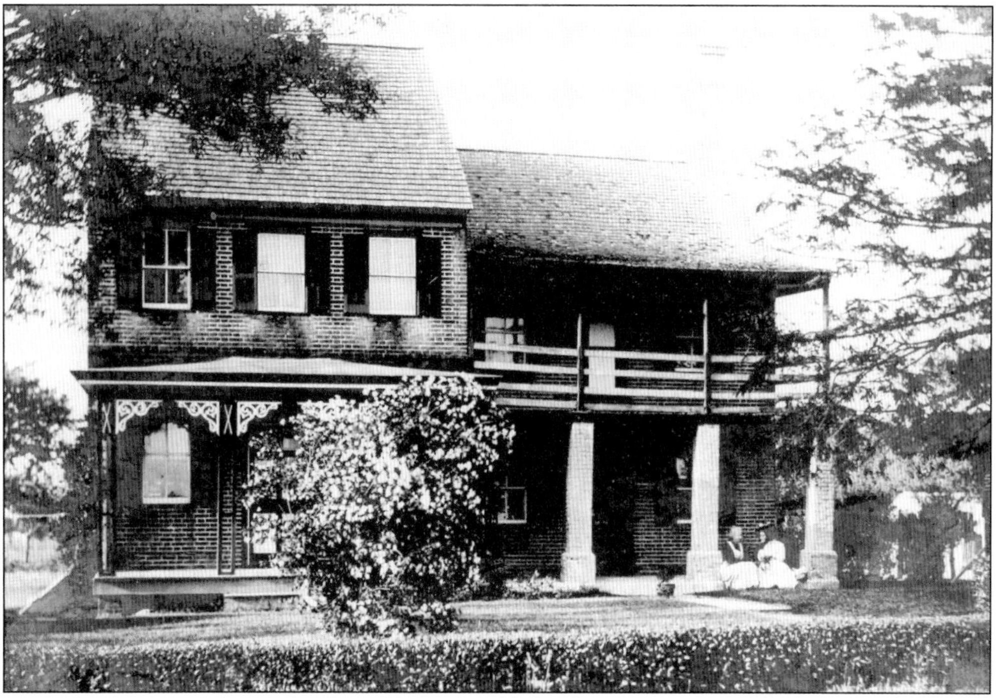

Samuel Somers built his classic brick home on Central Avenue *c.* 1800 just up the road from the gristmill built by his father, James "the Miller" Somers. The Somers property deeds predate the American Revolution, and Samuel's home remained in the family for more than 200 years.

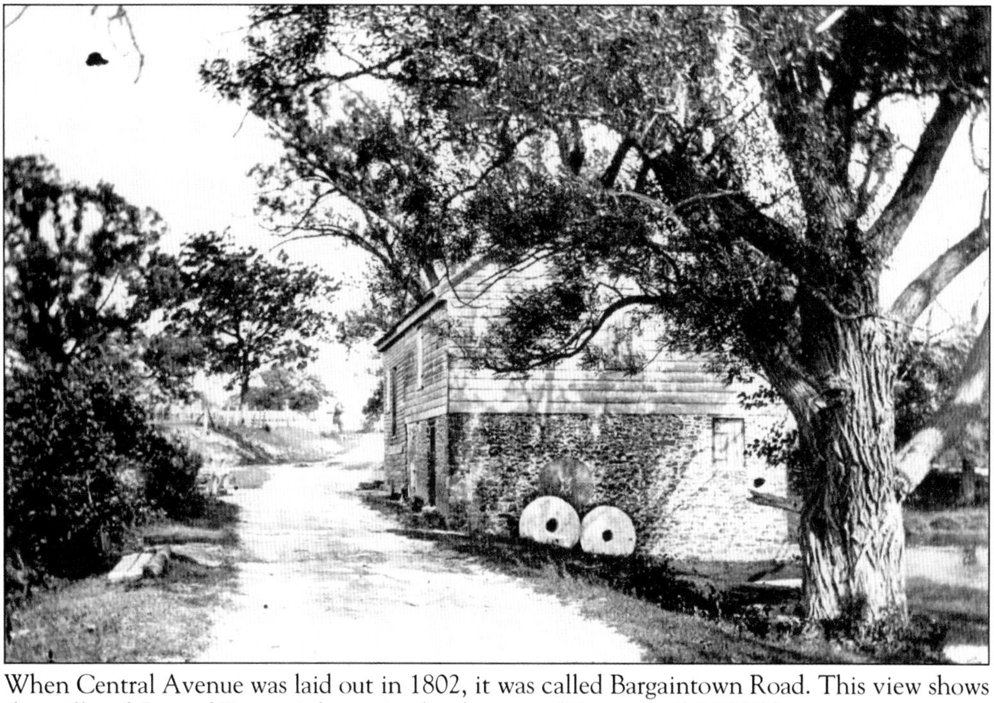

When Central Avenue was laid out in 1802, it was called Bargaintown Road. This view shows the mill and Samuel Somers's home in the distance. (Courtesy of ACHS.)

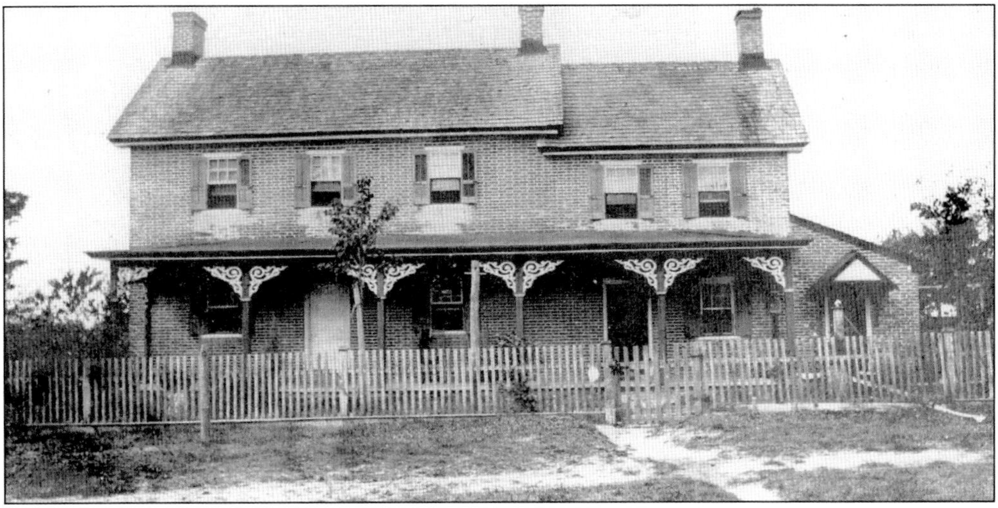

Not far from Samuel Somers's home, down on Bog Road (Oak Avenue), are the homes said to have been built for his sons, George Washington Somers and Constant Somers. Although no definite construction dates have ever been confirmed, both homes clearly represent old Leedsville. The Constant Somers home (above) became the farmhouse of the Krumm family in 1882. The kitchen in George Washington Somers's home (below) was a store on Shore Road at the time of the American Revolution. Ongoing research indicates this home may be much older than originally thought. In front of the home, from left to right, are Bertha Hieringer, Lewis T. Bryant, and Elizabeth Hawk.

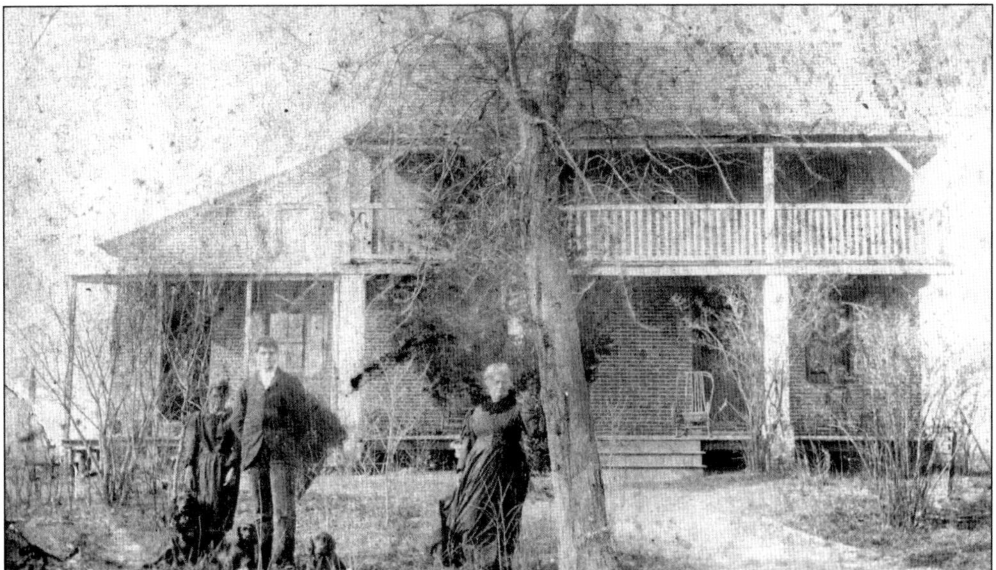

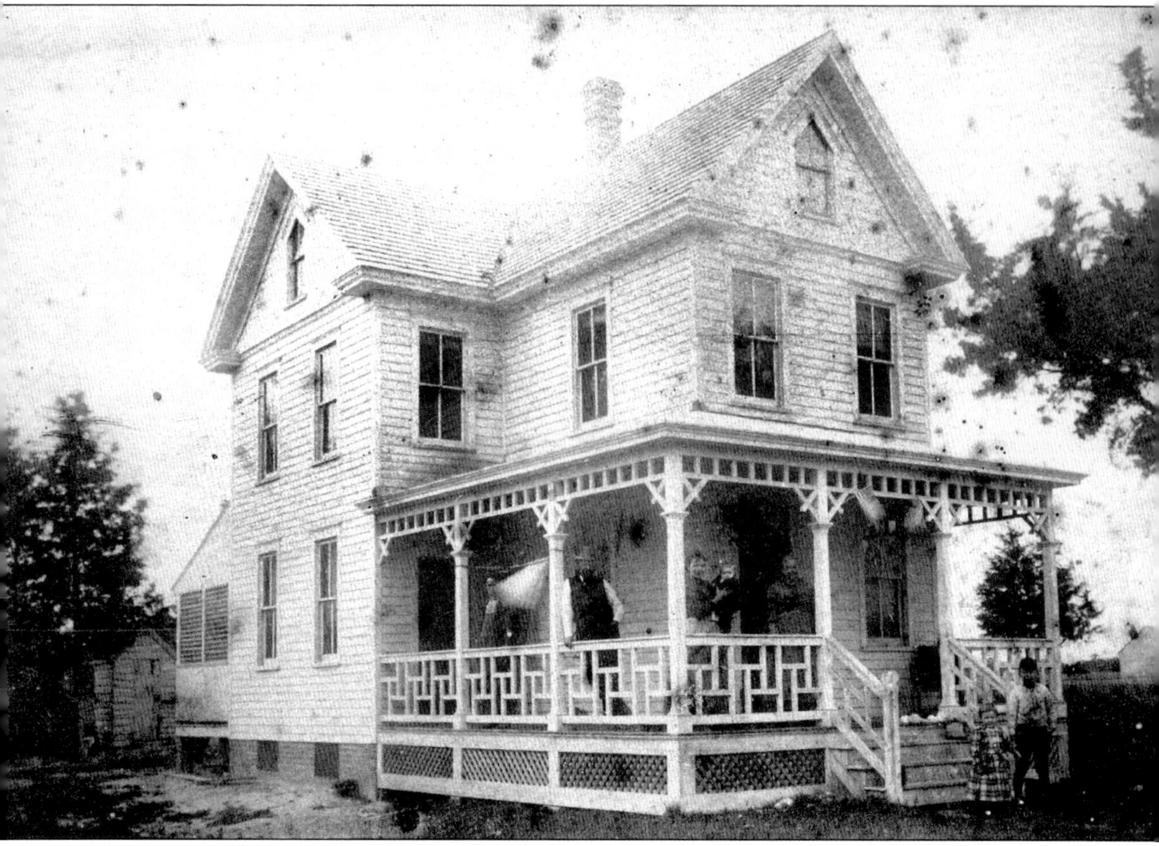

Members of Benjamin Broadhead's family are pictured on the porch of their Shore Road home. Benjamin's parents, Joseph and Sara Broadhead, lived in Gettysburg, Pennsylvania, at the time of the great Civil War battle. Sara's diary of those terrible days was privately published. The Broadheads moved to Linwood in the late 1800s, and Joseph and Sarah became active members of the community. A passage, dated July 3, from Sara Broadhead's diary reads, "Nearly all afternoon it seemed as if the heavens and earth were crashing together. The time that we sat in the cellar seemed long, listening to the terrific sound of the strife; more terrible never greeted human ears. We knew that with every explosion and the scream of each shell, human beings were hurried, through excruciating pain, into another world and that many more were torn and mangled, and lying in torment worse than death."

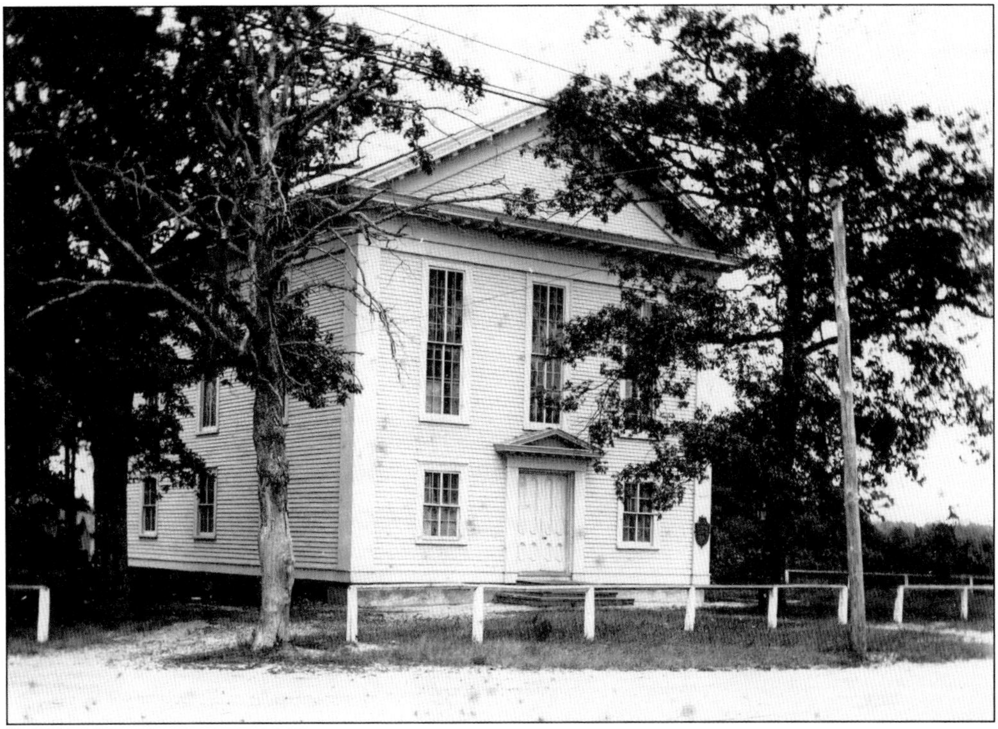

After Capt. John W. Tilton suggested the construction of a centrally located church, meetings were held at the Leedsville Academy on Maple Avenue to discuss the idea. Francis Somers offered to donate land where Bargaintown Road met Sea Shore Road. The offer was accepted. On June 19, 1860, a cornerstone was laid for a new church to be named Central Methodist Episcopal Church. Eventually, Bargaintown Road became known as Central Avenue. In 1939, the church changed its name to Central United Methodist Church. The old church building (shown above in 1908) was replaced in 1968 with a new brick church. Rev. James Morrell (right) was the first minister at the church. (Courtesy of Central United Methodist Church.)

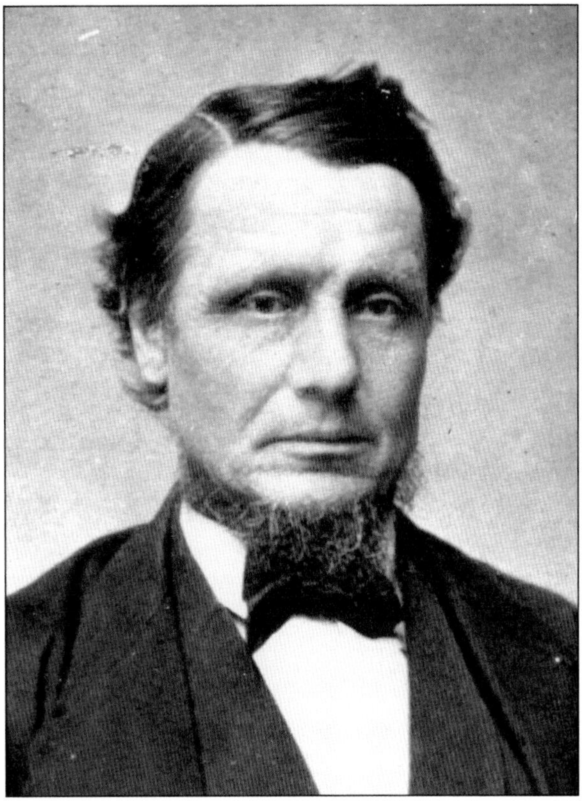

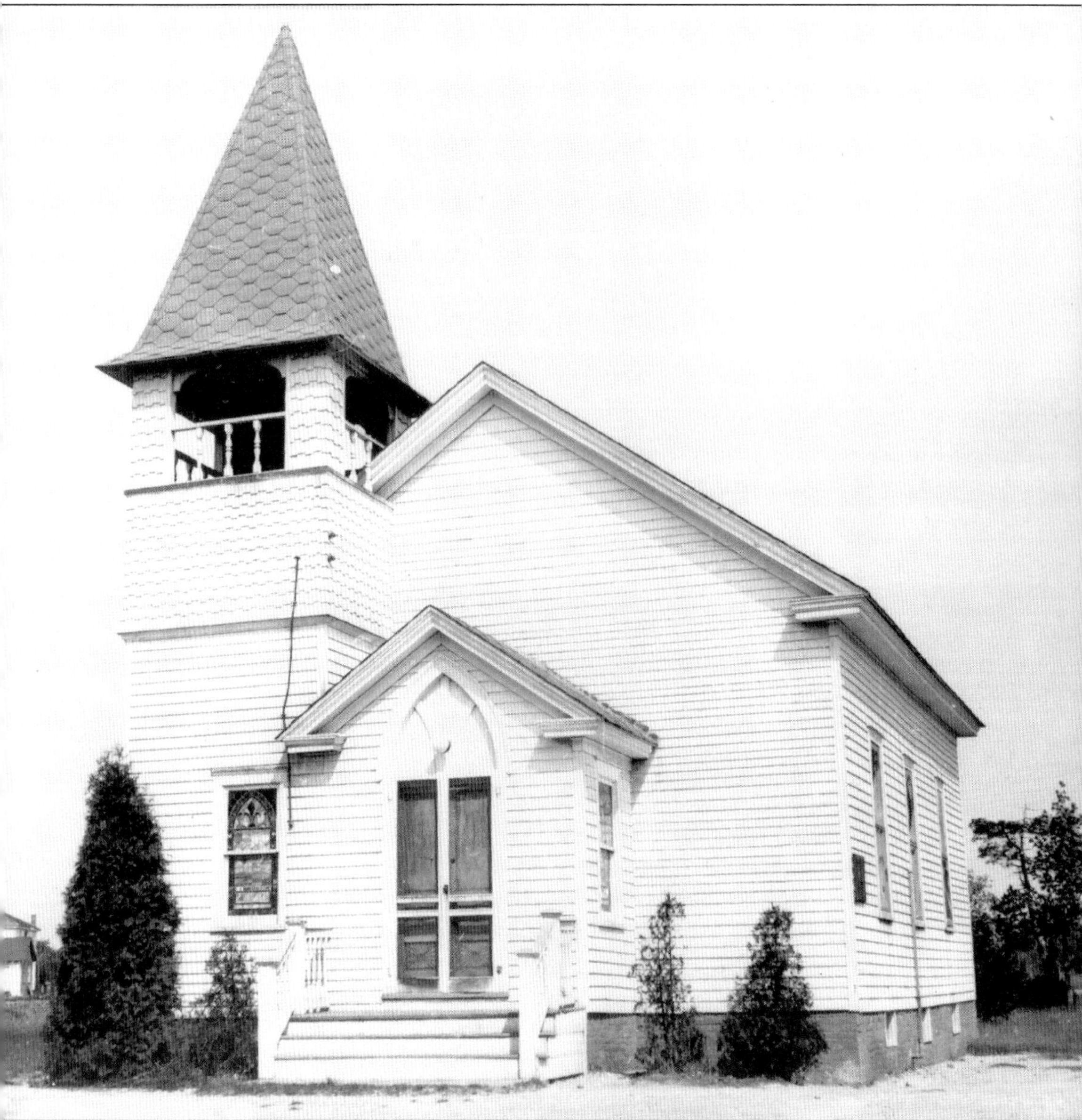

In 1845, people in the southern part of Leedsville had been attending services at the Cedar Grove School, near Garfield Avenue. Services were conducted by circuit preachers and a few of the folks wanted something more organized but closer than the Zion Church in Bargaintown. In 1848, Bethel Methodist Episcopal Church was organized, and Capt. Elmer English donated land for the building. Nicknamed the Old Mariner's Church, it was active throughout most of the 20th century. After 1939, the church was named Bethel Methodist Church. In the 1980s, the church closed and the building was sold to a pizza shop.

A report on Central and Bethel Methodist Episcopal Churches from April 24, 1880, contains interesting summaries of membership and finances. Approximately 80 families were listed as members at Central Methodist Episcopal Church, and over 120 are members at Bethel Methodist Episcopal Church. All of the family names were of the well-known leading citizens of Leedsville, such as VanSant, Rose, Scull, Steelman, Townsend, Adams, Risley, Smith, Somers, Ireland, and Frambes. The quarterly income reported for Central was $217.56 and for Bethel $143.97.

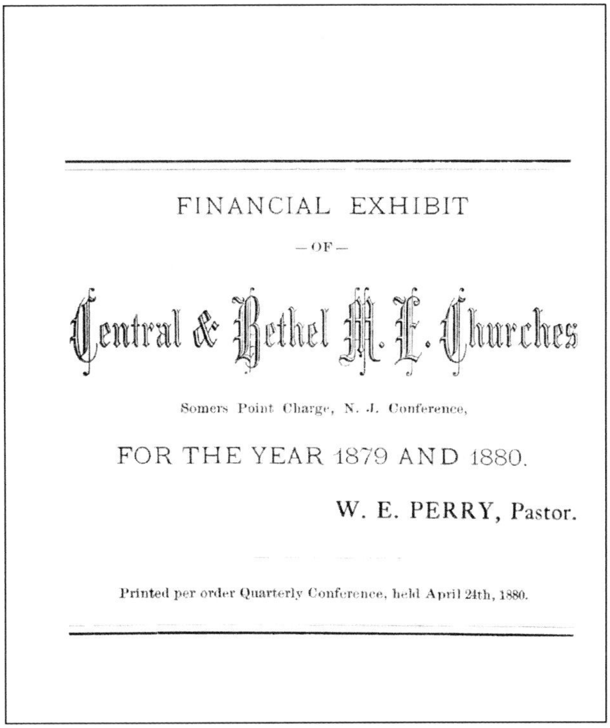

FINANCIAL EXHIBIT

—OF—

Central & Bethel M. E. Churches

Somers Point Charge, N. J. Conference,

FOR THE YEAR 1879 AND 1880.

W. E. PERRY, Pastor.

Printed per order Quarterly Conference, held April 24th, 1880.

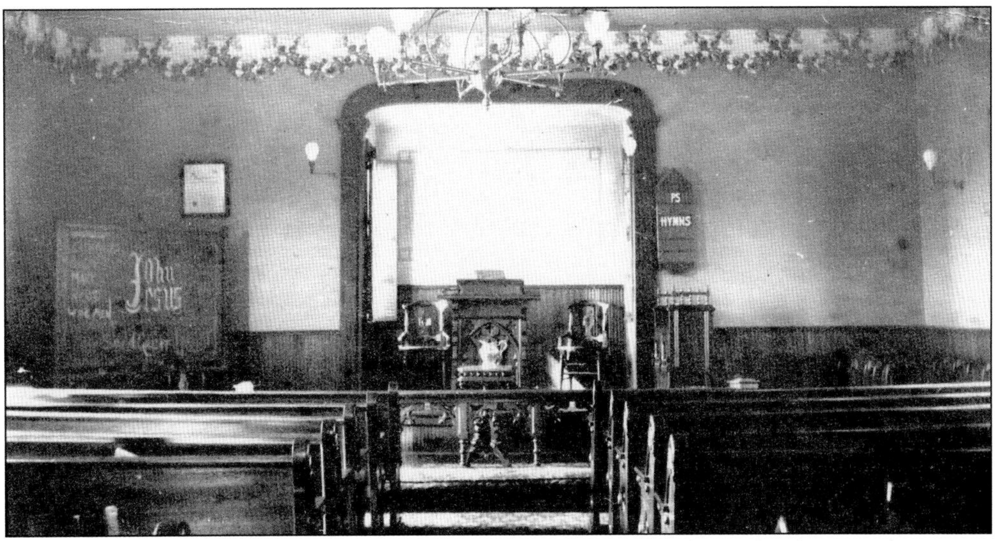

The interior of Bethel Methodist Episcopal Church is shown in this early photograph.

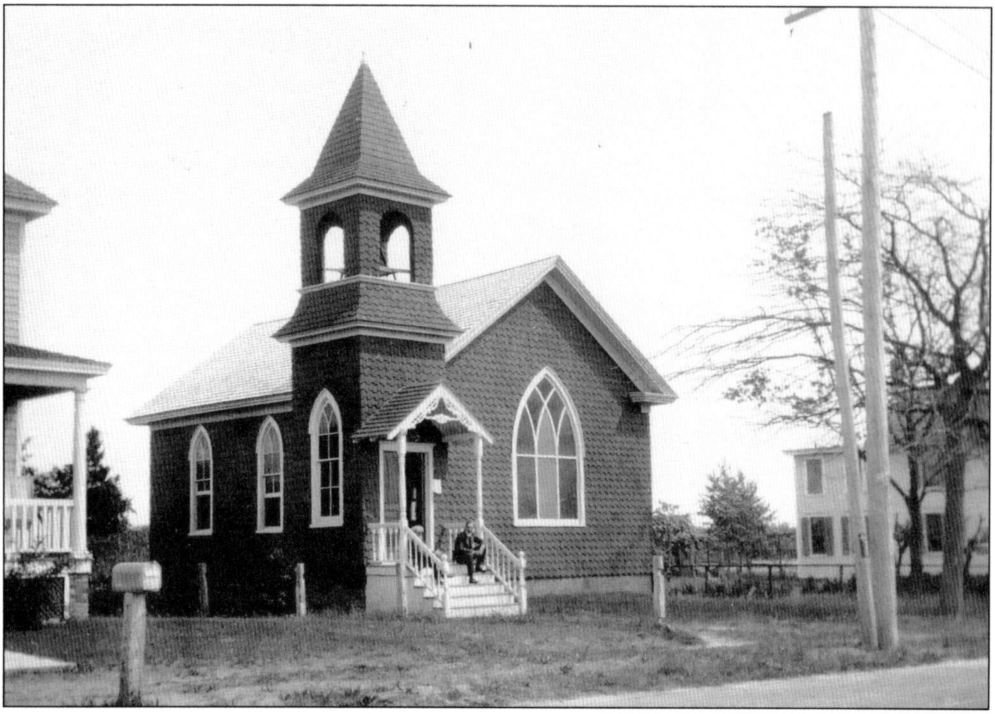

In 1881, the Union Congregation Hall, used by the Leedsville Baptists for services, was destroyed by fire. Church members decided to move the Bakersville Baptist Chapel to Leedsville as a replacement. The tower was added for a new bell shortly before this picture was taken in 1903. In 1961, the congregation built a new church and the old church became a private residence. (Courtesy of ACHS.)

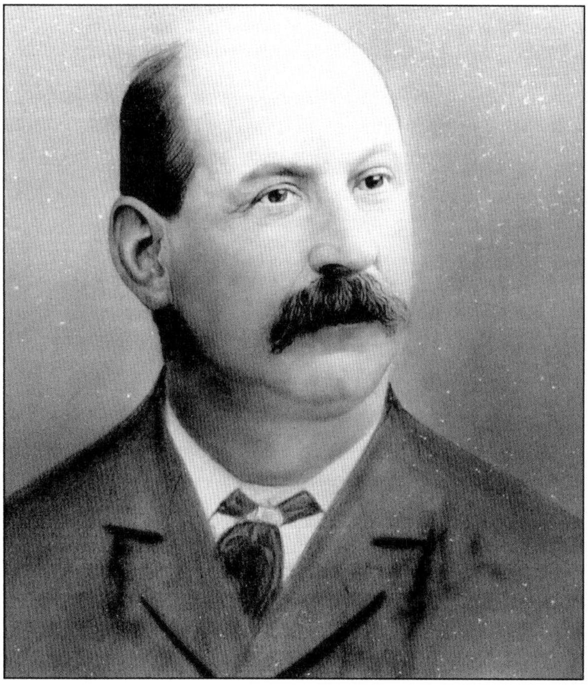

When visiting his daughter's family across the street from the Baptist church one Sunday, hotel owner Mark Malatesta learned that the church had no bell. He ordered one from a foundry in England. After too much time went by, he wrote to ask about the delivery. Shortly thereafter, two bells were delivered instead of one. The generous Malatesta kept both bells, giving the second one to Bethel Methodist Episcopal Church.

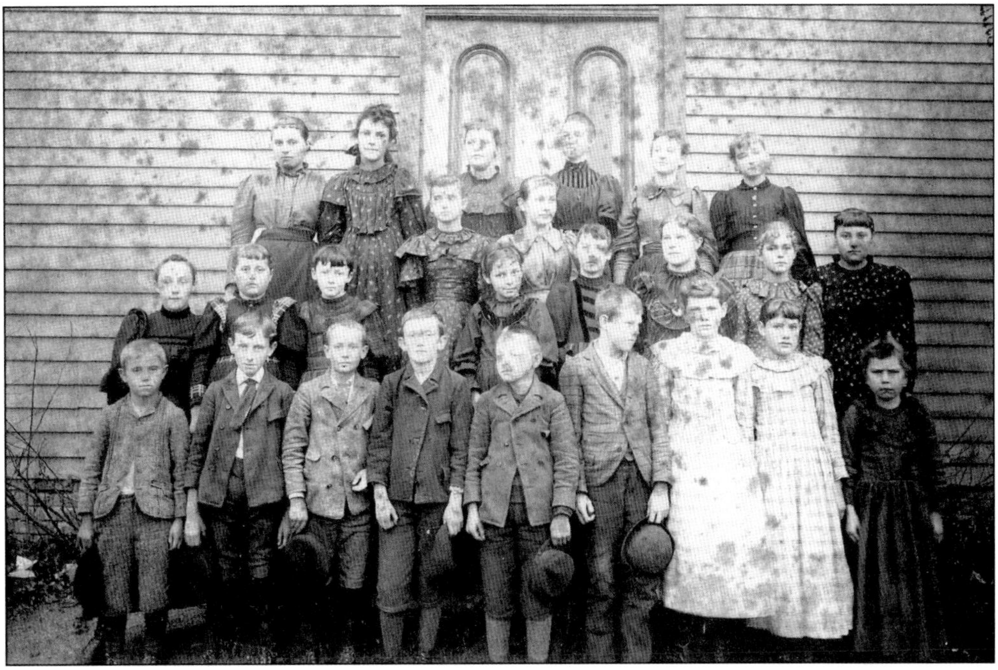

On March 25, 1843, trustees of the Leedsville Academy bought one twentieth of an acre of land from Robert and Elizabeth Risley on Maple Avenue for $7.50 to build a school. The school often served as a community meetinghouse. It was replaced in 1873 by a new school on Poplar Avenue. Anna Elizabeth Risley was the teacher here for many years. In 1871, she married Civil War veteran Capt. Samuel Cavileer. Cavileer held several public posts including county sheriff and state senator. Tragically, he was lost at sea off of Cape Hatteras in 1876.

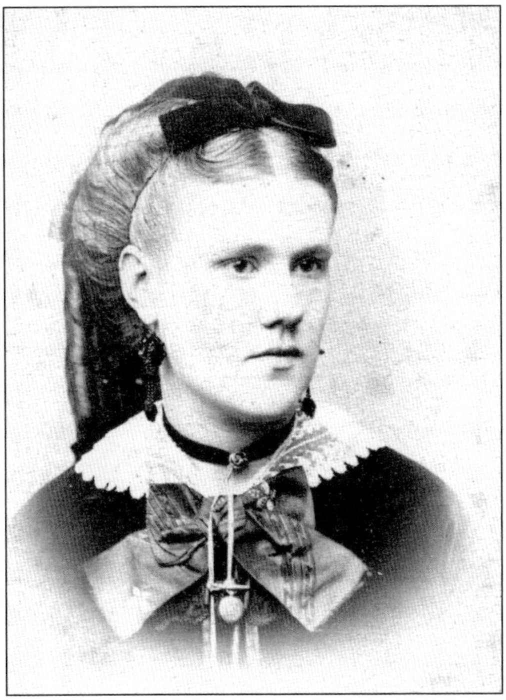

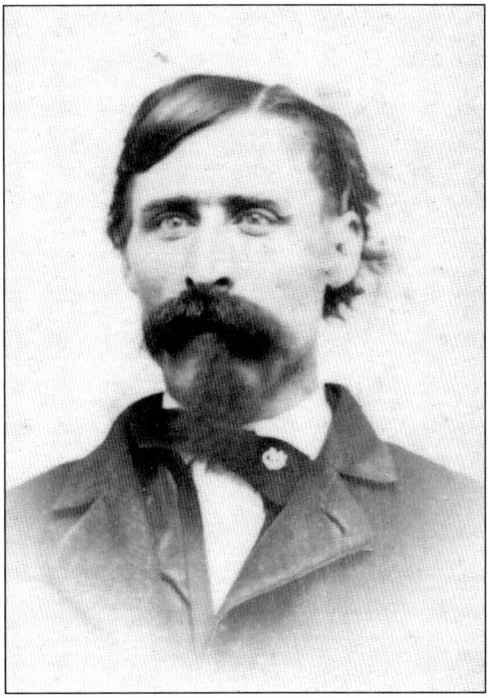

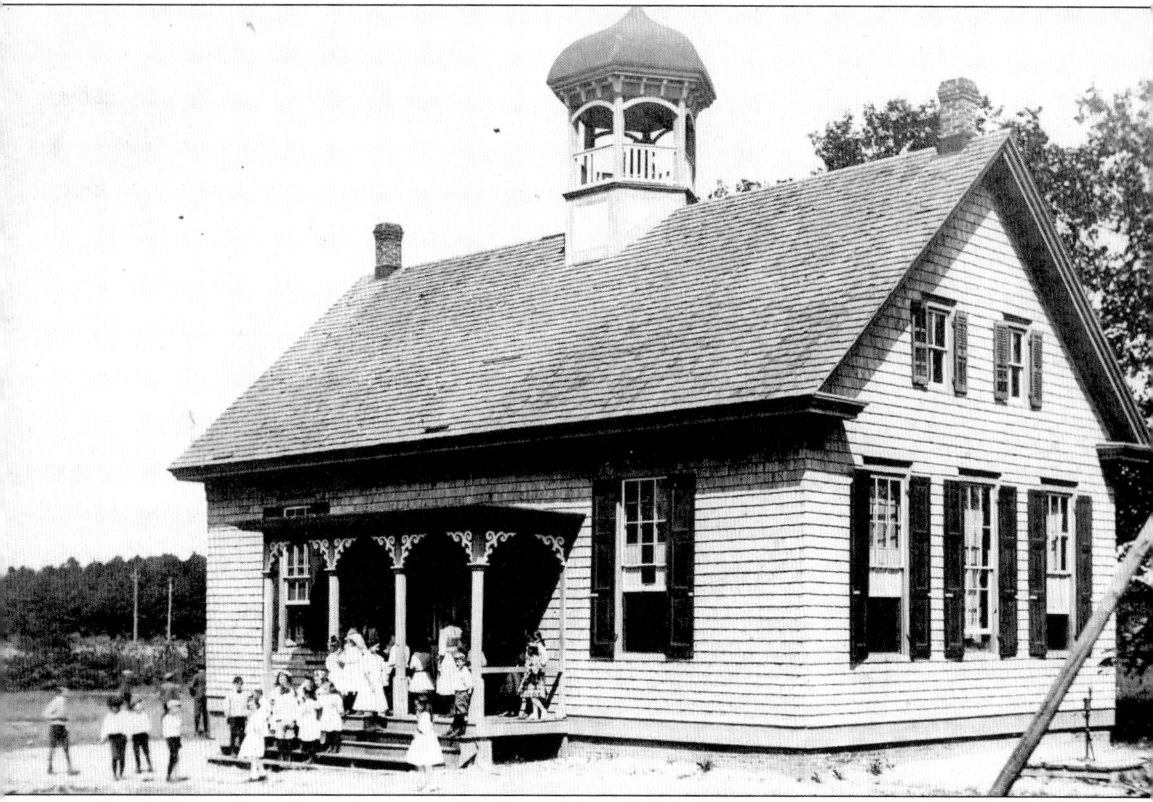

In 1873, children from the Leedsville School District No. 19 of Egg Harbor Township attended school in the old Leedsville Academy. This included children who lived in the area from Poplar Avenue to Belhaven Avenue. Capt. John Sanders donated a tract of land on Landing Lane (Poplar Avenue) for a new schoolhouse. The Meneely Bell Company of New York was commissioned to make a bell for the cupola. The school register for 1872–1874 described the school as a one-room, ungraded school with a single teacher for 66 students ages 5 to 19. In 1895, it was divided into two classes, primary and upper grammar and high school. There were two teachers. A male principal received a salary of $56 per month and his assistant, a female, received $30 a month. An 1894 note from W.E. Kern, a teacher, to James Farish, Esq., reads, "I wish you would send that man Murray here again to see if the well rope is in the well. It disappeared mysteriously."

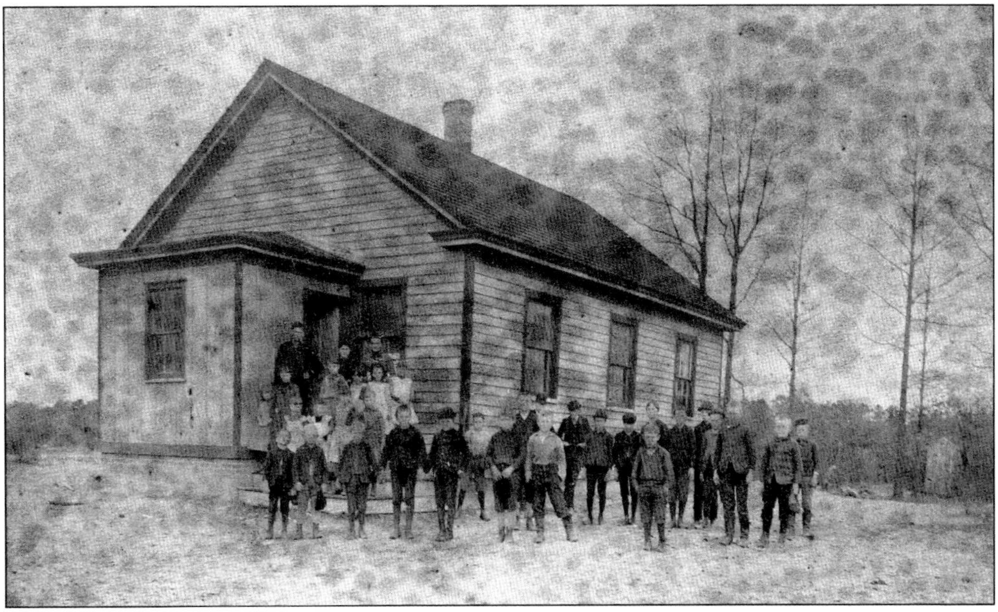

Children who lived south of Belhaven Avenue were assigned to the Somers Point School District No. 20, and their school was called the Sea View School. In 1887, Capt. James Steelman donated land to build a new schoolhouse to replace the original 1861 building. The new building cost $1,800. In 1873, there were 43 students between the ages of 5 and 18 in one ungraded classroom.

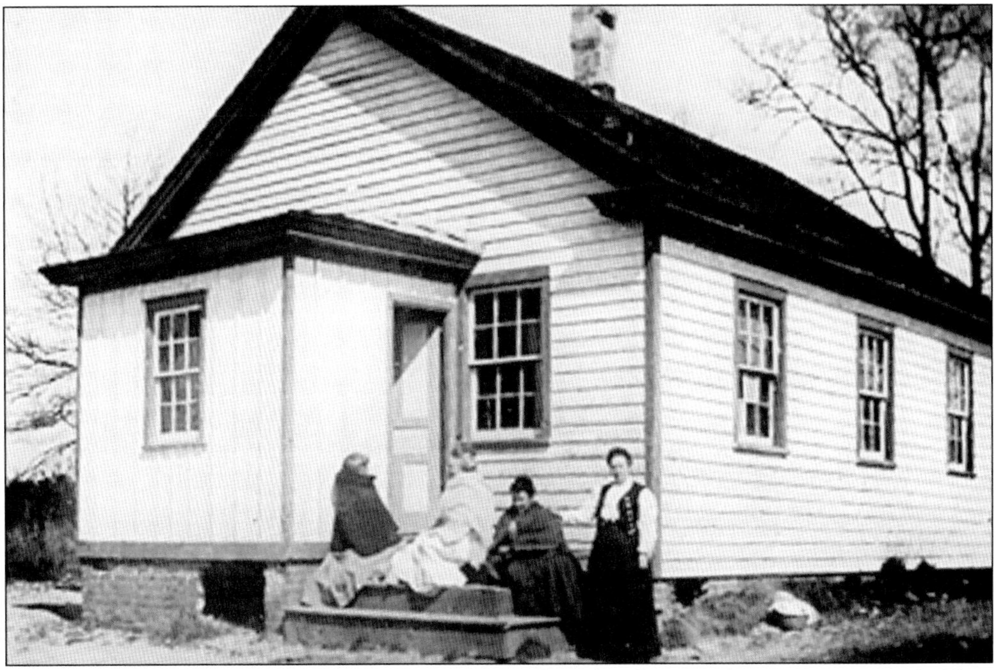

The "Minet Book" of District No. 20 indicates that the district's last meeting was held in 1894, when the new Linwood Board of Education was organized. When Belhaven School opened in 1908, the property was sold and it became a home. The people on the back step are unidentified. (Courtesy of ACHS.)

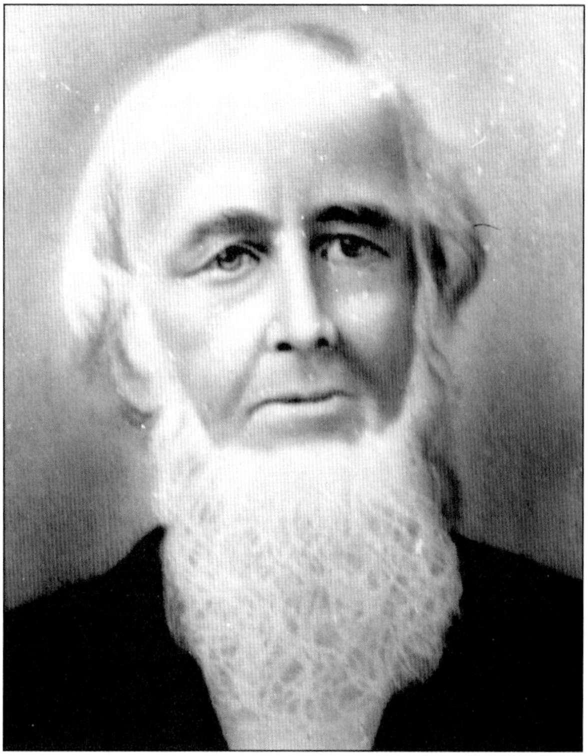

Most of Job VanSant's ancestors were 18th-century shipbuilders. His grandfather Christopher had a shipyard on Patcong Creek in 1796. In 1840, Job VanSant opened his shipyard on the bay in Somers Point. He built the *Emma Cottingham* in 1875 and kept a day-by-day record of its construction in his time book. For 45 years, he walked to work each day from his Poplar Avenue home to the shipyard until his death in 1885.

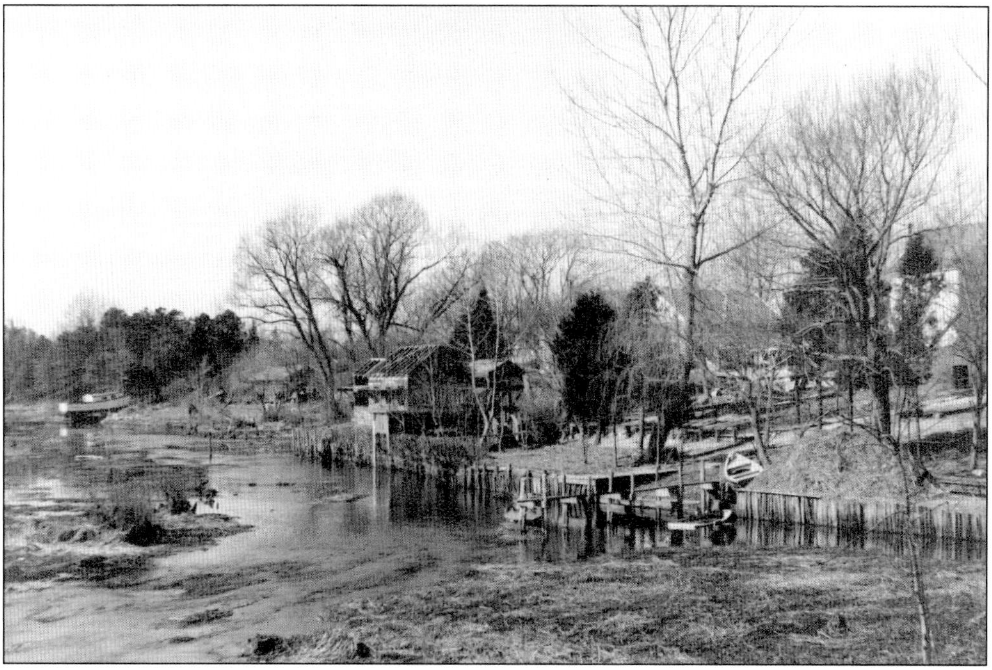

Looking at this picture, it hardly seems possible that anyone could have had a shipyard on Patcong Creek, but this is just about where Christopher VanSant's shipyard was located. There were other yards nearby, but the construction of bridges across the creek in 1817 and 1819 forced the yards to move to Somers Point.

Job VanSant married Sarah Risley, daughter of Robert B. Risley, and they moved to Leedsville in 1841. The Risleys were among the early settlers in the Leedsville area, and many of the family members were leaders in community churches and other organizations. Like the Somers family, descendants of the VanSants and the Risleys continue to live in Linwood and maintain an active community presence.

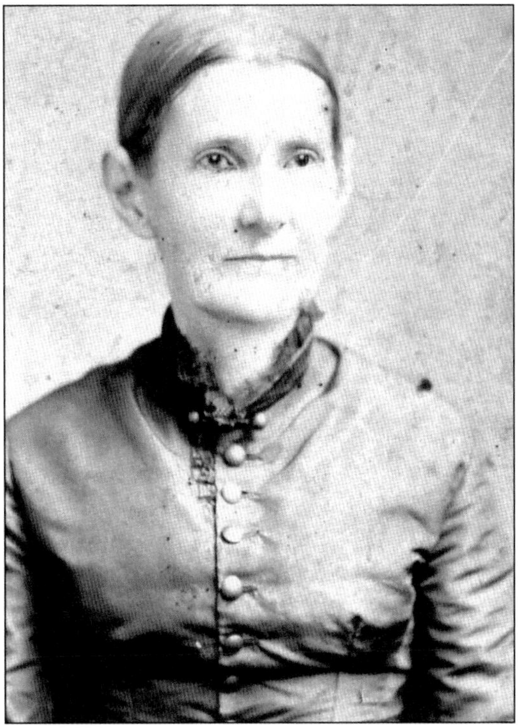

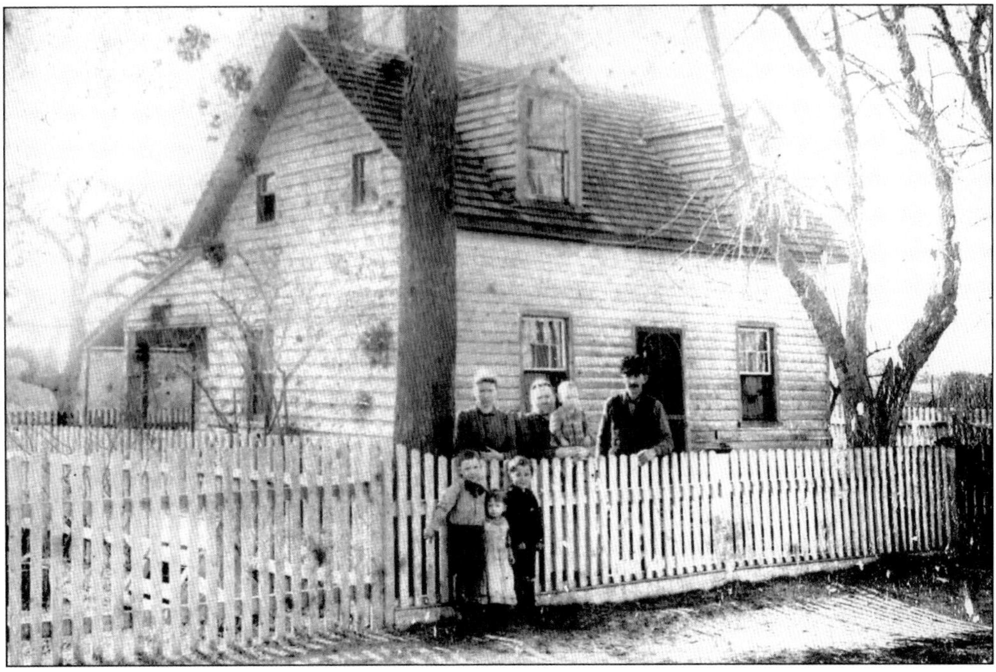

The VanSant home on Poplar Avenue has been altered many times over the years. Job and Sara VanSant's son, John, and his family are seen here. Pictured are, from left to right, Maggie Sutton Price; John's wife, Sally Sutton VanSant (holding young Walter VanSant); and John VanSant. Children outside of the fence are, from left to right, Somers Price, Flora Price, and young John VanSant. (Courtesy of ACHS.)

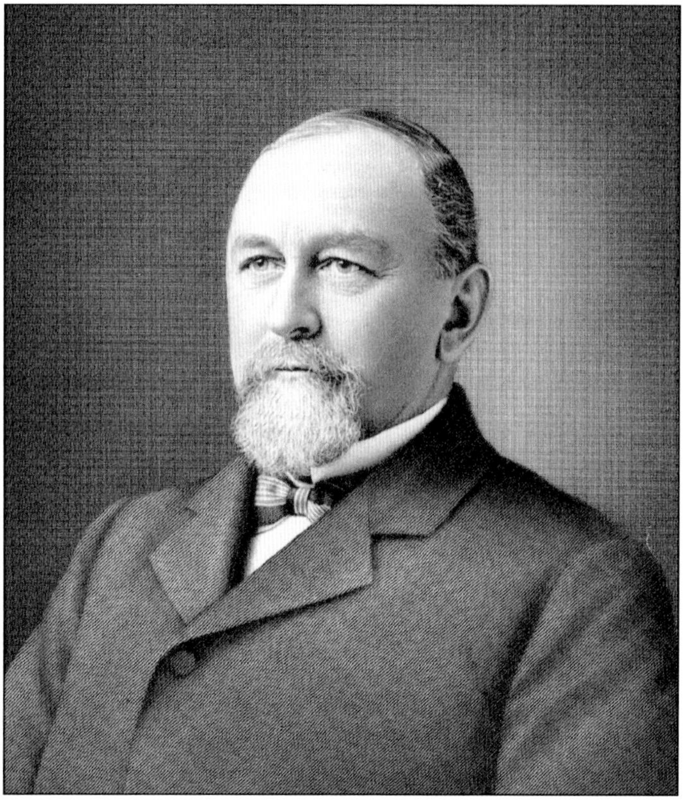

Israel G. Adams's grandfather Jesse was one of the early Quaker settlers to the county. Adams (1843–1918) became a captain by the age of 21 and was engaged in trade with West Indian and Mexican ports. In February 1865, he was shipwrecked in a violent storm off of Cape Lookout. On his way to Abraham Lincoln's second inauguration, Adm. David Porter found the shipwrecked men and sent a crew to rescue them.

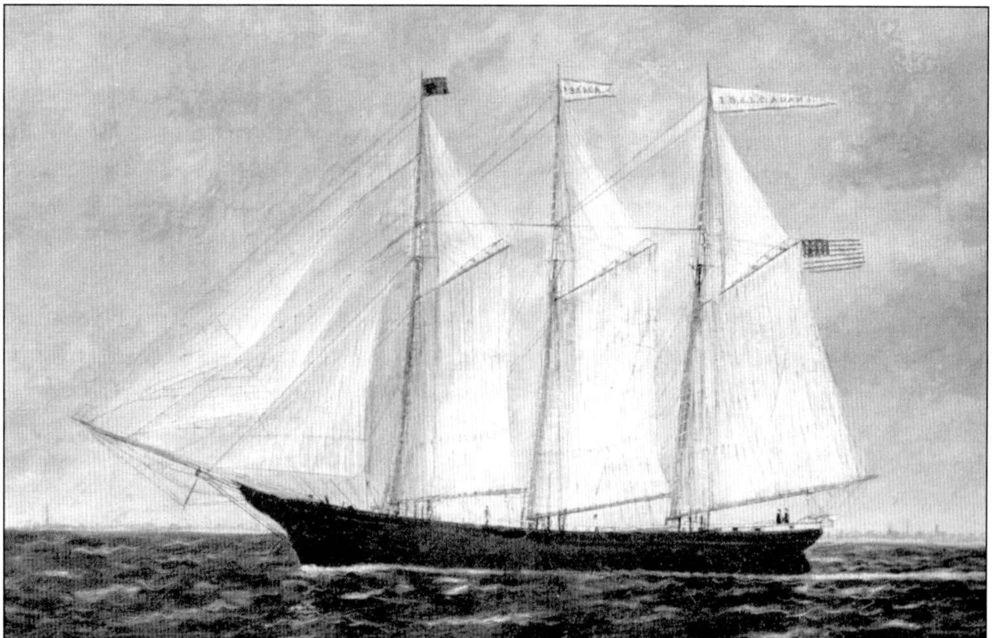

Captain Adams's ship, the *I.S. & L.C. Adams*, named for his parents, is pictured here. It was built in Port Republic in 1866. The ship was nearly destroyed in 1867 during a hurricane at sea.

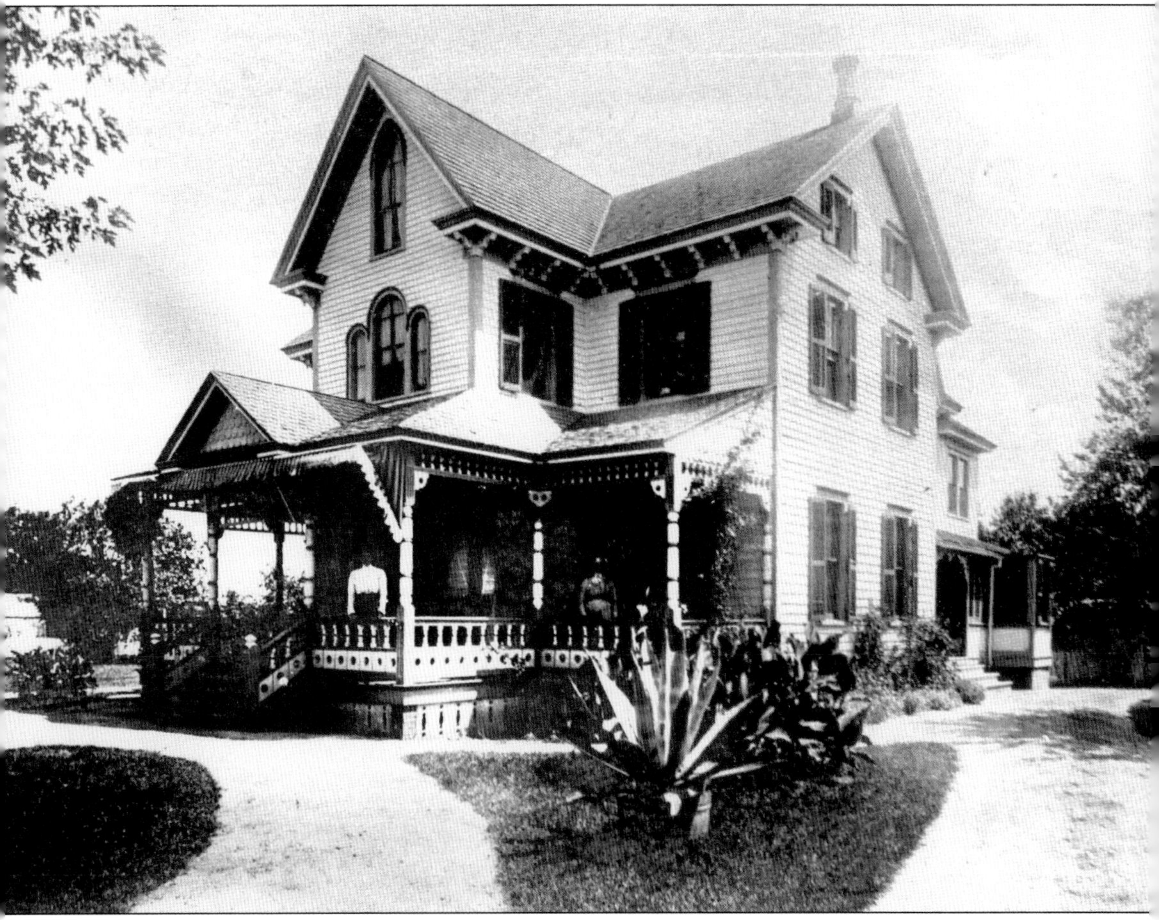

The Shore Road home built by Joseph Risley for Capt. I.G. Adams remains one of Linwood's notable Leedsville treasures. Captain Adams was a graduate of Pennington Seminary and, like his father and grandfather before him, he followed the sea. Adams had his home built sometime between 1870 and 1872. In 1880, his wife died, leaving five children to raise. Shortly afterward, he quit the sea and became an influential Atlantic City businessman. He was a director and on the board of many banks and other local firms and was very active in the Central Methodist Episcopal Church. He served as mayor of the borough of Linwood from 1893 to 1894. In a letter to the district clerk, James Farish, on May 17, 1893, Adams wrote, "Be sure to get a good school teacher and don't engage one unless you know he is OK."

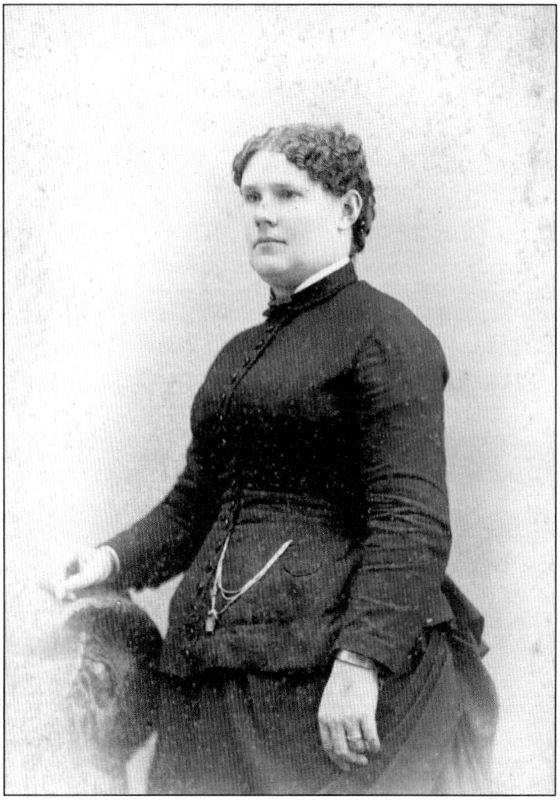

After the death of her first husband, Captain Cavileer, Lizzie Risley (left) married Capt. Peter Reed (below), who was engaged in coastal trading. She often traveled with her husband on his voyages. In November 1896, one of Captain Reed's ships was given up as lost at sea. The ship carried a crew of seven men and a cargo of 950 tons of coal. The captain was Lewis H. Reed, who was born in Leedsville in 1845.

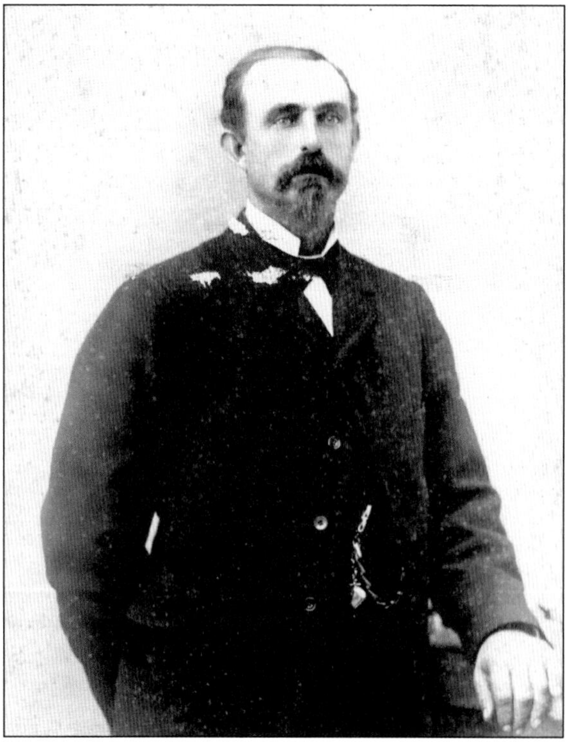

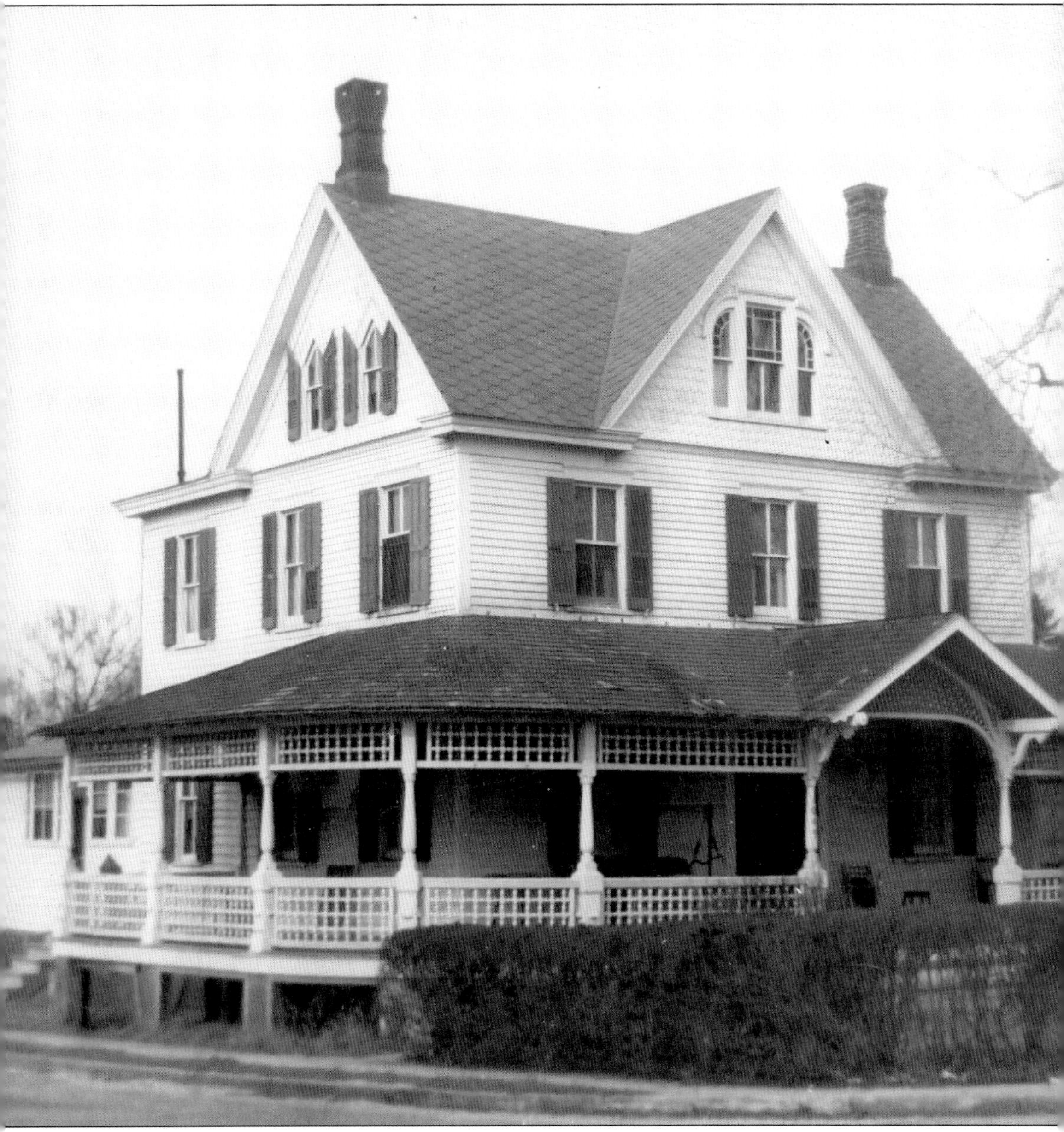

The Reeds built their home in 1880 on the corner of Maple Avenue and Shore Road. Edgewood Avenue had not yet been created, so theirs was a nice property, set well back from the road. It was originally part of the land that Lizzie's grandfather Robert Risley had purchased in 1836. The home was identified as the Linwood Inn in the 1932 *Sanborn Atlas*. An old postcard referred to it as the Levin residence. The original spindle work and balustrade on the wraparound porch is an outstanding example of Queen Ann Victorian style.

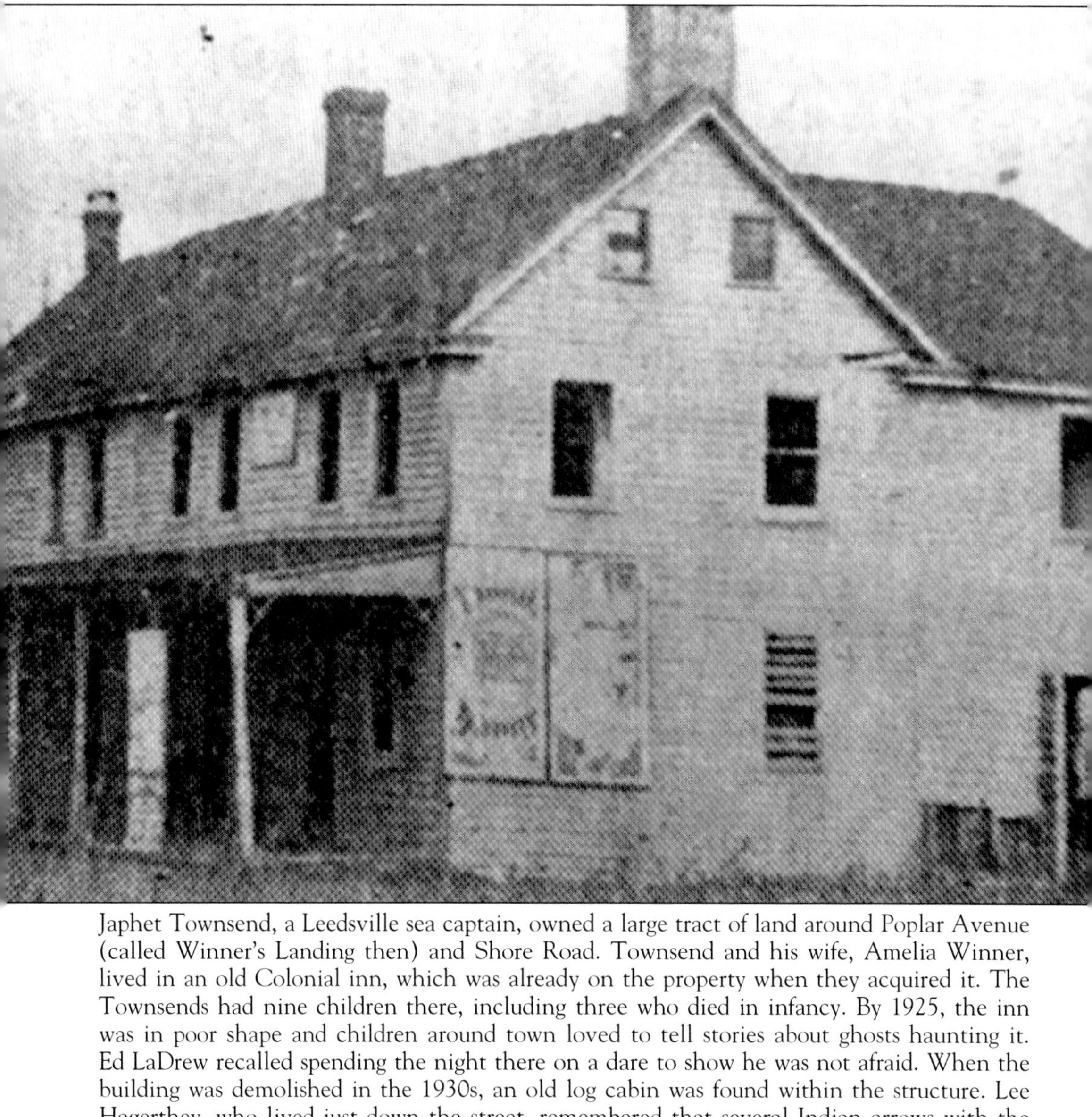

Japhet Townsend, a Leedsville sea captain, owned a large tract of land around Poplar Avenue (called Winner's Landing then) and Shore Road. Townsend and his wife, Amelia Winner, lived in an old Colonial inn, which was already on the property when they acquired it. The Townsends had nine children there, including three who died in infancy. By 1925, the inn was in poor shape and children around town loved to tell stories about ghosts haunting it. Ed LaDrew recalled spending the night there on a dare to show he was not afraid. When the building was demolished in the 1930s, an old log cabin was found within the structure. Lee Hagerthey, who lived just down the street, remembered that several Indian arrows with the feathers intact were found under the cabin.

To *Mulford Townsend*

Your Tax for the year 1869, in the TOWNSHIP OF EGG HARBOR, has been assessed as follows:

Rate of Assessment, for State Tax,	$0.08	on $100	valuation.
" " County,	0.30	"	"
" " Township Bounty,	1.00	"	"
" " Township,	0.40	"	"
" " School,	0.40	"	"
Total,	2.18	"	"

Acres of Land.	Value of Real Estate.	Val. Personal Property.	Total Taxable Estate.	Debts.	Net Val.	State.	County	Township Bounty.	Township.	School	Dog.	Poll	TOTAL.
10	600	10	610		610	.32	1.95	6.10	2.60	2.60		4.65	$18.63

Commissioners of Appeal in cases of Taxation meet at the INN OF JAPHET TOWNSEND, in Leedsville, November 23d, 1869. Return Day, 20th day of December. All that is not paid then will be charged 12 per cent. interest until paid.

D. B. SOMERS, Collector.

Received Payment of the above Tax in full,

.... Collector.

DOUGLAS & BARCLAY, Printers, Patriot Office, Bridgeton, N. J.

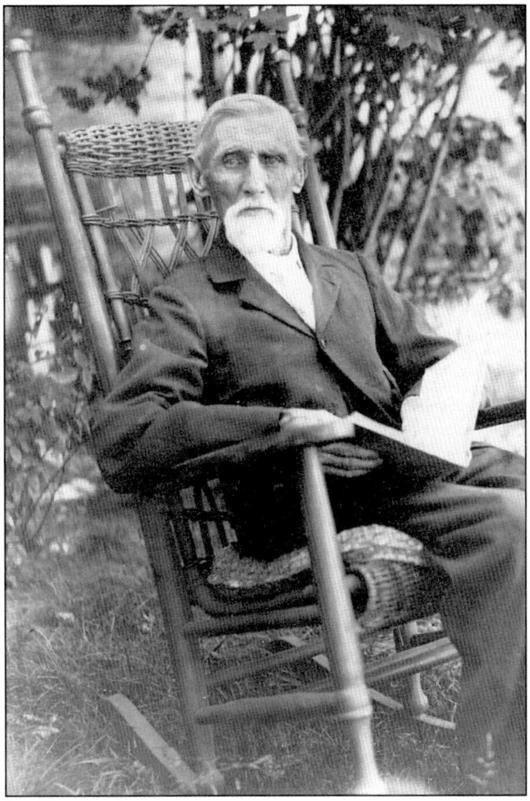

Like his brother Japhet, Mulford Townsend (right) was a sea captain. In 1898, he was keeper in charge of the Great Egg Harbor Life Saving Station in Longport. Townsend owned a home on Bog Road (Oak Avenue), and his 1869 tax bill in the amount of $18.63 (above) was due to be paid at his brother's establishment, the Inn of Japhet Townsend. The inn was often used for such business by the township and by Linwood borough. Other names for the inn were Dan Grey's Hotel and the Linwood Hotel.

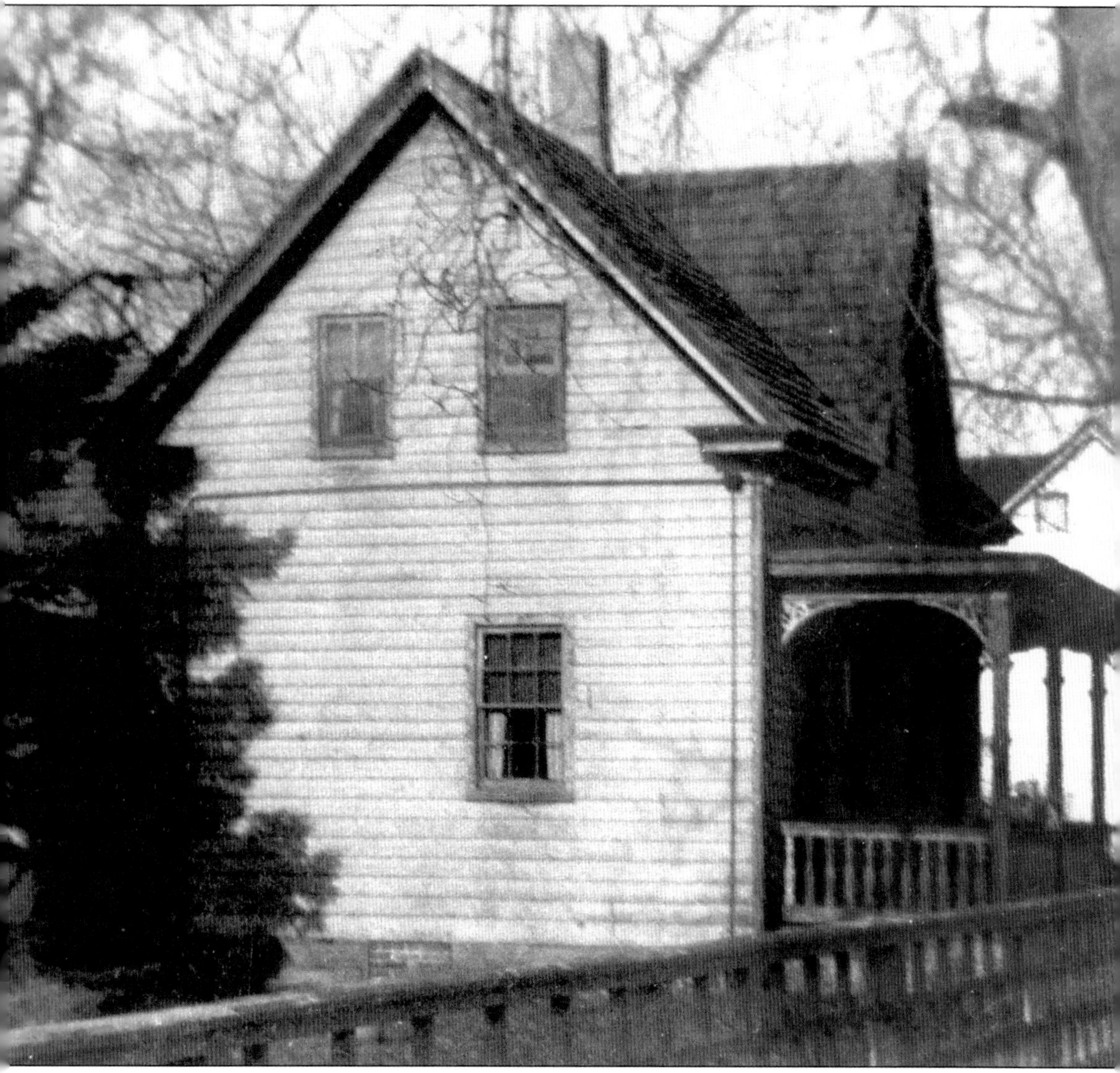

Maple Avenue could be called the main road from Leedsville to Linwood, and the Risley home there was surely a primary link. Robert B. Risley (1788–1863) bought the property from Phillip Smith in 1836, and it was the family home for four generations. Risley was a justice of the peace and very active in community affairs. On February 2, 1845, he received a commission from Pres. John Tyler to serve as the collector of customs for the port of Bargaintown. His commission is on display at the Leedsville School Museum. Risley owned most of the land on the south side of the block and he subdivided it among his children and grandchildren. The home served as a post office for Linwood for many years.

By 1881, villagers in Leedsville believed that the town was large enough to have its own post office and they petitioned the government to establish one. Because there was another Leedsville in New Jersey, a name change was required. After a lengthy discussion, the name Linwood was chosen. Robert Risley's son, Joseph (1825–1897) (right and below), who acquired his father's home in 1861, was appointed as the first postmaster, and the post office was in his home until his death in 1897.

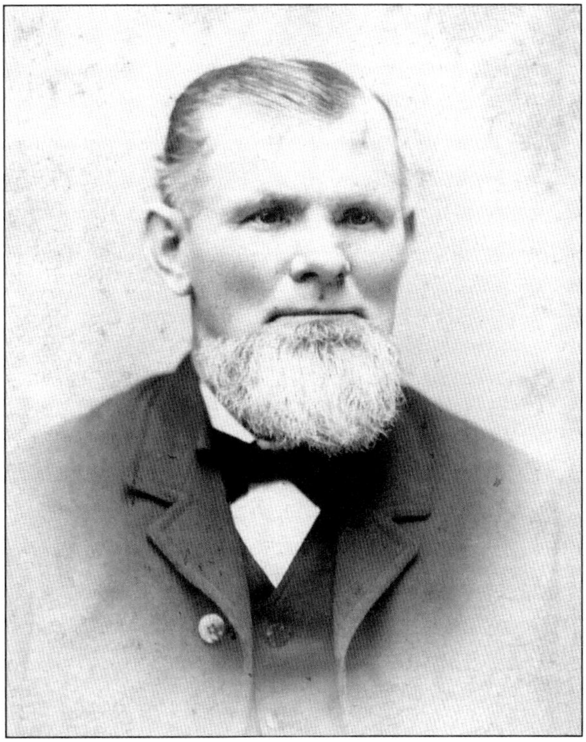

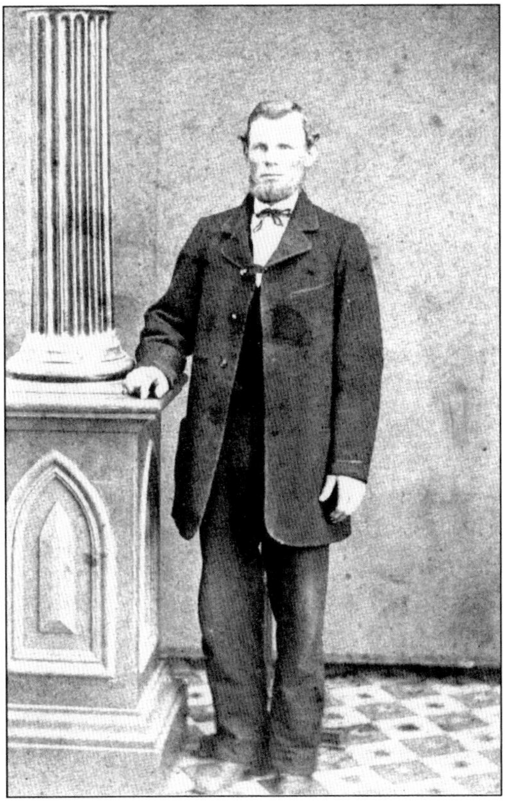

A Joseph R. Risley diary entry reads, "February 12, 1869 Got up this morning at Six oclock. went down to Somers Point to wirk on the Aid. wind South East. Wether Plesant. the Mary Dixton went out. jung the Aids Rudder. Davis Garwood took up fishers Post. Smallwood came to Corking. this afternoon thare was a schooner came in and ashore. thare was one came down the River loded with wood. Ezra Price Got loded. he is Reddy to go out. at home all evening. Wind South Clear and Cool. So ends this day."

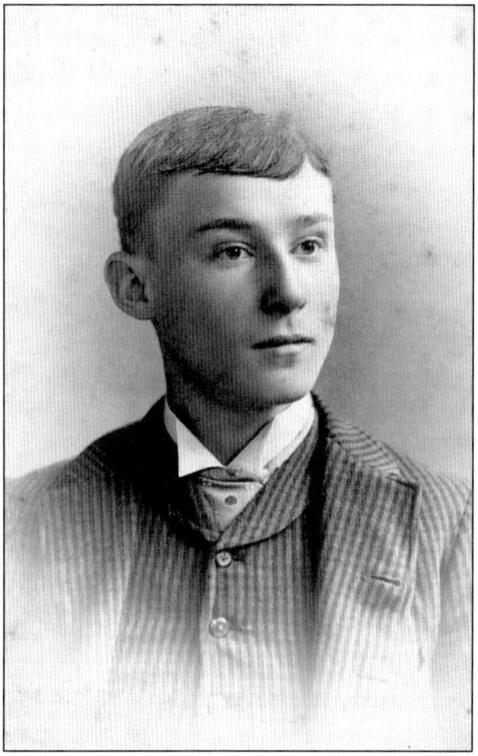

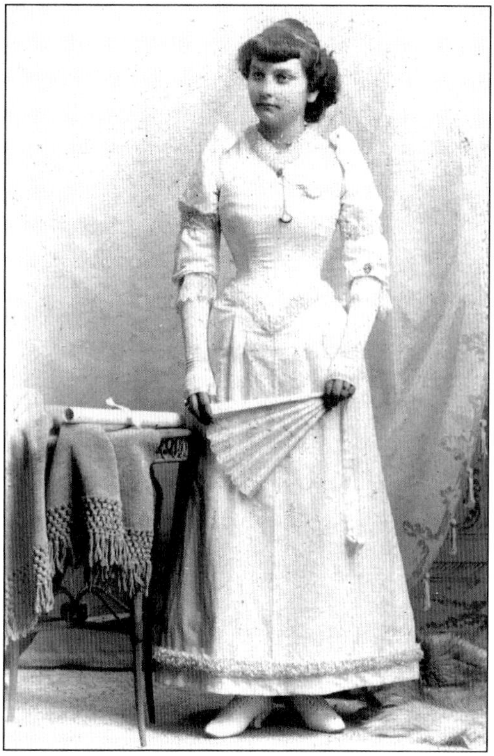

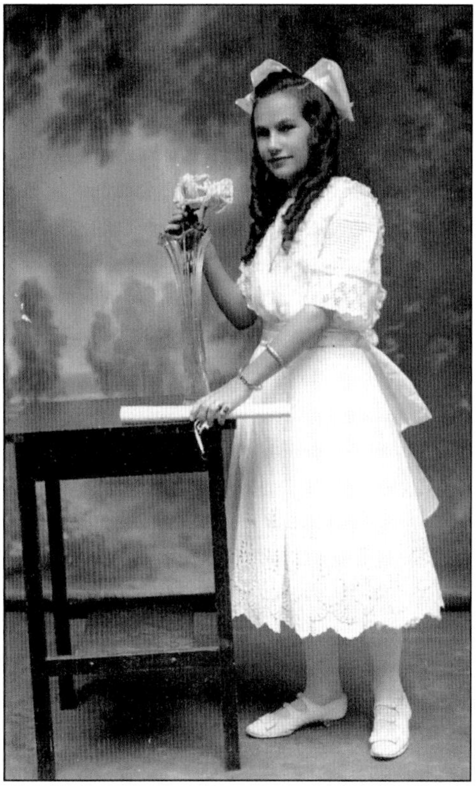

When Joseph Risley died in 1897, the Risley home became the property of his grandson Joseph H. Cavileer (upper left), who was born there in 1871. Joseph married Mamie Turner (upper right) of Bakersville. They were the parents of two children, James and Marie (lower left, at age 14). James died of appendicitis in 1914, a few weeks before he was to graduate from high school. Joseph died in 1918, and the following year Mamie was appointed as the new Linwood postmaster. She ran the post office from her home until 1926. Mamie, who was always very active in the community, died in 1948. Marie Risley married Stanley Gandy and they lived in the old homestead. Marie was another one of the links connecting the centuries. She had attended the Leedsville School and was one of Linwood's beloved elder citizens until her death in 1981.

Two

LIFE IN THE BOROUGH

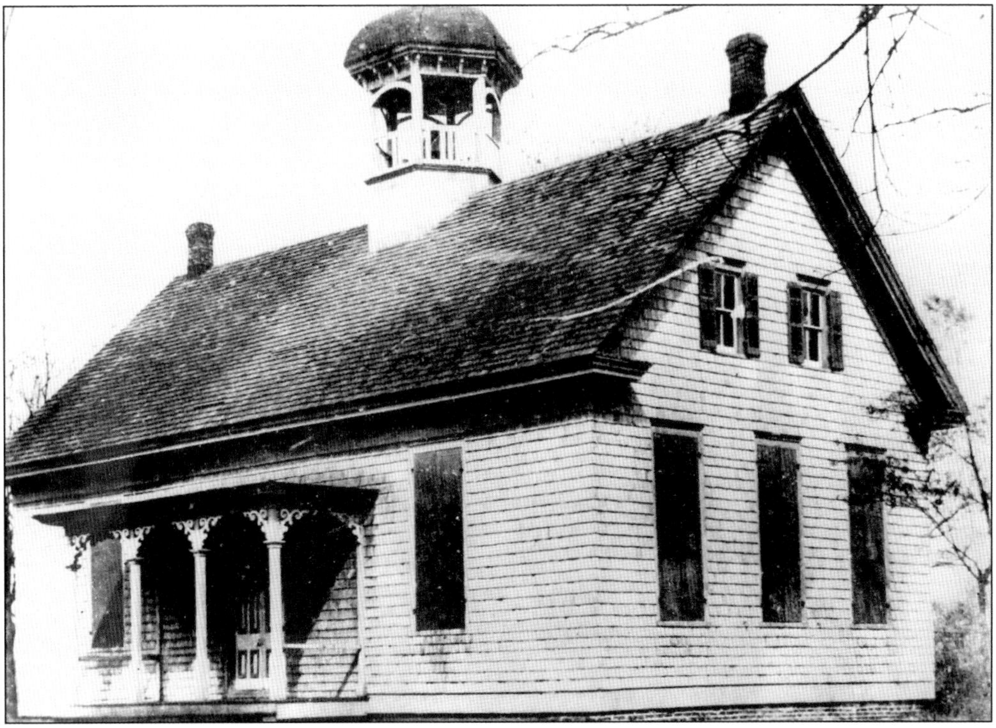

Less than two decades after Leedsville changed its name to Linwood, residents were ready for the next step—creating their own government. In 1889, they formally withdrew from the township and established the borough of Linwood. After renting office space for several years, the borough finally had an official town hall when the old Leedsville School closed in 1908. The town developed a strong sense of community spirit. Life at the beginning of the 20th century looked good for the citizens of Linwood. (Courtesy of ACHS.)

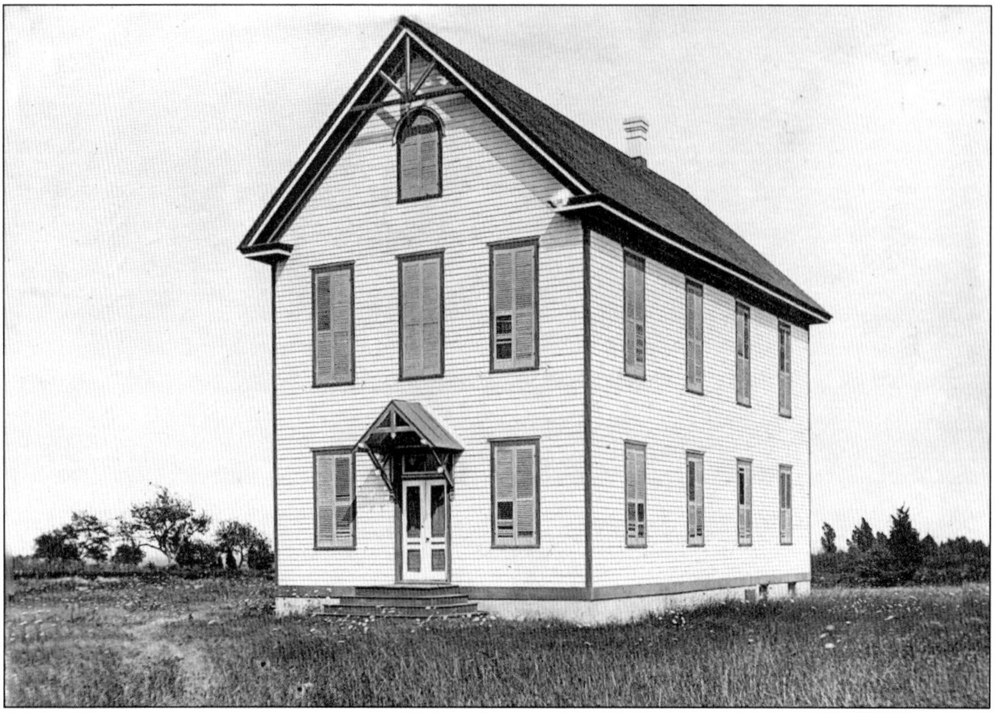

The Keystone Masonic Lodge was organized in January 1883, and the members built their lodge hall on Shore Road at Poplar Avenue. The building was often rented out to organizations and the newly created borough council held its first meeting there on March 13, 1889. In 1904, members of the council received permission to put their safe in the lower hall. They continued to use the hall until 1906, when they moved to Mechanics Hall. (Courtesy of ACHS.)

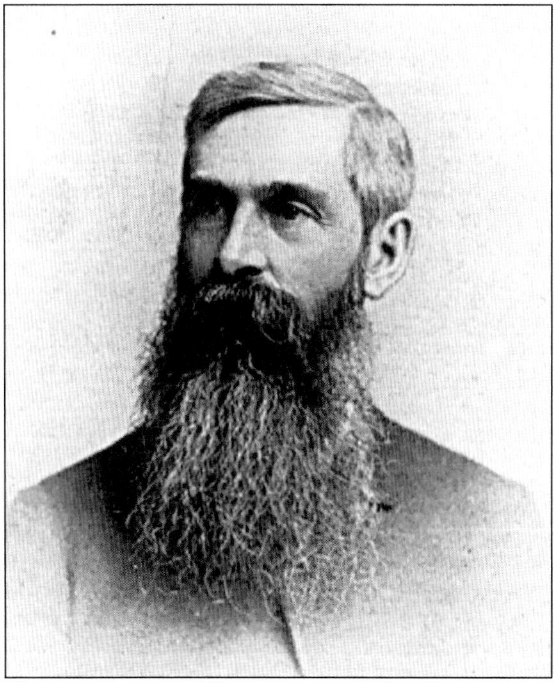

Dr. Job Somers, the first master of Keystone Masonic Lodge, held meetings in his home across the street until the building was constructed. He was also the first president of the Atlantic County Medical Society and the mayor of Linwood borough from 1891 to 1892.

The election ticket was a method of casting ballots that came into practice in the mid-19th century. Preprinted ballots for each party were used to make it easy for people to cast their votes, hence the term "party ticket." Regulations called for the tickets all to be printed on paper that was the same color and size to maintain secrecy. This is an 1889 election ticket for Frank Somers in Linwood's first borough election. Somers lost to Mark Townsend.

LINWOOD

BOROUGH TICKET,

1889.

For Mayor,
FRANK SOMERS.

For Council,
JAS. SOMERS, } 1 year.
R. L. SOMERS, }
JOHN D. SANDERS, } 2 years.
JOS. BROADHEAD, }
G. W. HAGGERTHY, 3 years
PETER B. REED, 3 years.

Chosen Freeholder,
JOSEPH STEELMAN.

Assessor,
LEWIS E. SOMERS.

Collector,
LEWIS STEELMAN.

Judicious Freeholders,
JAMES JEFFRIES,
SOMERS SNELL,
S. R. RISLEY.

Overseer of Poor,
RICHARD I. SOMERS.

Pound Keeper,
GEORGE MYERS.

Judge of Election,
ELISHA S. SMITH.

Inspectors of Election,
JETHRO V. ALBERTSON,
DANIEL E. TILTON.

Constable,
THOMAS SAMSON.

Justice of Peace,
WILLIAM H. HAWK.

APPROPRIATIONS.

For road purposes,	$200.00
For Borough purposes,	300.00
School Tax, per scholar,	1.50
Dog Tax,	1.00

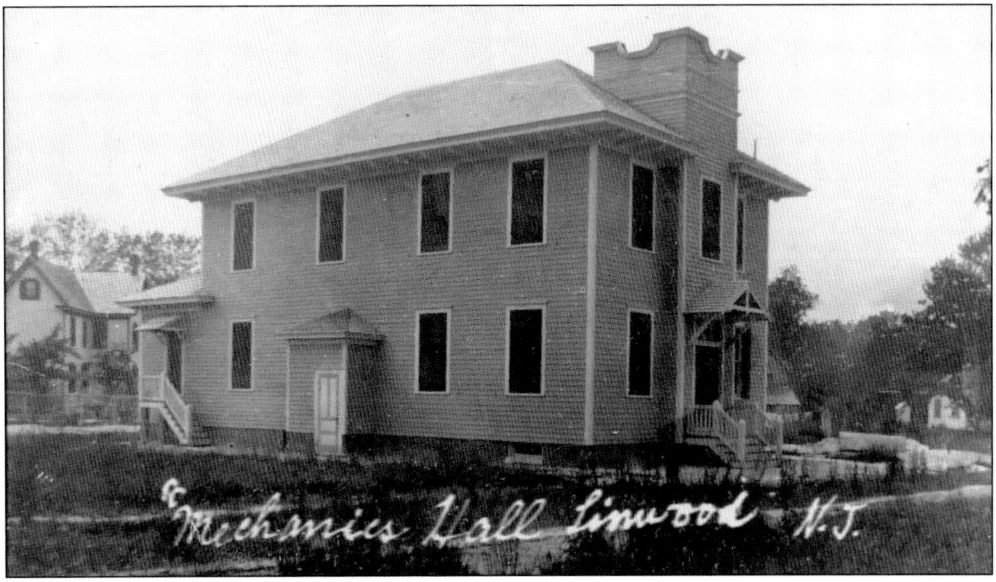

Mechanics Hall on Elm Avenue was built *c.* 1906 by the Junior Order of United Mechanics, and the building also served as a community meeting hall. In 1906, the borough rented the audience room for municipal purposes for $65 a year. Borough officials were permitted to put a jail cell in the basement but had to pay extra for heat and electricity when it was used. (Courtesy of Lee Hagerthey.)

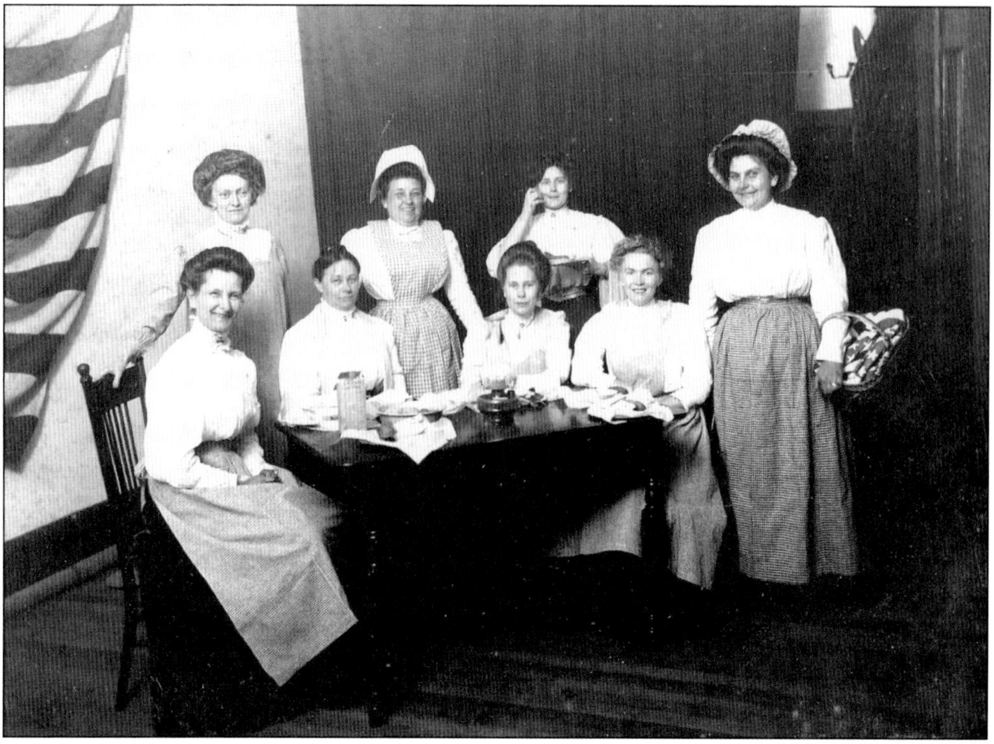

This photograph was taken at Mechanics Hall. The ladies appear to be working on costumes for the patriotic dancers shown below, and they all seem to be having a great time.

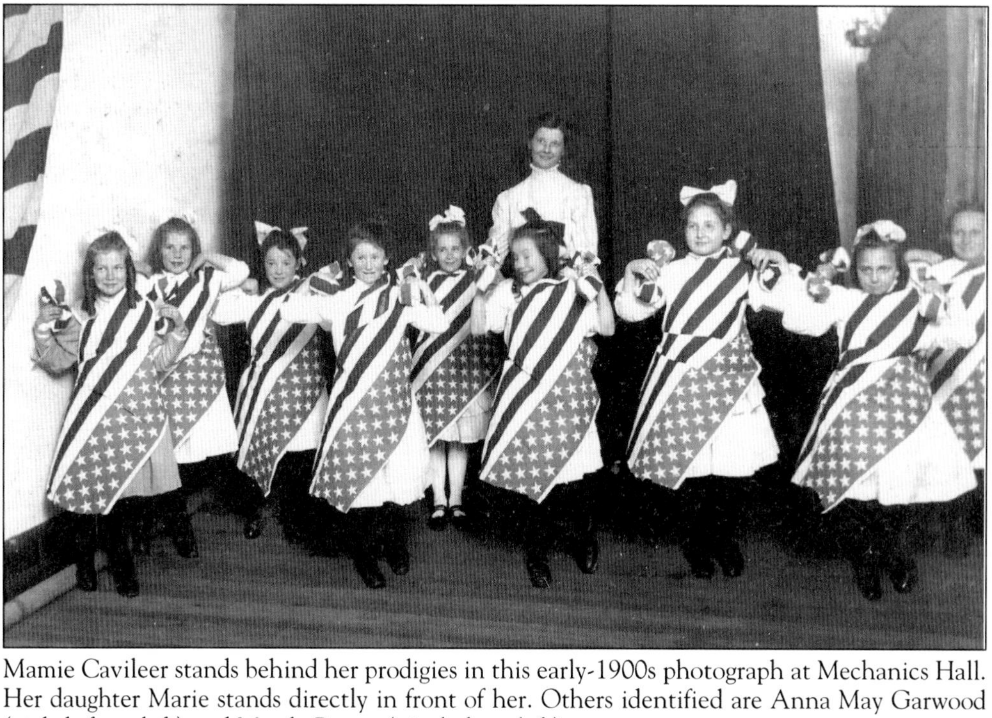

Mamie Cavileer stands behind her prodigies in this early-1900s photograph at Mechanics Hall. Her daughter Marie stands directly in front of her. Others identified are Anna May Garwood (eighth from left) and Myrtle Potter (ninth from left).

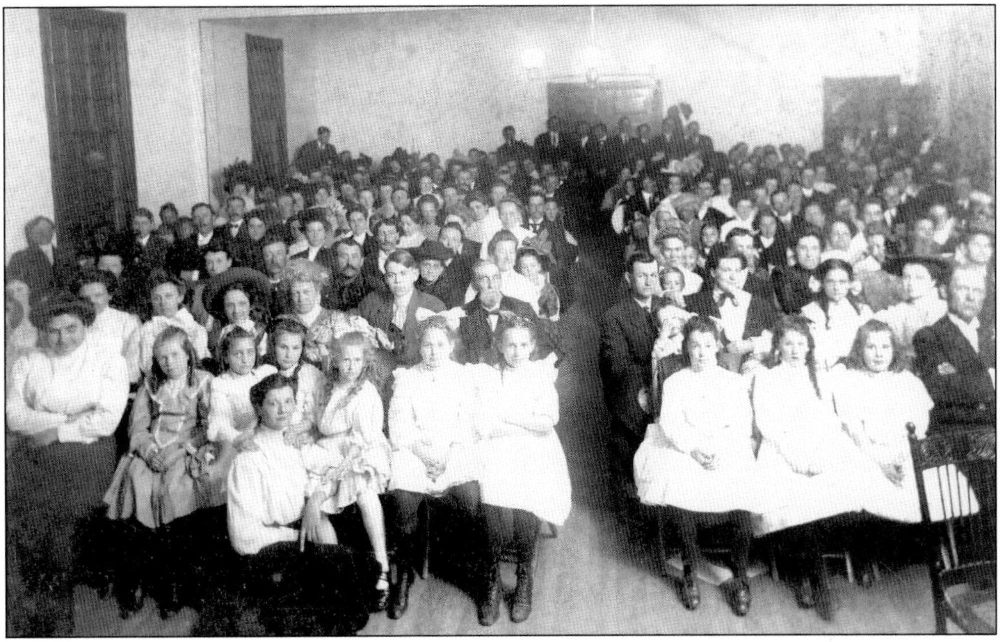

A huge crowd fills the hall in this *c.* 1908 photograph. Zilpha Brandis Hopf is kneeling in the front, and Marie Cavileer is seated third from the left, with her hand on Hopf's right shoulder. No record of this event has been found.

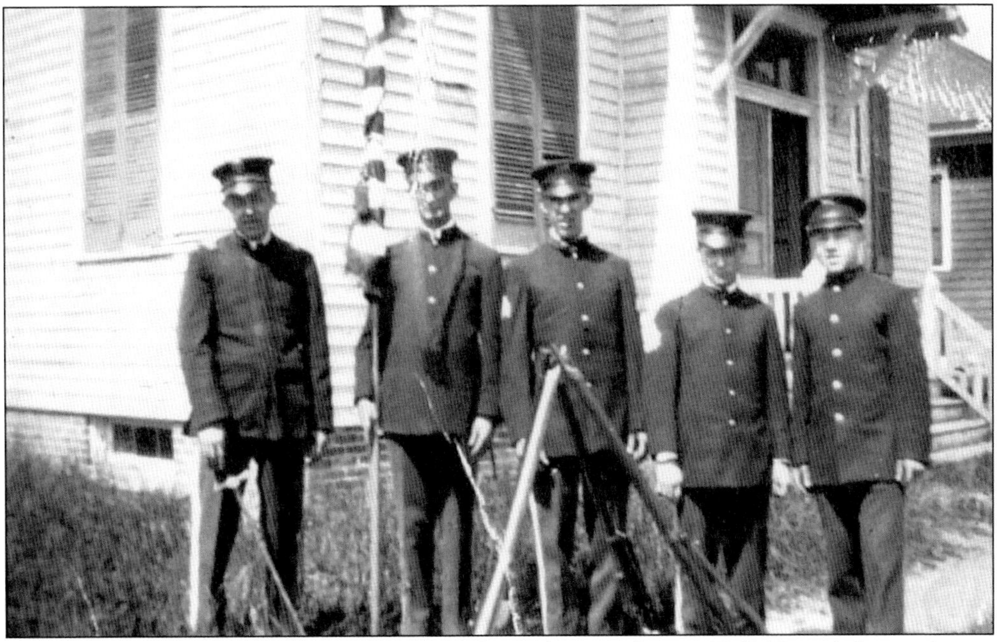

Members of what appears to be a color guard stand at Mechanics Hall. From left to right are Harry Wolfbrandt, Duke Force, unidentified, Mulford Potter, and unidentified. Wolfbrandt was the stationmaster at Linwood Station for many years. Mulford Potter was Linwood's first automobile mechanic.

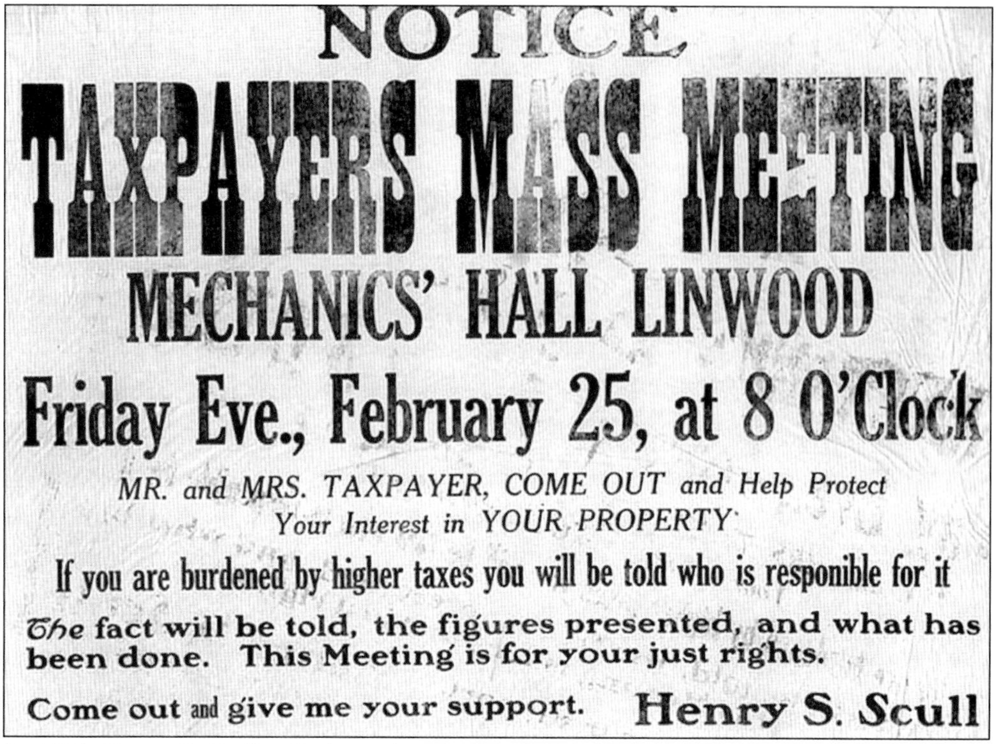

In 1904, Henry S. Scull called people together at Mechanics Hall, obviously for a political message. Scull, born in Leedsville in 1862, was the son of Captain Rolon and Elizabeth VanSant Scull. He often accompanied his father on his trips to sea. Scull was active in the Democratic Party and, in 1914, was appointed chief probation officer for Atlantic County. He was a member of many community organizations, including the fire department and the Kiwanis Club.

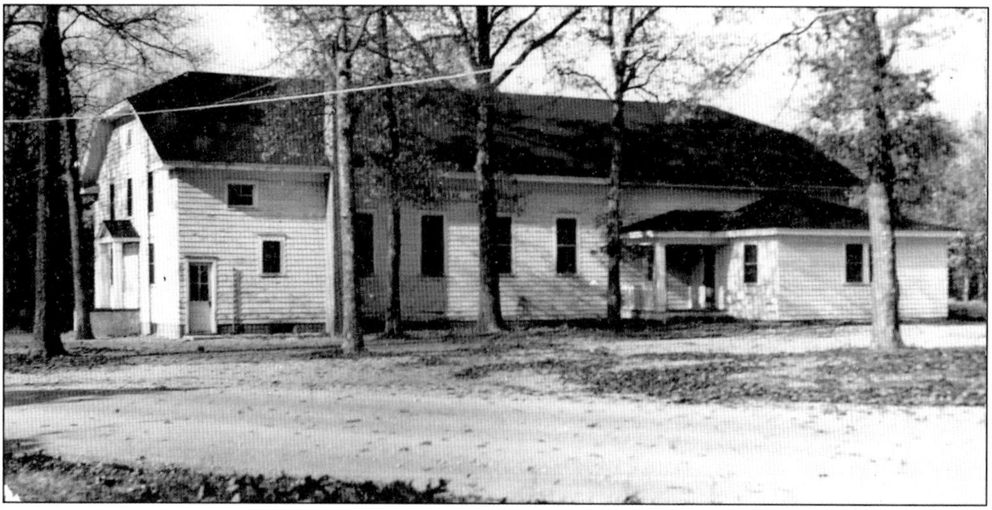

Adams Hall at Central Methodist Episcopal Church served as a community center for many affairs, including eighth-grade graduation ceremonies, well into the 1950s. The hall was built in 1926 at a cost of $23,500. Mabel Adams donated $10,000 in memory of her father, I.G. Adams. She later married Edgar Miller, who was pastor of the church from 1933 to 1937.

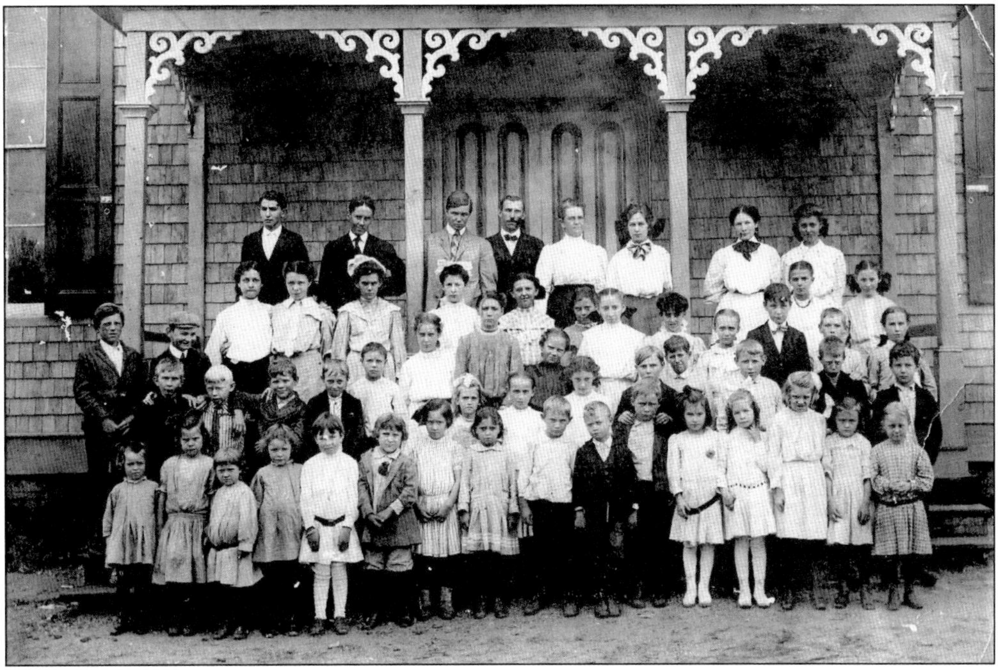

At the beginning of the 20th century, the Leedsville School was known as the Poplar School. This photograph was taken *c.* 1906.

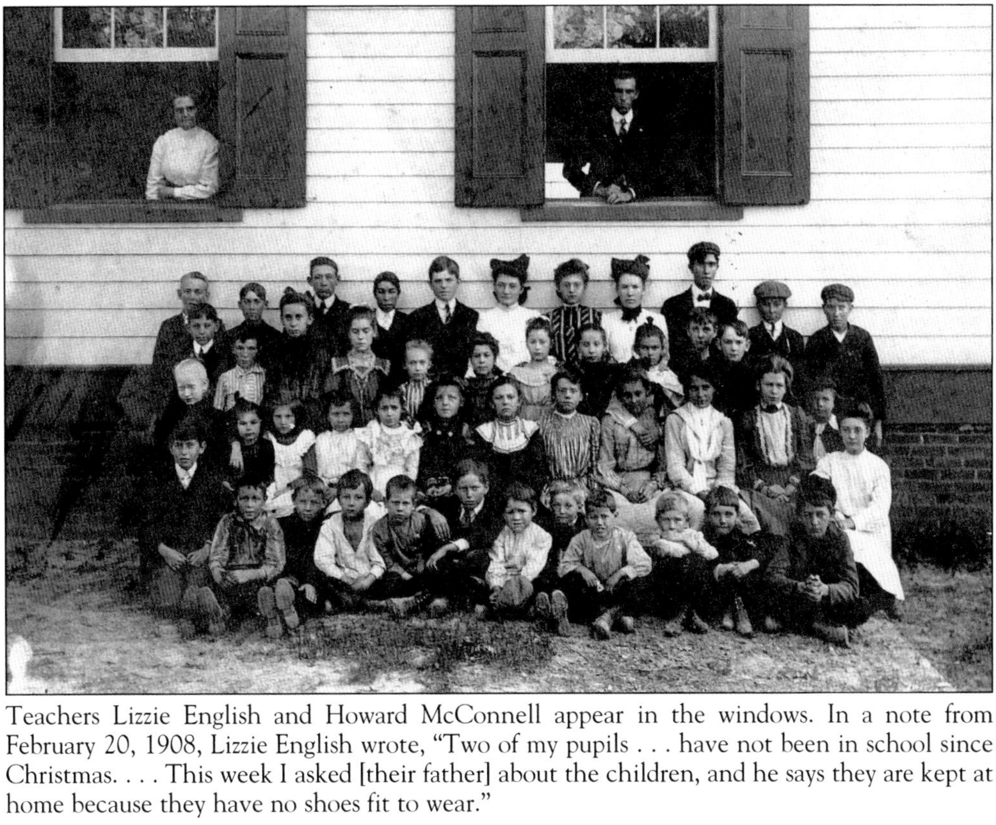

Teachers Lizzie English and Howard McConnell appear in the windows. In a note from February 20, 1908, Lizzie English wrote, "Two of my pupils . . . have not been in school since Christmas. . . . This week I asked [their father] about the children, and he says they are kept at home because they have no shoes fit to wear."

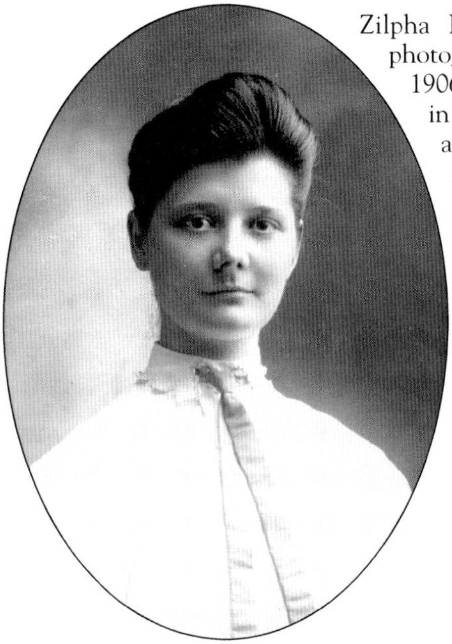

Zilpha Brandis Hopf, shown in her 1904 graduation photograph, came to teach in the Sea View School in 1906. After she left Linwood, she became a principal in Bargaintown and Scullville. Her accomplishments as an educator had far-reaching results. She founded the Parent-Teacher Association in Atlantic County and the Atlantic County Library. She was also instrumental in establishing school lunch programs. (Courtesy of Janet Way Dingler.)

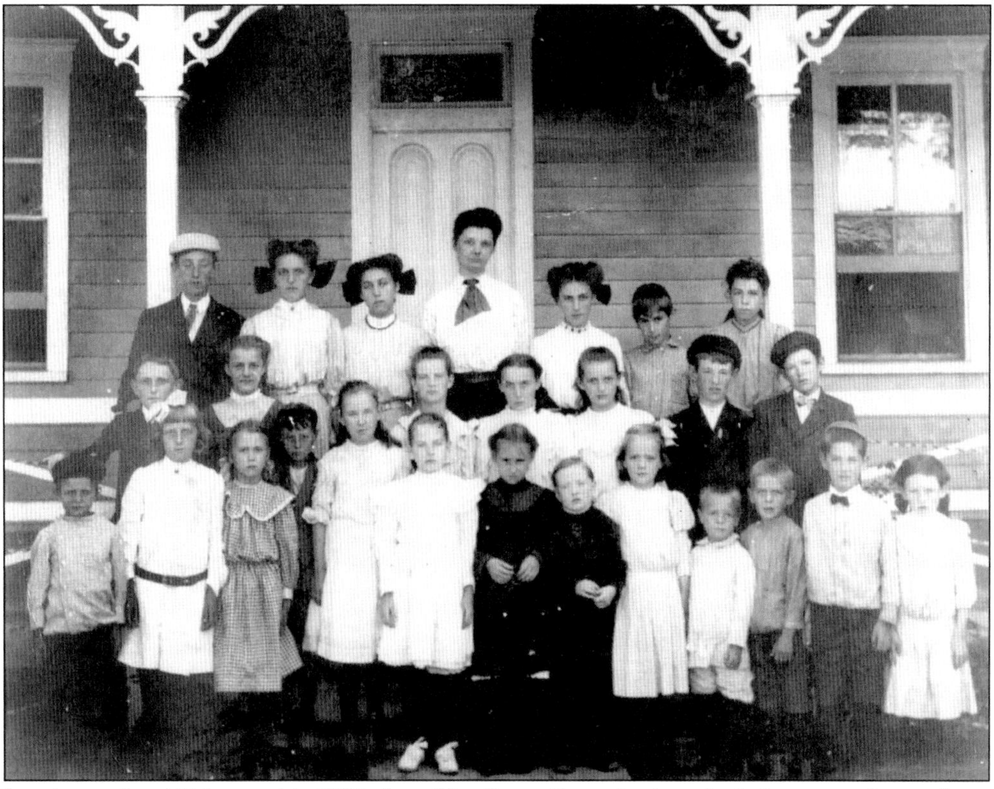

In a letter dated February 14, 1907, from Hopf's pupils to the board of education, the students wrote, "We wish Miss Brandis to be our teacher the remainder of this year and next. Will you kindly acknowledg (sic) our request and not her resignation. Yours truly, Scholars of Linwood School No. 2."

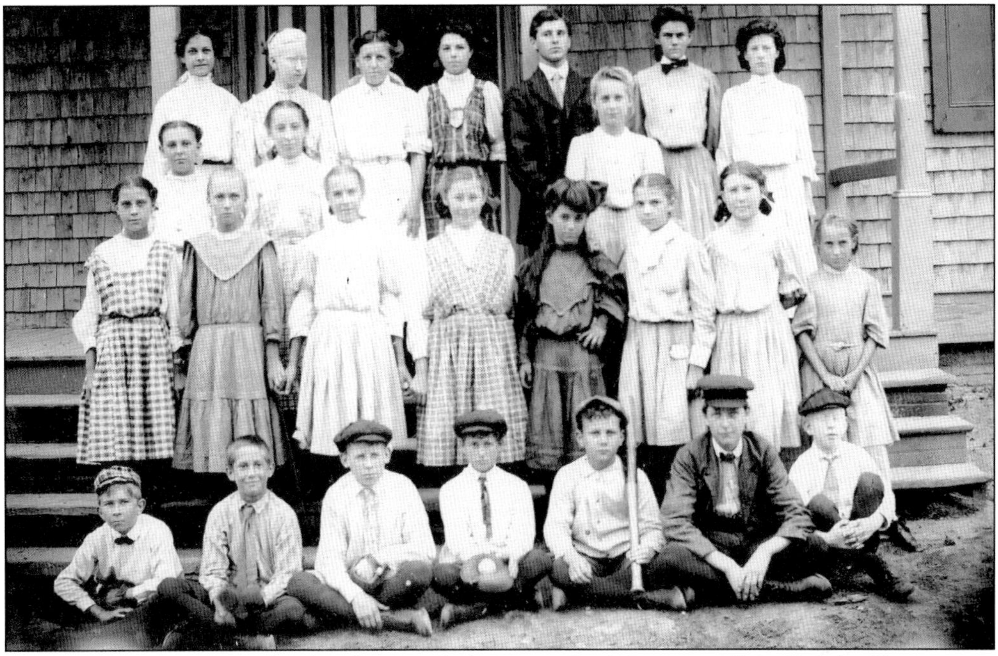

In a note to James Farish, the district clerk, Lizzie English wrote, "Mr. Farish, Please get a plumber here today. The pipe is burst and we are in a great mess." The note was signed, "Lizzie English by order of Mr. Weintrobe."

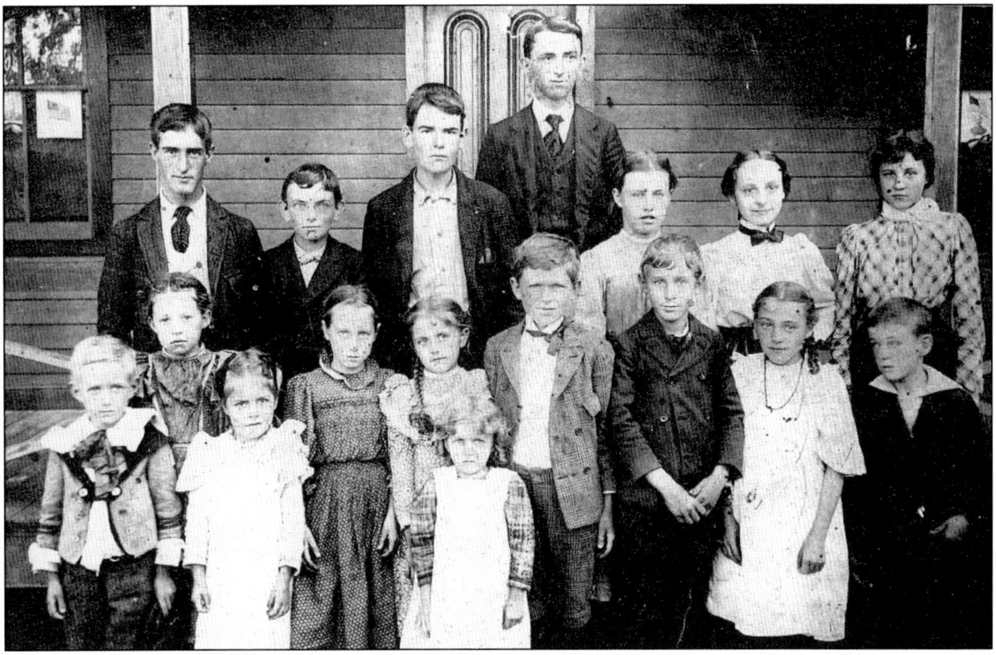

On May 9, 1893, teacher Charles Tomlin wrote to James Farish, "I suppose you will repair those water-closets before I come so allow me to request that locks be put on them and that in the boys there be placed a spout or trough in which they can deposit their urine and not be tempted so to do upon the seats. Have the trough with a slant so as to carry the water off. If you put a tight board fence around the boys, the trough had better be in one corner of the yard."

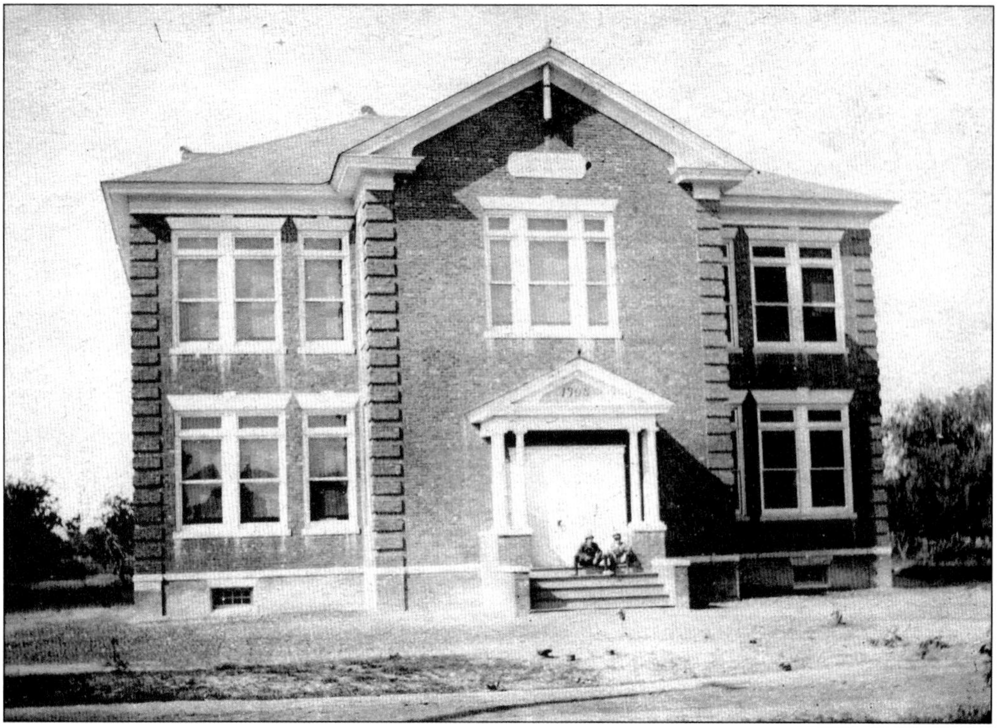

By 1907, townspeople thought that it was time to replace the old Leedsville and Sea View Schools and educate all of Linwood's children in one building. The board of education purchased land on Belhaven Avenue for $600 and set aside $12,000 for the construction costs, equipment, and furniture. This photograph may be the first one taken of the new school.

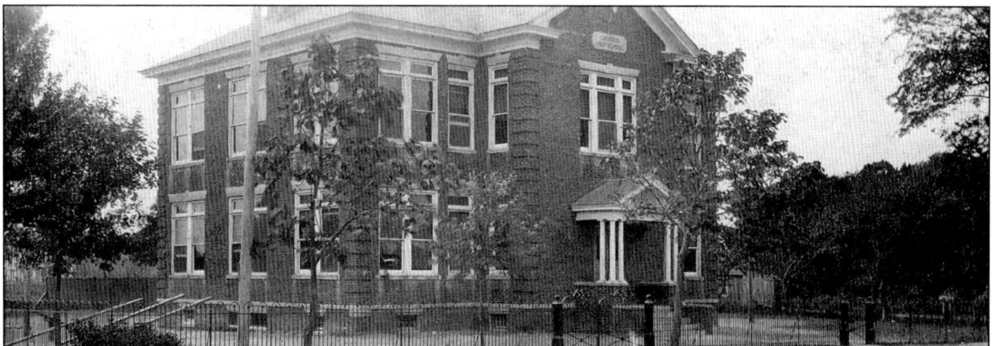

In August 1908, James Farish, district clerk, wrote, "The Board of Education has not yet decided when school will re-open, probably about the middle of September. All scholars will be transferred to the new building."

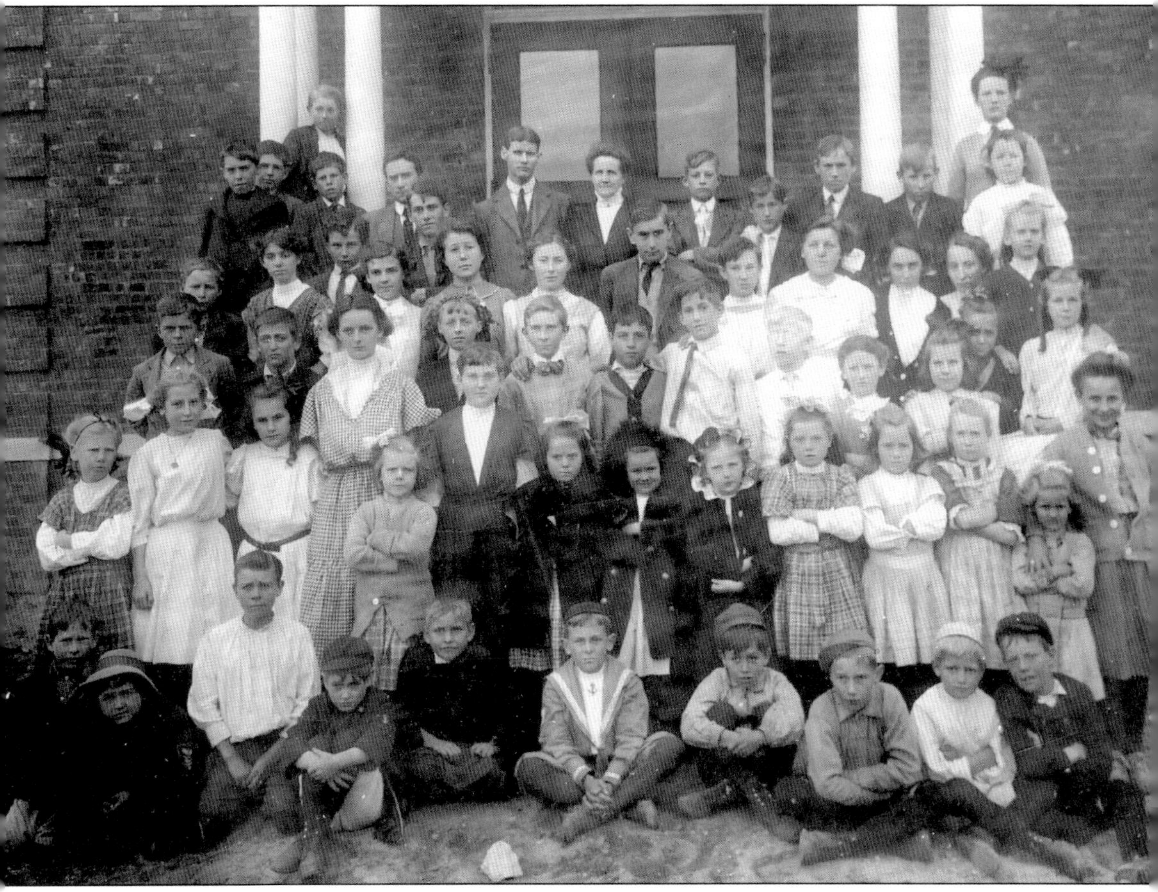

For more than 50 years, students at Belhaven School stood for class pictures on the front steps of the building. The signature double columns of the front facade have always identified the building. This photograph is believed to be the first one taken of students in the new school. Many of the children pictured here are seen in earlier class pictures taken at the Poplar School and at the Sea View School. The building originally had only four classrooms, with two grades assigned to each room. In 1925, the board of education added four rooms to the back, allowing each grade to have its own classroom. Although in the early years ninth-grade classes were held here, no one knows why the building's nameplate in the front gable reads Linwood High School.

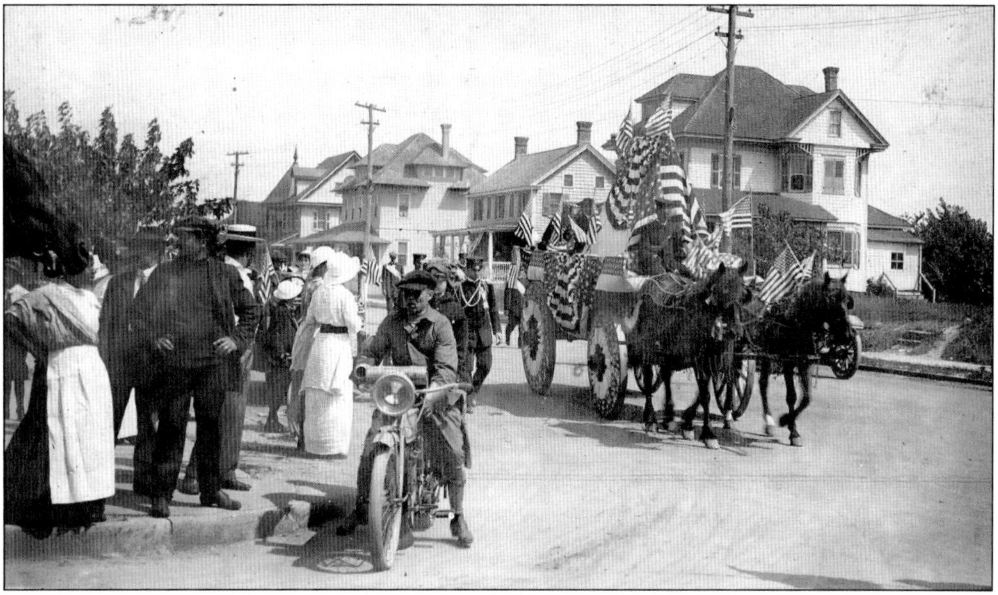

The Patriotic Order of Sons of America had an active chapter in Linwood in the early 20th century. Walter VanSant is shown marching to the right of the motorcyclist in the 1914 Fourth of July parade.

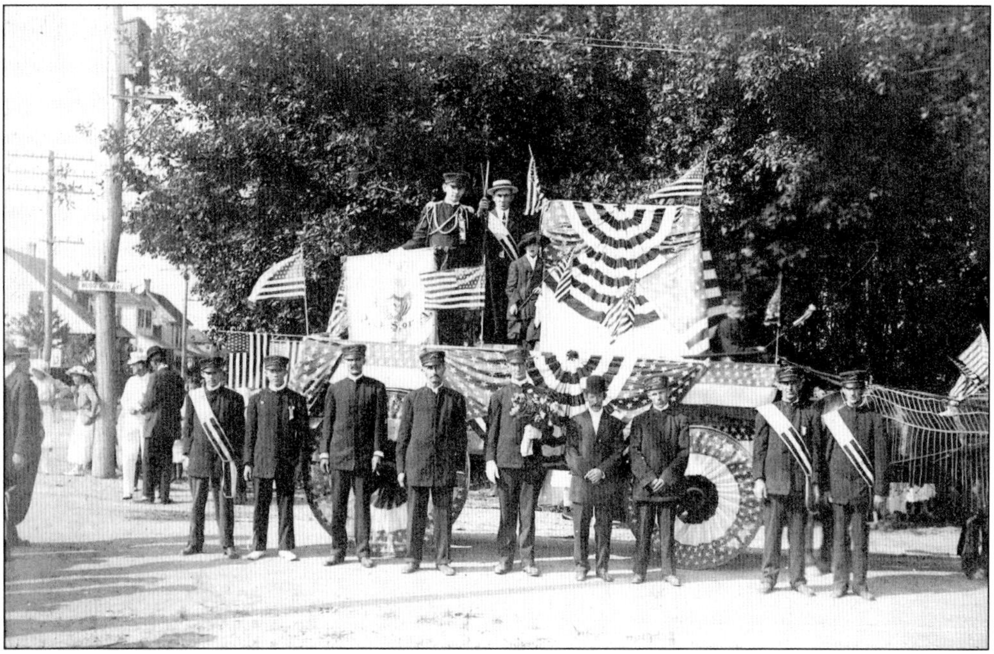

Standing in front of a 1914 Fourth of July float, from the left to right, are the following: (front row) unidentified, Cotten Ireland, Tom Keen, Ben Broadhead, Lawrence Force, ? Robinson, Mulford Potter, Jessie Ad, and Clarence Keeler; (back row) Walter VanSant, John R. VanSant, Harry Garwood, and Joshua Garwood (driver).

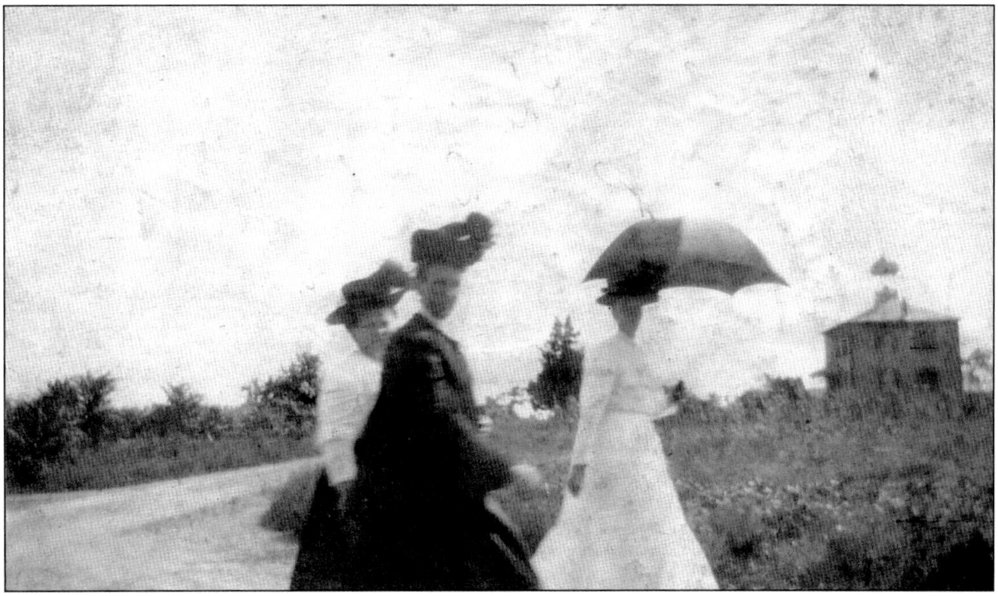

Residents of the borough walked pretty much everywhere they wanted to go. From left to right are Phine Sutton, Clara Carmen, and Priscilla Sutton, walking to the Zion Church over in Bargaintown. The Bargaintown School is on the right.

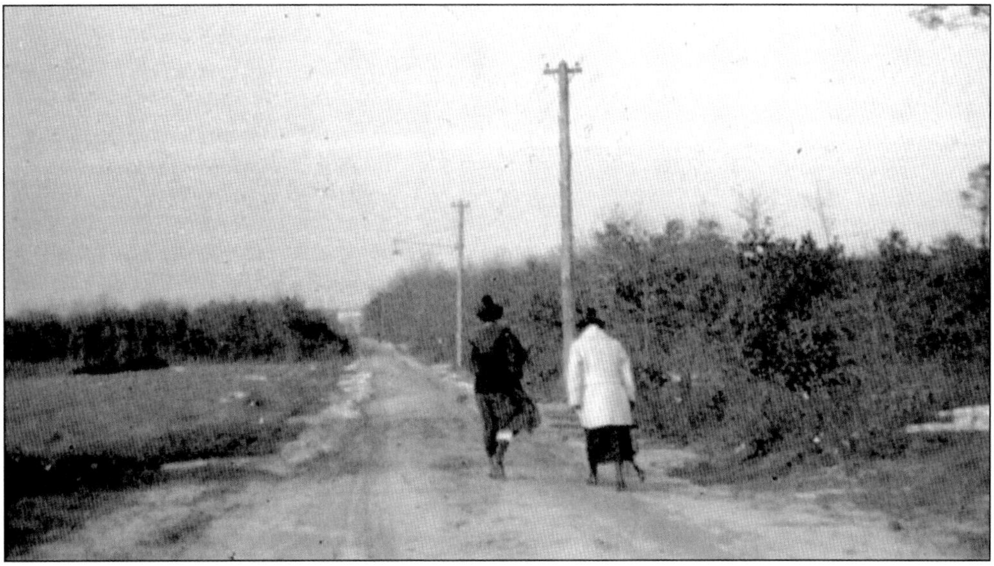

Marie Cavileer and Myrtle Potter walk down Central Avenue on the way to the Mill Pond in 1917.

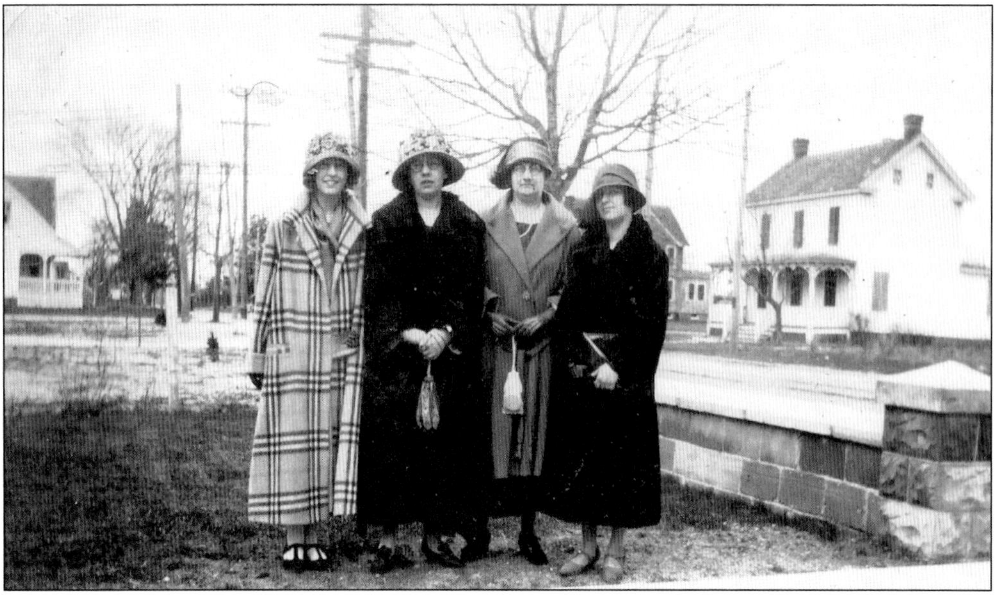

All dressed up for an Easter trip to the boardwalk, from left to right, are Betty Fenton, Lourene Fenton (Betty's mother), Sallie Smith Sparley (Betty's cousin), and Ethel Dry (friend). The Fentons lived in the home built by Lourene's mother, Elizabeth Caroon, on Shore Road in 1905. (Courtesy of Betty Fenton Martin.)

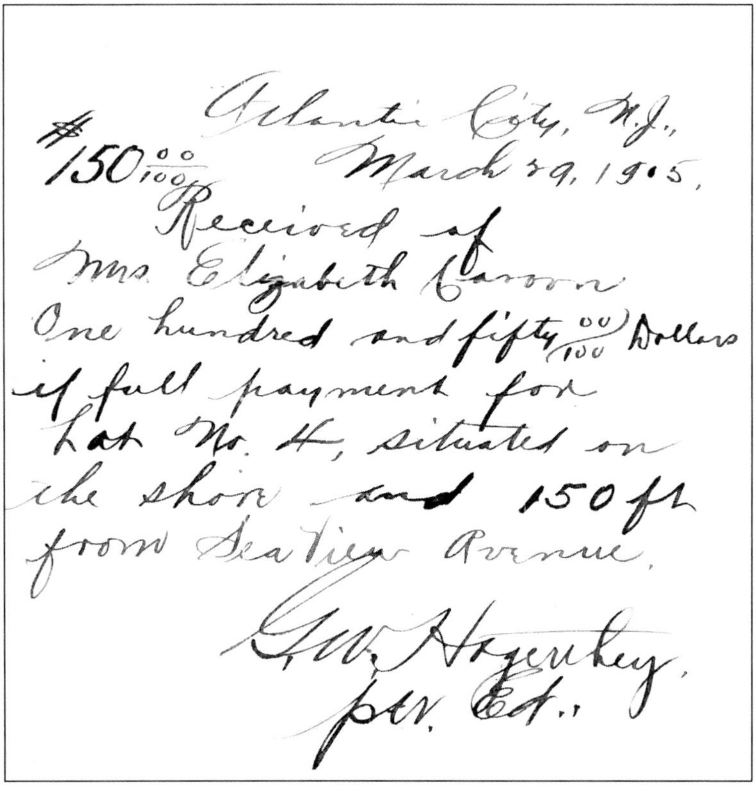

Atlantic City, N.J.,
\$150 00/100 March 29, 1905.
Received of
Mrs. Elizabeth Caroon
One hundred and fifty 00/100 Dollars
in full payment for
Lot No. 4, situated on
the shore road 150 ft
from Seaview Avenue.
G.W. Hagerthey.
per. Ed..

Elizabeth Caroon purchased the land for her home from George W. Hagerthey. This receipt gives some idea of the cost of buying land in Linwood in the early 20th century. (Courtesy of Betty Fenton Martin.)

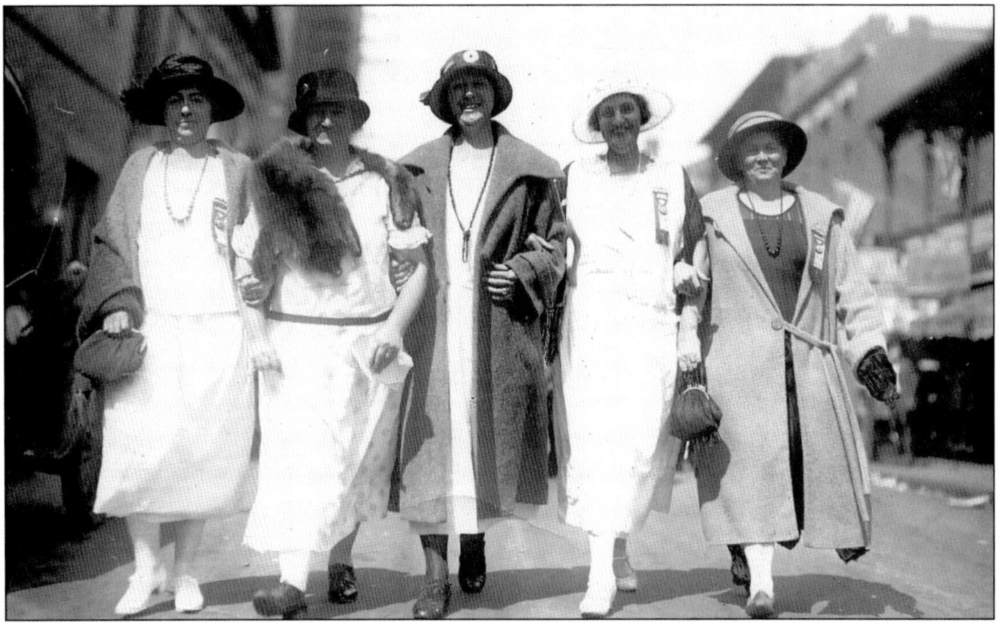

Some Linwood members of the Daughters of the American Revolution enjoyed a day in Ocean City. From left to right, in this undated photograph, are Anna Horan Risley, Clara Wolfbrandt, Margaret Scull, Florence James, and Sally Sutton Keeler.

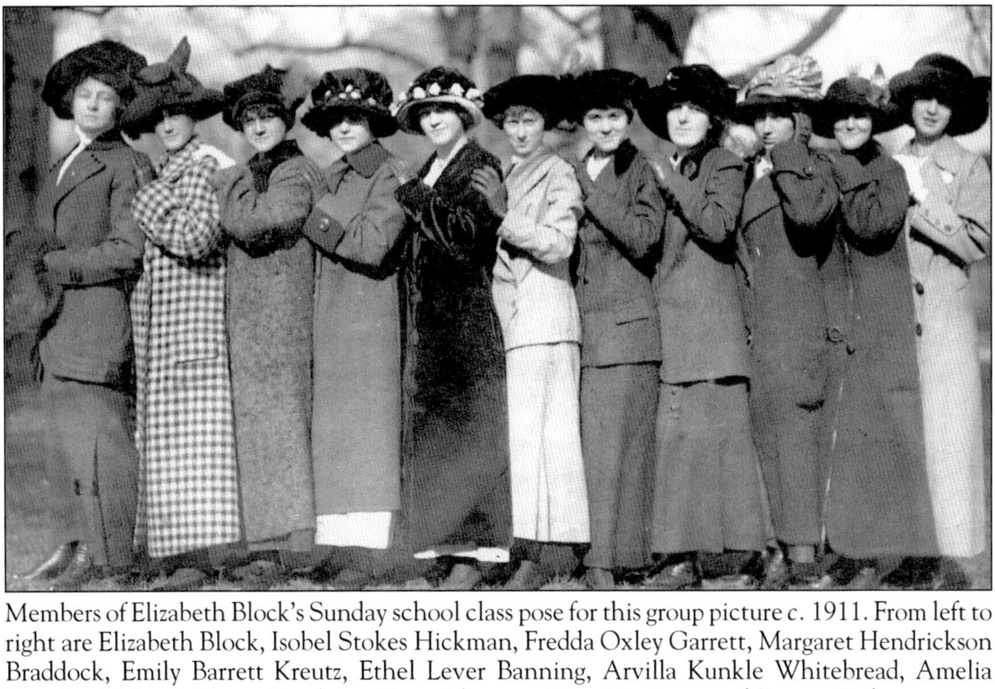

Members of Elizabeth Block's Sunday school class pose for this group picture c. 1911. From left to right are Elizabeth Block, Isobel Stokes Hickman, Fredda Oxley Garrett, Margaret Hendrickson Braddock, Emily Barrett Kreutz, Ethel Lever Banning, Arvilla Kunkle Whitebread, Amelia Doughty Nyborg, Hanna Steelman Gant, Florence Price VanSant, and Emma Graham.

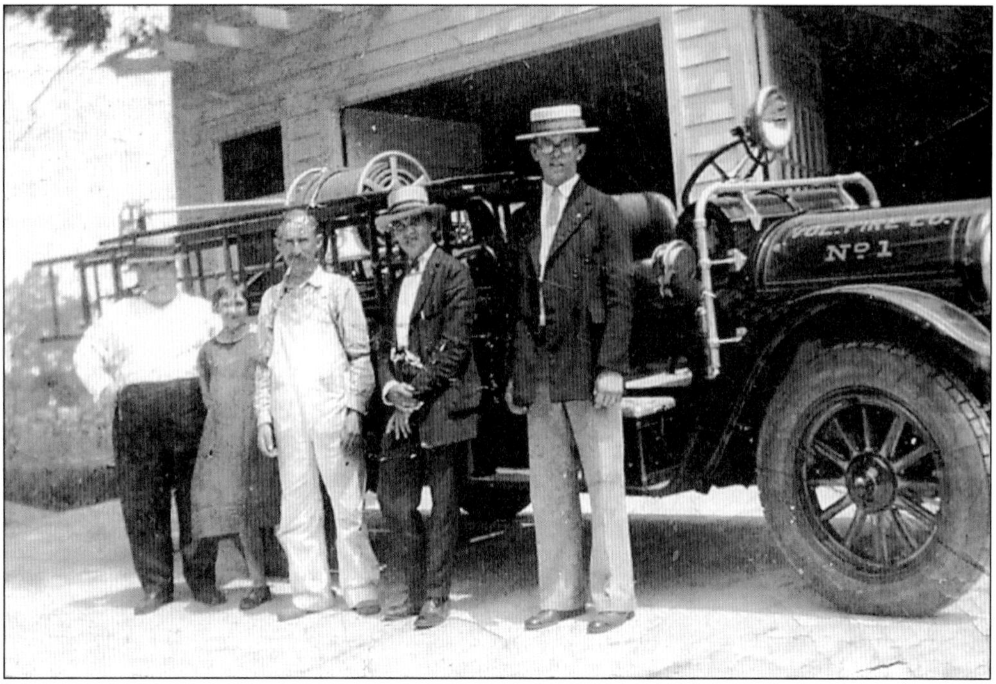

The Linwood Volunteer Fire Company was organized in 1924. Pictured in front of the new pumper c. 1929, from left to right, are Jake Naglee, Ethel Naglee, unidentified, Jake Naglee Jr., and Winfred VanSant.

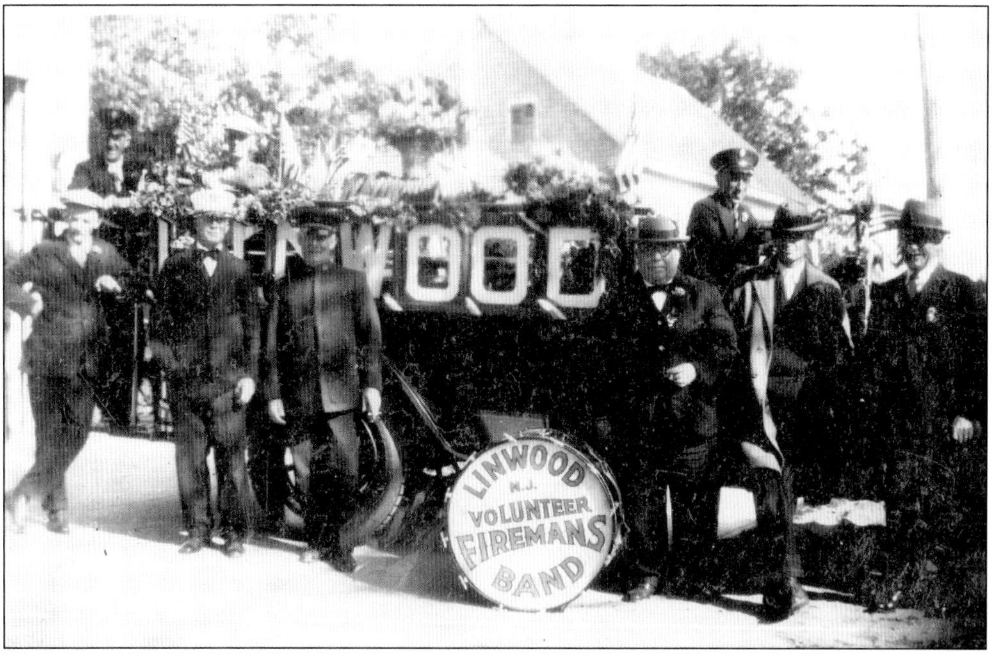

Members of the Linwood Volunteer Fireman's Band c. 1928 pose by the firehouse and city hall. From left to right are Mercer H. Wilson, a freeholder; Edmond Somers; Walter Scull; J.H. Naglee Sr., a judge; Lawrence Force; Delbert Dubois; Clarence Potter, seated; George Dunbar; and John Marlsboro.

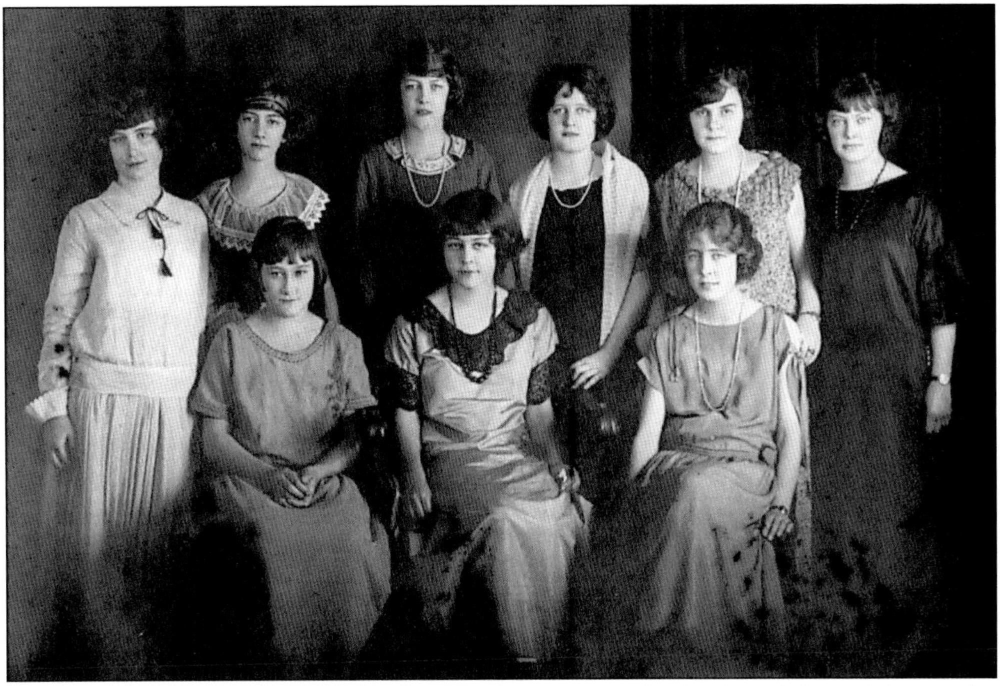

The new fire department held a beauty contest to raise funds. From left to right are the following: (front row) Helena Scull, second runner-up; Verna Sowers, winner; and Elizabeth Fenton, first runner-up; (back row) Emma Burroughs, Joetta Wilson, Amy Millagin, Abbie Sanders, Mildred VanSant, and Eleanor Camp.

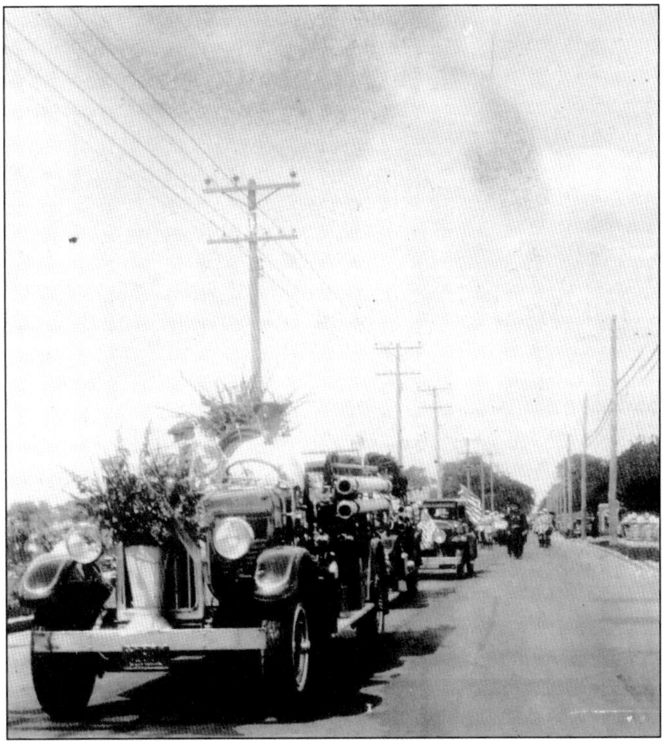

The new 1930 Hahn fire truck is proudly displayed in a parade down Shore Road.

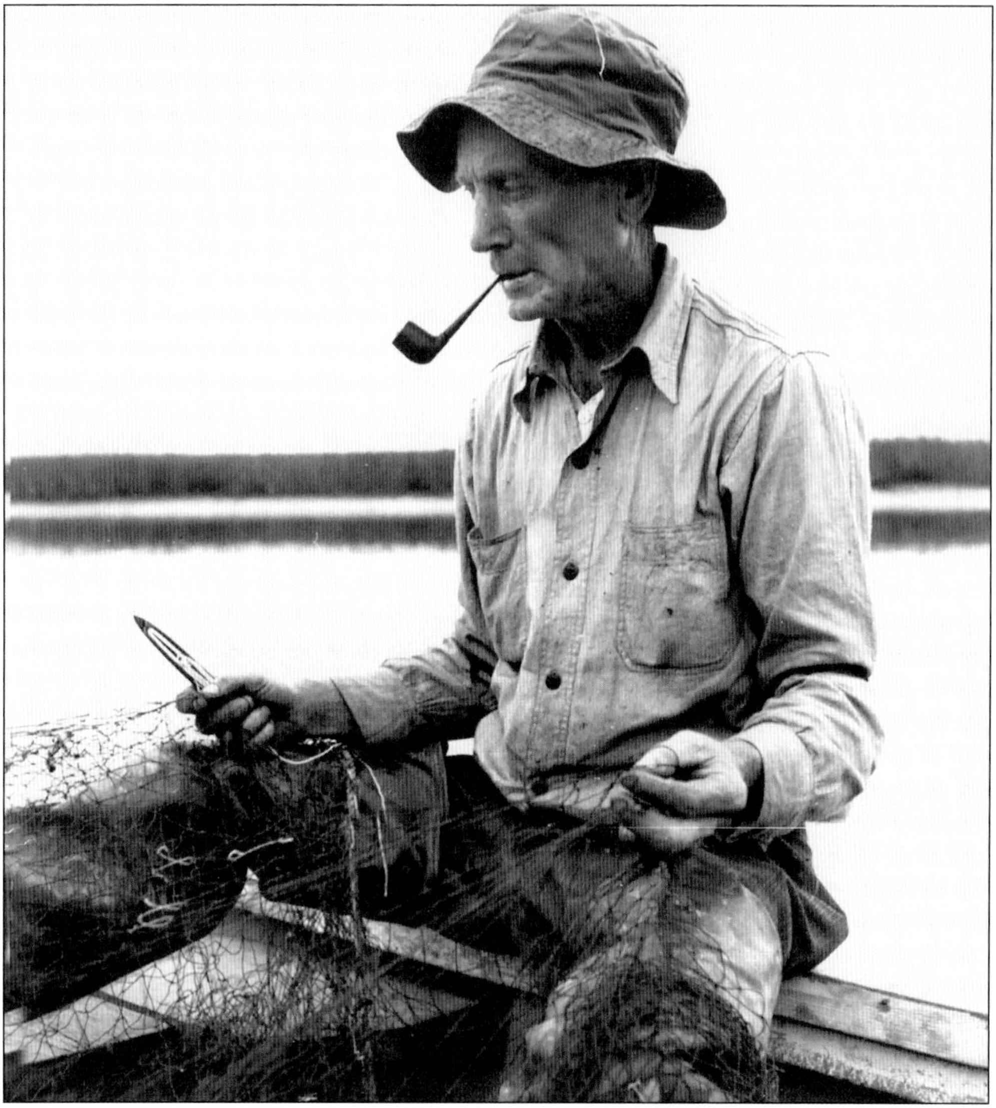

Up to the mid-1900s, there was still enough marine life in Scull's Bay to enable baymen to earn a decent living. This bayman working on his nets was caught in a classic pose by Win Boileau *c.* 1939. Many local families were able to survive the Great Depression on the food they brought home from the bay.

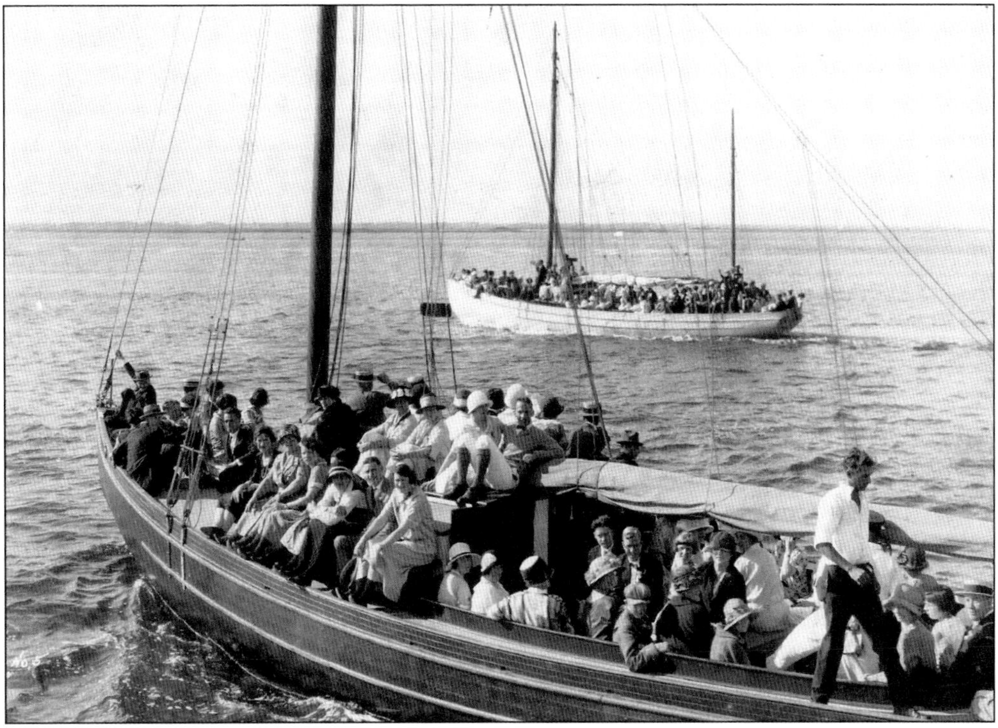

Sailing in the bay and moonlight cruises were popular activities at the shore, and boat captains made the most of that popularity. Capt. Lewis Risley, whose boat appears in the background (above), had a long career on the water. His new boats were always named *Cap Lew*. His nephew L. Chattin Risley stands at the wheel of his own boat (below).

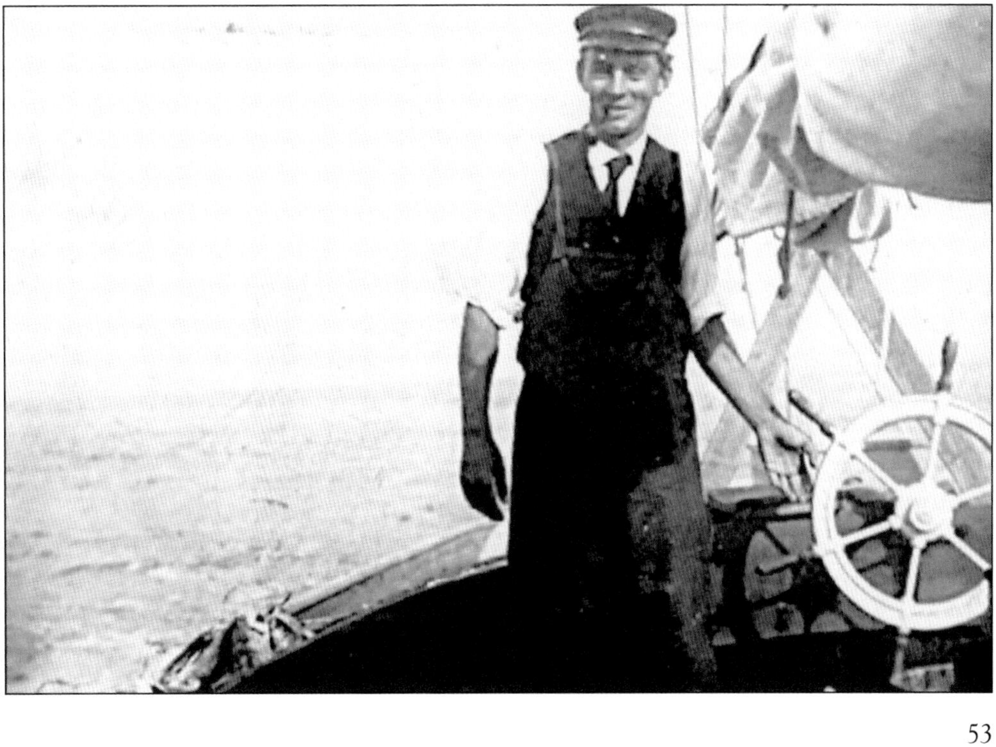

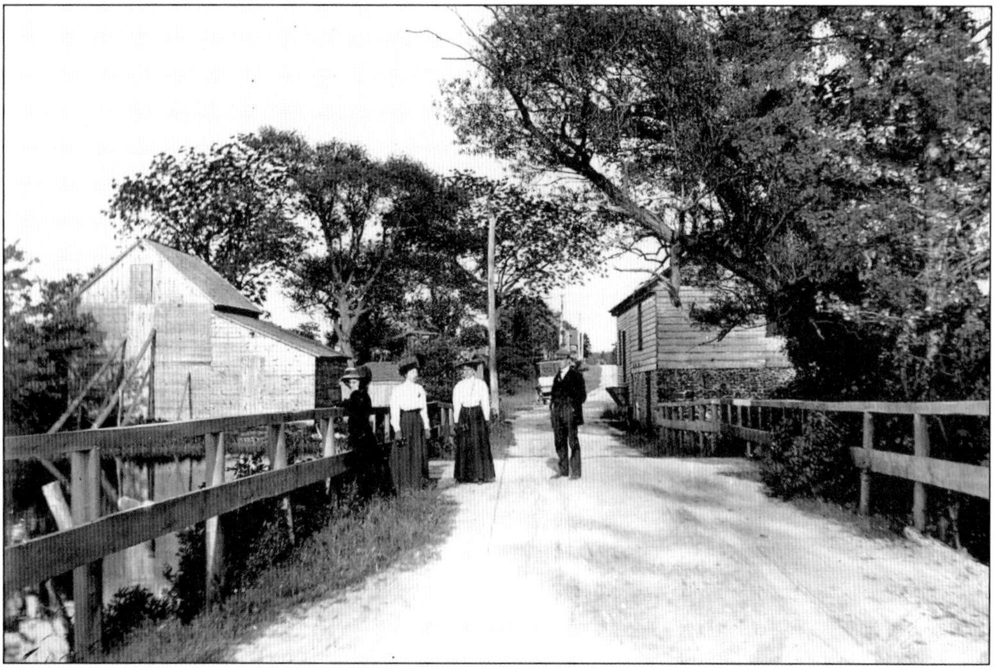

The Central Avenue Mill Pond was an important business center for many generations. The first gristmill was built here by James "the Miller" Somers in the early 18th century. This 1910 photograph shows the second mill built on the site (right). The icehouse of Daniel Collins (left) continued in business until 1917. Another sawmill was located across the pond in Bargaintown. (Courtesy of ACHS.)

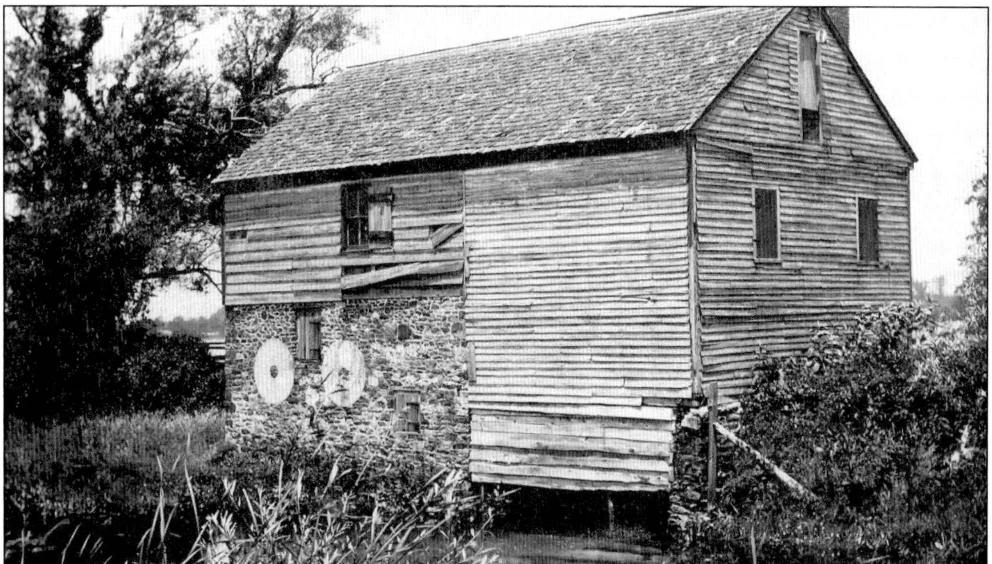

The pond was a year-round recreational area for picnics, swimming, and skating. The millstones shown in the side wall of the mill came from the original 18th-century gristmill. By 1920, the old mill was badly deteriorated and, a few years later, it burned down.

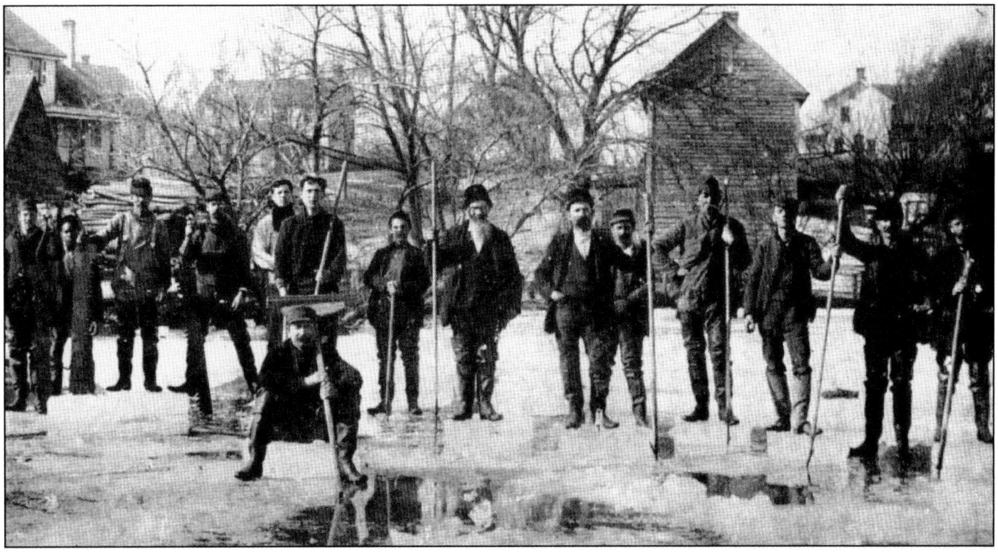

Ice cutting was a major Mill Pond industry. From left to right, the ice cutters are as follows: (front row) Joseph Price; (back row) Joseph Thoman, Joshua Tinley, Hosea Sutton, Frank Hackett, Herman Schauffler, Robert Lloyd, John Doughty, Fred Myers, Joshua Dueble, William Byrd, Smith Sutton, Joshua Garwood, Benjamin Sutton, and Gus Brower.

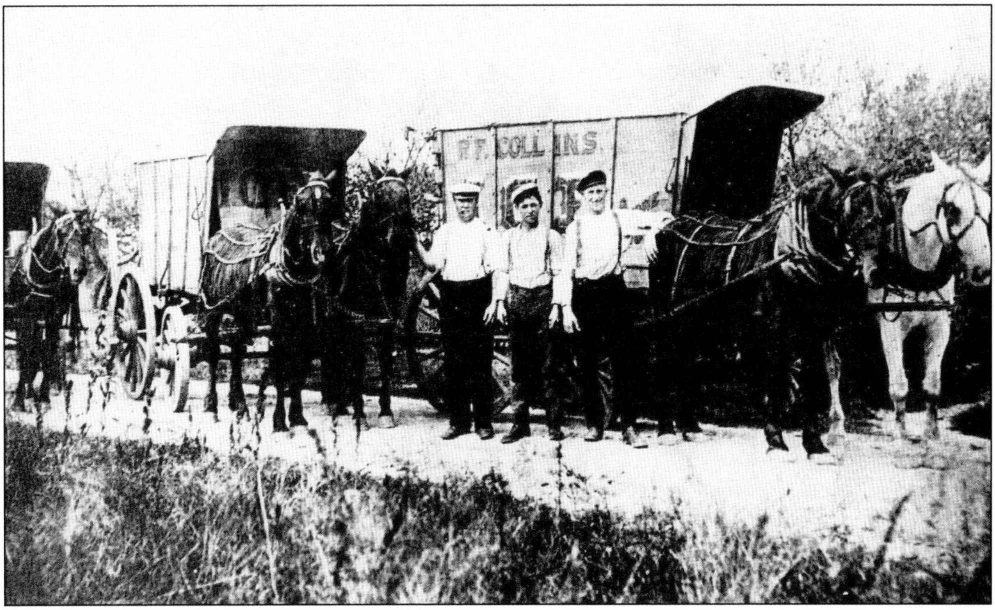

The Collins brothers delivered ice by horse-drawn wagons to nearly 200 customers on the mainland and in Atlantic City. From left to right are drivers Henry Rankin of Bargaintown, Roy Collins of Bakersville, and William Barrett of Linwood. (Courtesy of ACHS.)

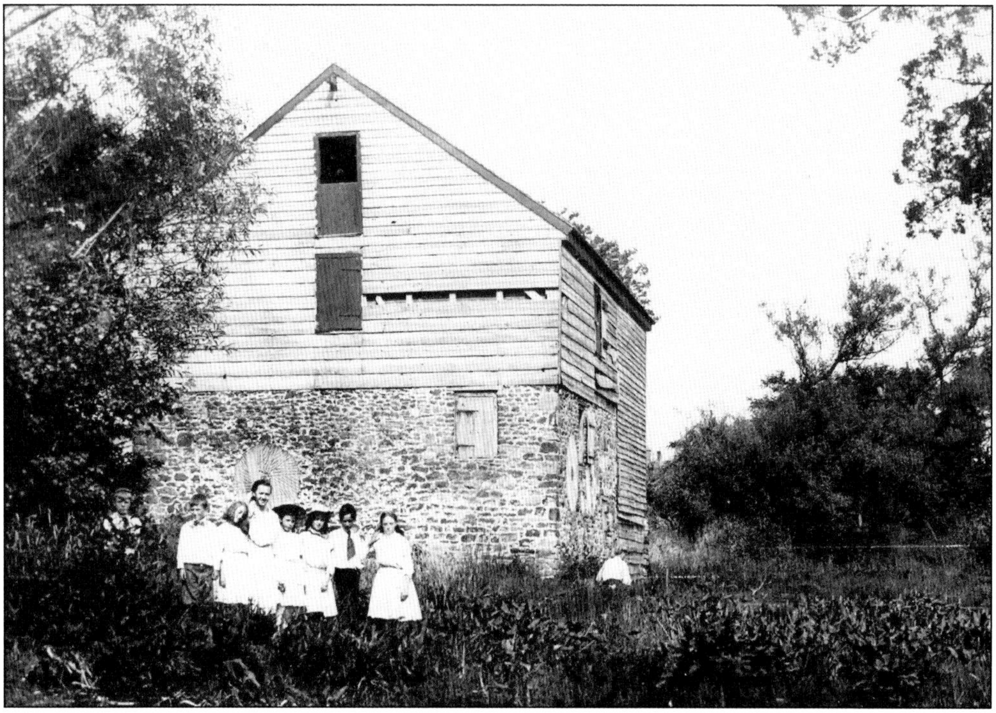

The Mill Pond was a picturesque spot for photographs of group activities and postcard views.

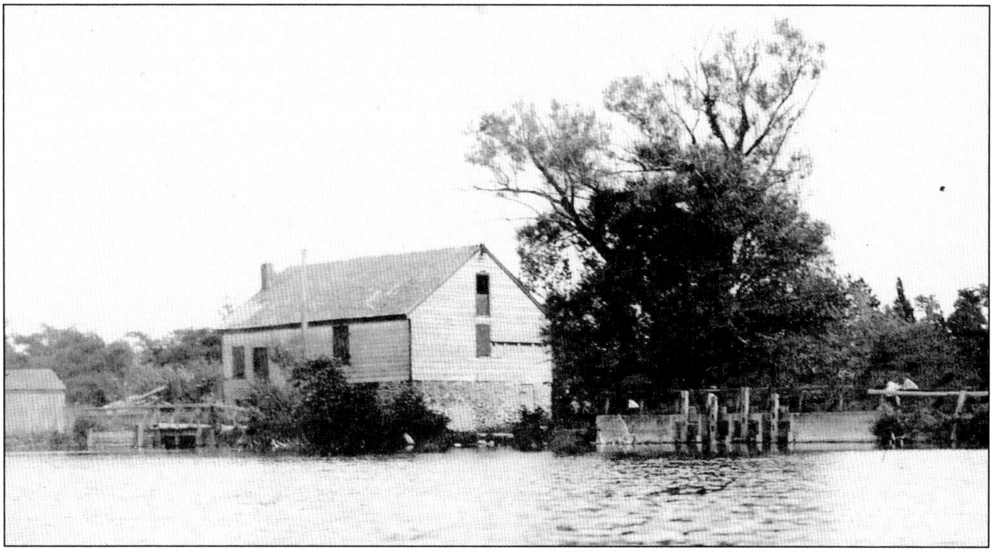

On June 18, 1921, the Linwood council received a petition from the Women's Christian Temperance Union that read, "The WCTU of Northfield petition your council to take some action to abate the nuisance at the gristmill at Bargaintown dam. We are informed people are awakened at 2 and 3 o'clock in the morning by screaming and laughing coming from the place, and we feel such a place should not exist in our community. Thanking you in advance for any action you might take to abate this nuisance."

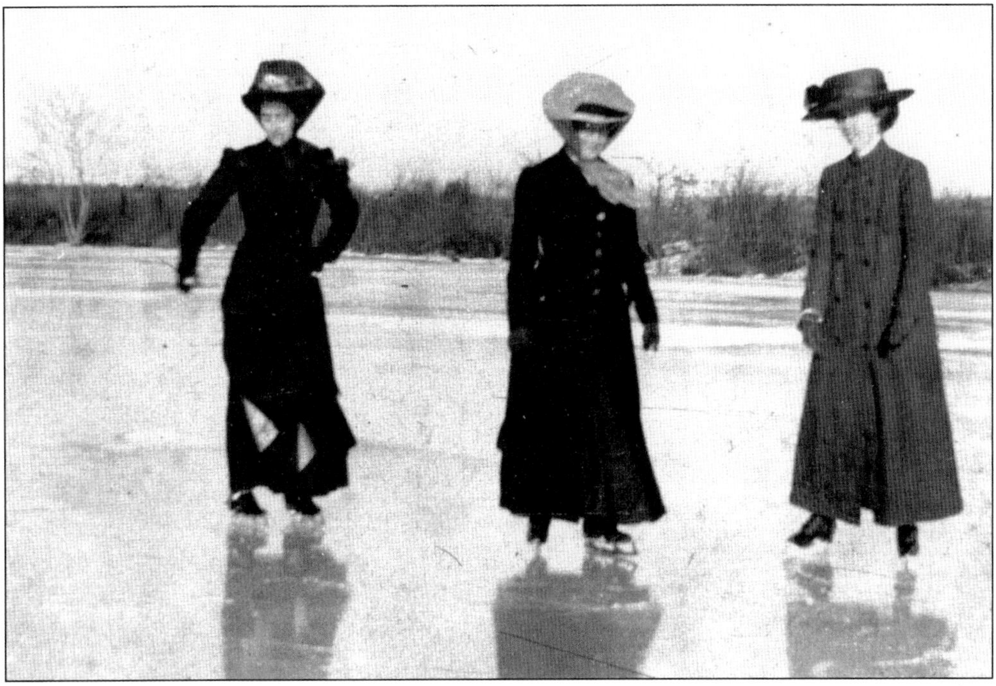

Members of the Farish family who lived just up the street provide a picturesque scene as they enjoy themselves on the ice in this *c.* 1890 photograph.

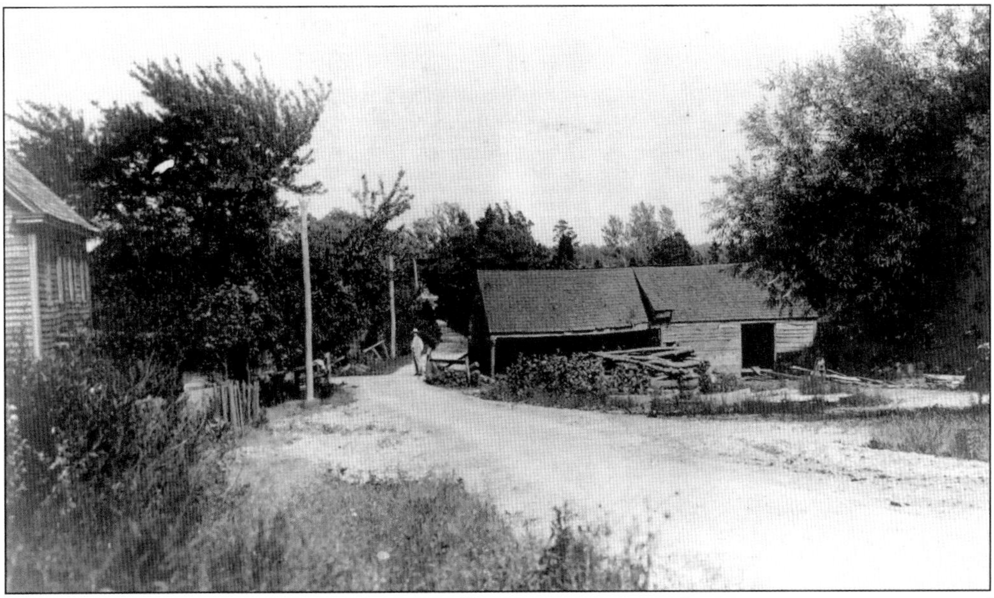

This view facing eastward shows the sawmill in Bargaintown and an interesting perspective of Central Avenue. Also shown is the building that served as the customs house for the port of Bargaintown after Robert Risley was appointed customs collector in 1845.

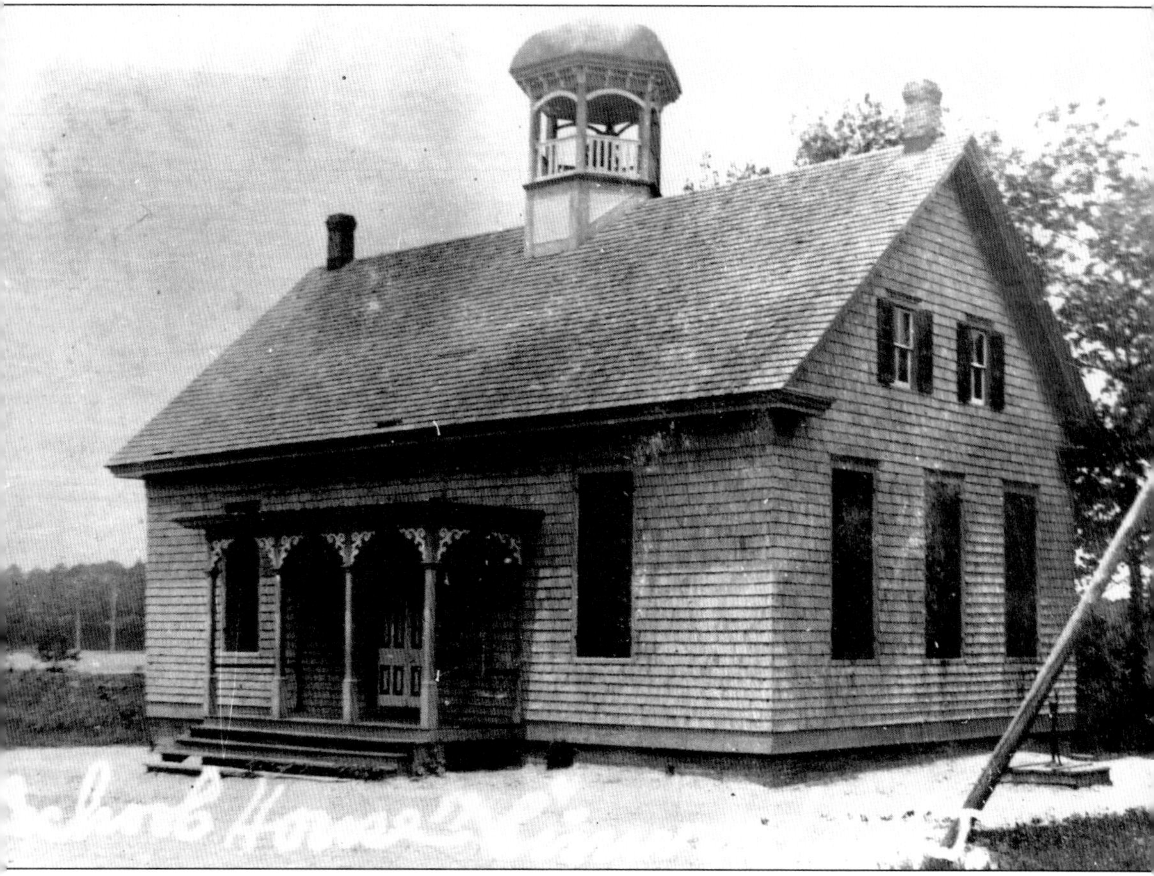

When Belhaven School opened, the borough of Linwood purchased the old School No. 1 building for $1. This historic treasure has been in continuous public use since it was built in 1873. It was a school from 1873 to 1908. Then, the building was used as borough hall and, later, it was used as city hall until 1965. When Linwood built a new city hall, the Linwood library moved into the old school. A new library opened in the old Crestlea Park School in 1987 and the building then became the headquarters and museum for the Linwood Historical Society. The city council removed the cupola sometime during the 1930s and gave the bell to the Methodist Camp in Seaville. After a nationwide search for a replacement, the historical society traded the replacement to bring back the original bell and put it on display. In 1986, the building was listed on the National Register of Historic Places.

Three

PROPRIETORS AND PROPERTIES

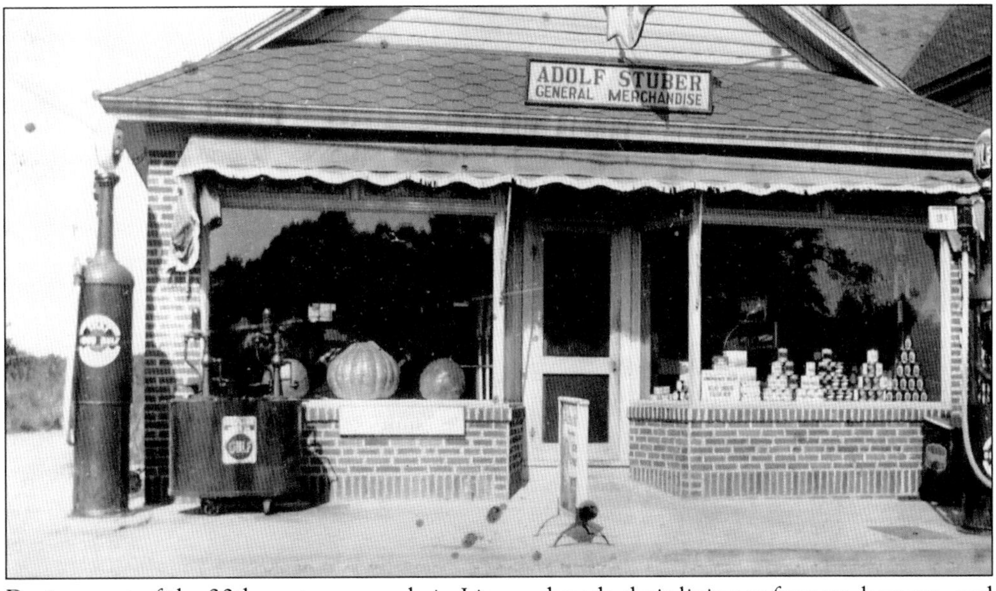

During most of the 20th century, people in Linwood made their living as farmers, baymen, and as shop owners providing services to the community. Of the many corner stores, only Stuber's old store survived and celebrated its 100th anniversary as the Linwood Market in 2001. Barely three acres of grape arbors remained to give testimony to the town's agricultural history as the 21st century began. The bay no longer provides the rich harvests so prevalent in 1900, but recreational fishing and some clamming are still popular on Scull's Bay. Fortunately, many photographs were saved to tell the stories of these old proprietors and their properties.

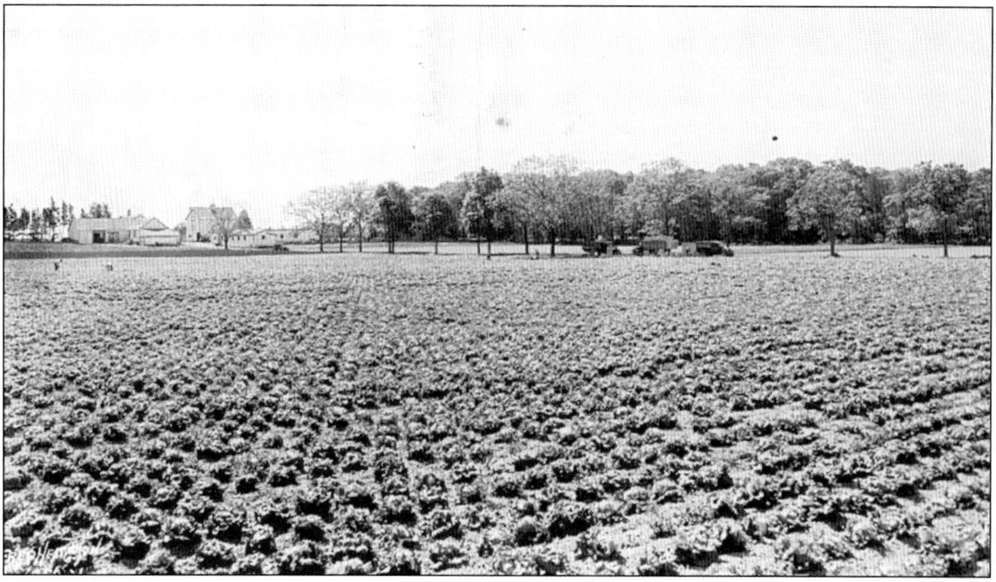

The Dennis Farm was originally part of an 18th-century plantation owned by John Scull, and it was a productive operation well into the 20th century. Owned by several Atlantic City hoteliers over the years, it was known for the production of lettuce and other vegetables for the hotel restaurants. In 1945, it became part of the Brighton Farms. The new owners were dairy farmers who grew hay and alfalfa instead of vegetables. The charming barns that are seen in the distance (above) are also shown in a closeup view (below).

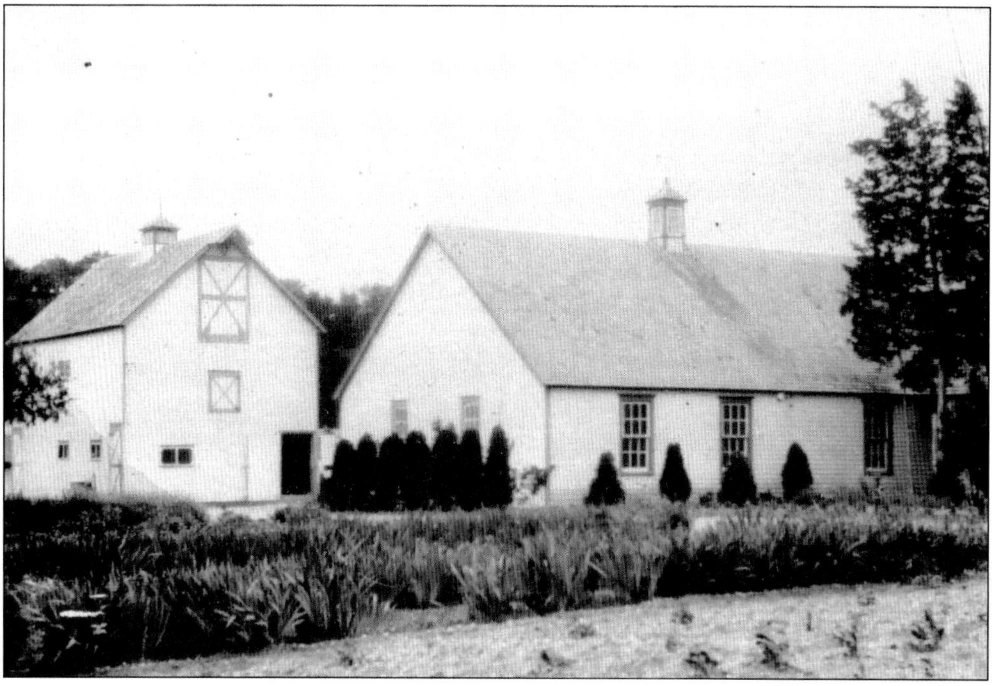

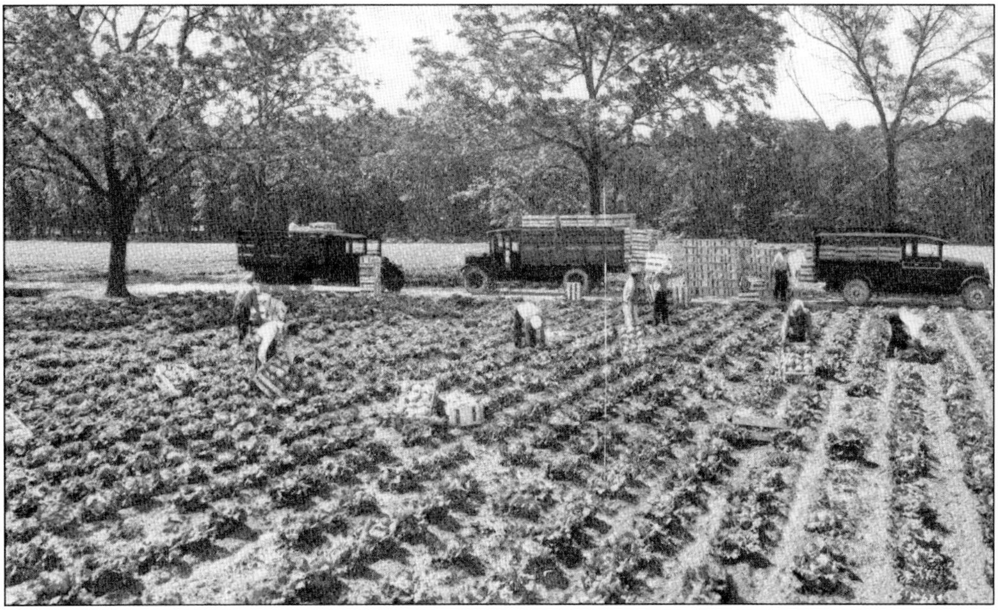

The 1920s postcard (above) shows farmworkers picking lettuce. No doubt the postcard was popular among the guests at the Dennis Hotel. Farm produce makes an interesting display in the hotel lobby (below).

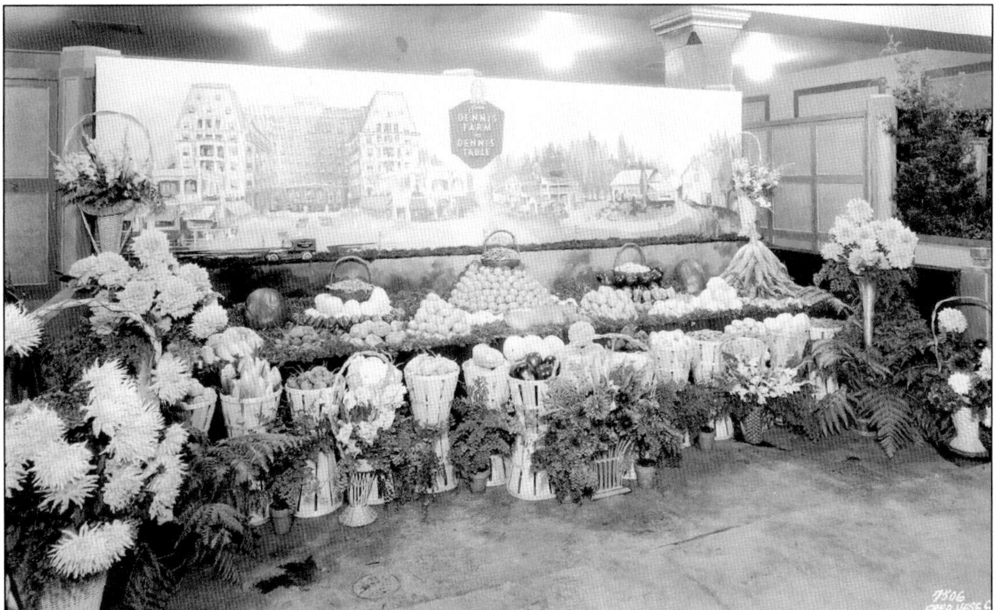

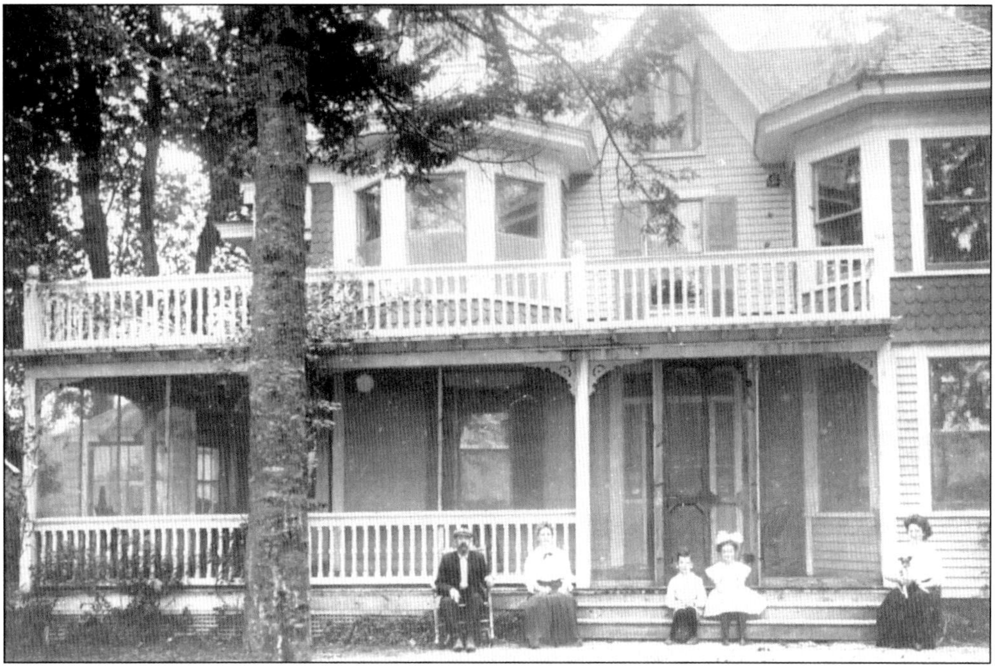

In 1895, the Dennis Farm was owned by hotelier Lewis T. Bryant. Bryant built a huge new home and called it Waverly, after his hotel. Both his home and the hotel are gone now, but the old brick farmhouse is one of the town's celebrated historic homes. From left to right in this 1908 photograph are Thomas and Margaret Allen, their son Everett, a niece Altha Allen, and their daughter Martha.

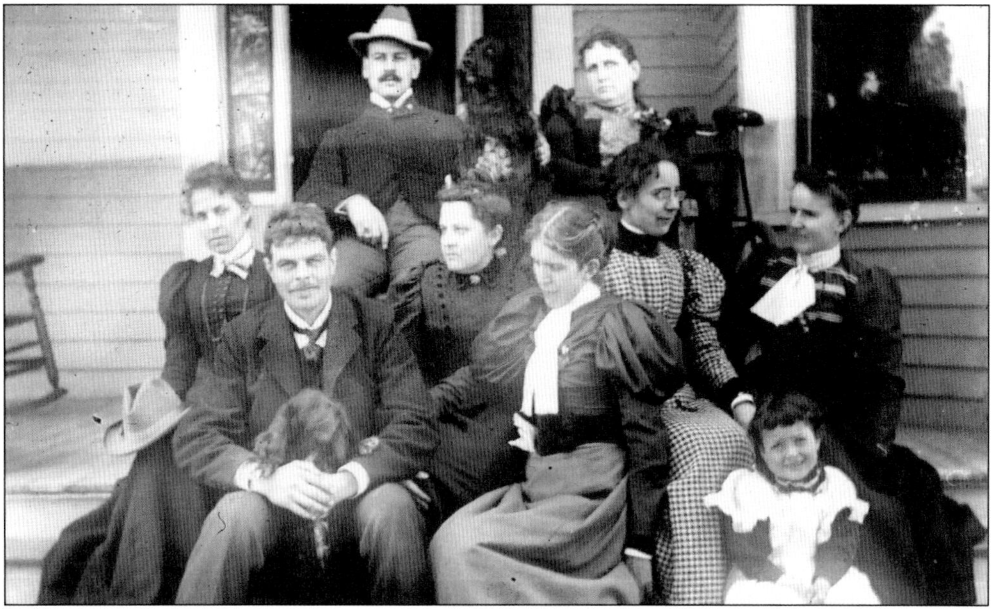

Gathered on the front porch, from left to right, are the following: (front row) Lewis T. Bryant, unidentified, and Elizabeth Allen; (middle row) Florence Nelson, Alberta Underwood, Mrs. Shriner, and Emma Underwood; (back row) Hubert Moore and Mrs. Silas Moore. (Courtesy of ACHS.)

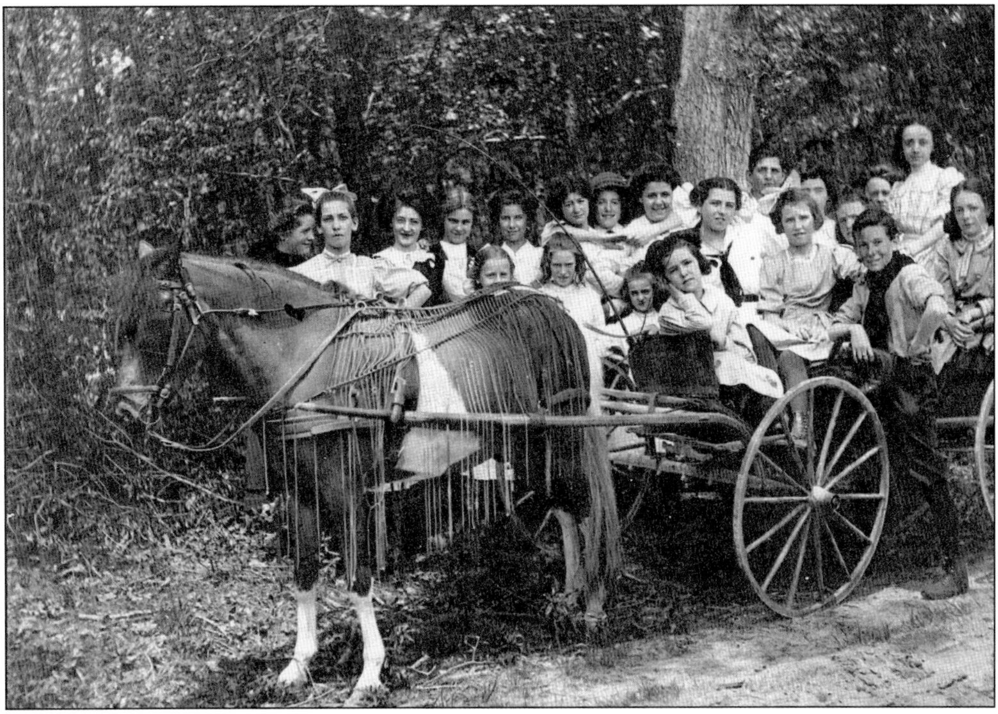

The Dennis Farm picnic grounds were popular among hotel guests and church groups alike. This group from St. Nicholas Church in Atlantic City seems to be having a wonderful time. The picture was taken by Father McFadden on June 17, 1906. The picnic grounds were large, and the facility was open to all free of charge.

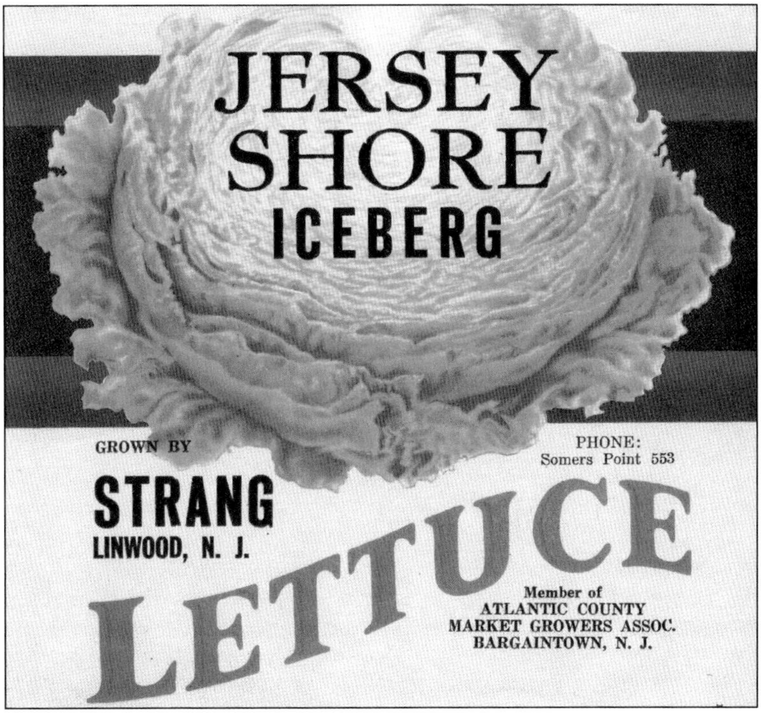

Earl Strang had a family farm off Poplar Avenue in the mid-1900s. His big crop was Jersey Shore iceberg lettuce. Strang also farmed several other parcels located throughout the city.

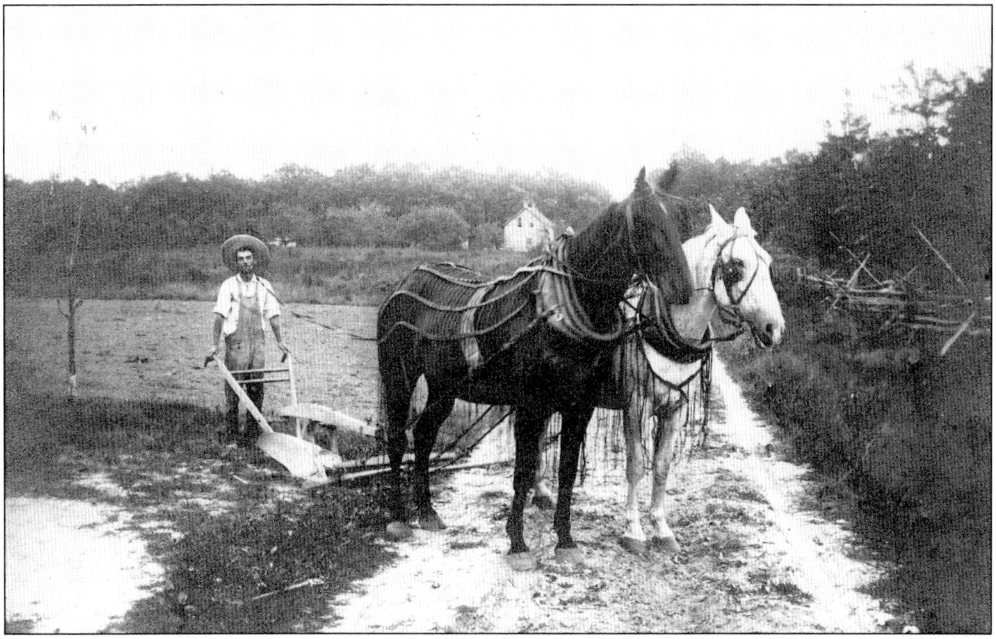

Joshua Garwood's farm, located on Central Avenue, was typical of the small farms throughout the town. This scene is about where the Village at Linwood and the Linwood Convalescent Center are now located. Garwood's family had a long history in Linwood. His father, Capt. Japhet Garwood, was a Leedsville ship captain who transported supplies for the government during the Civil War.

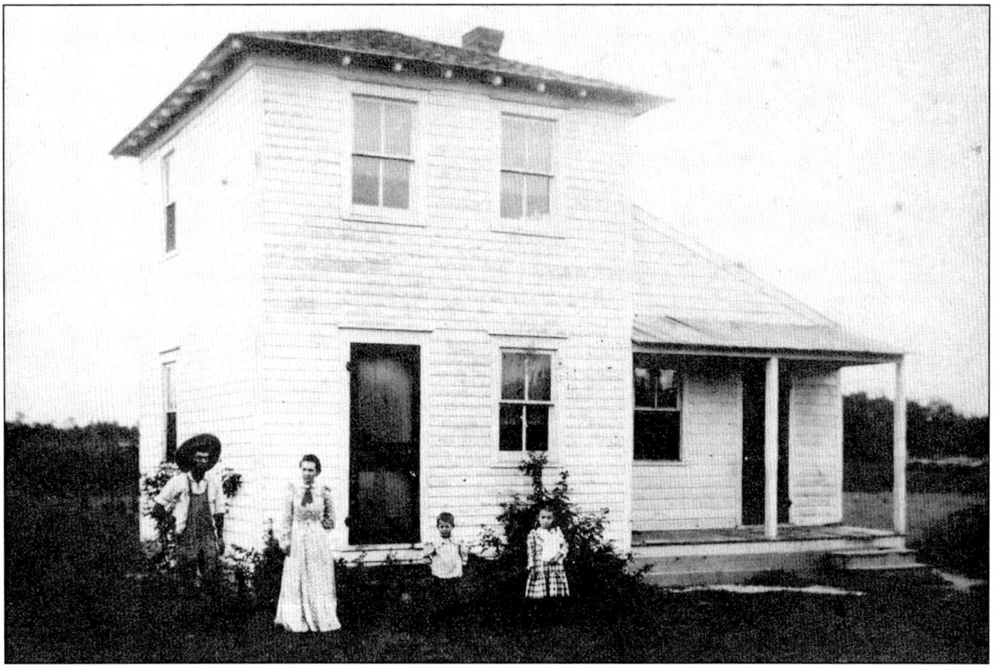

Members of the Garwood family are shown in front of their home. From left to right are Joshua and Roxanna Steelman Garwood and their children, Japhet and Annie. Annie later married Mulford Potter, son of blacksmith Harry Potter.

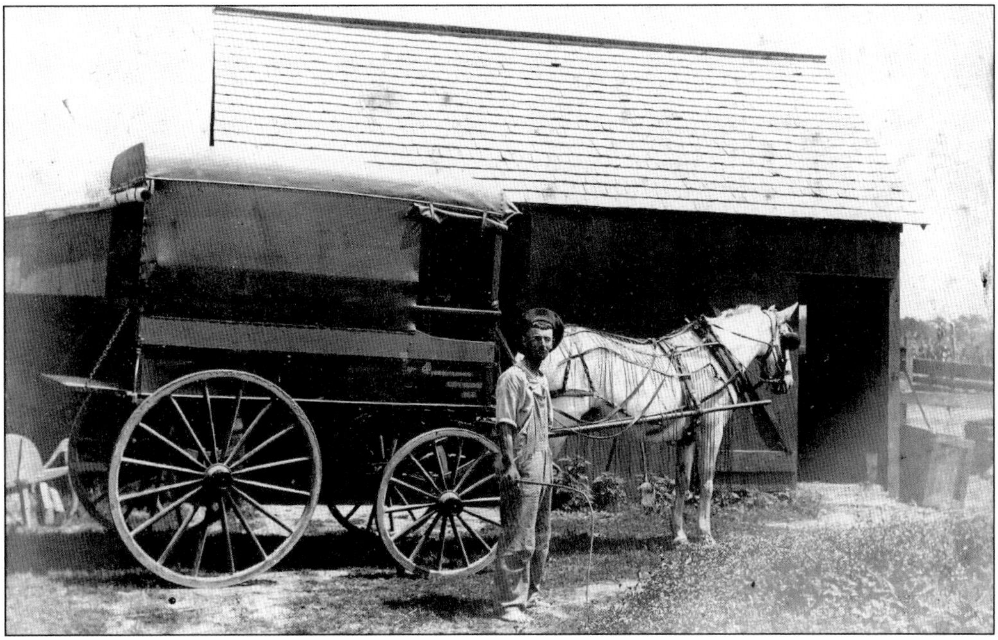

Joshua Garwood (above) had an altercation one day with a horse that was a special favorite of his son, Japhet. It seems that the horse kicked Joshua and he was so angry that he sold it that very day. When Japhet, age 14, came home from school and found the horse gone, he left home himself and went to Atlantic City to live with relatives. Japhet and his sister, Annie, are shown below. (Courtesy of Byron Garwood.)

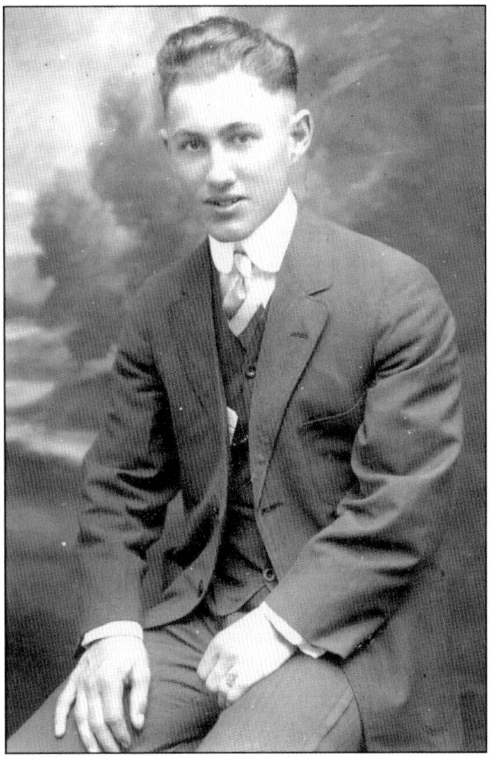

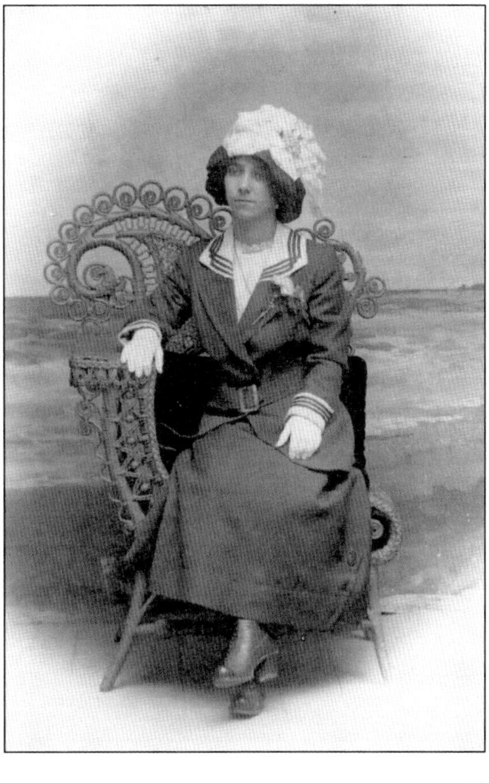

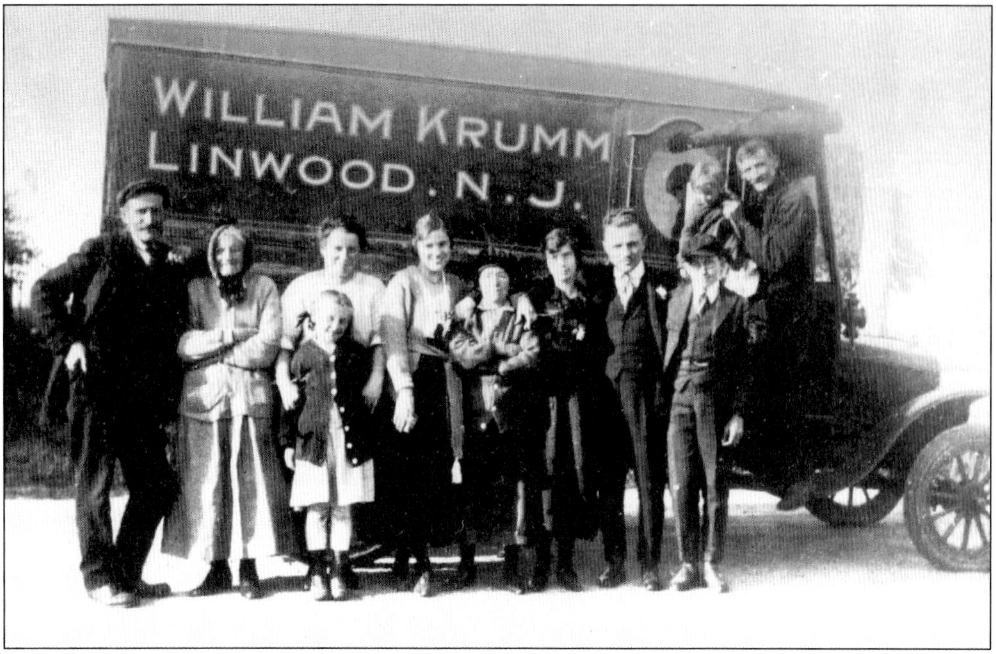

John George William Krumm came from Germany in 1882 with his wife, Caroline, and six children. He bought 50 acres of land and became a market gardener. The Krumms took products to Atlantic City and sold them on the street corner from the back of their wagons. From left to right are George, Caroline, Sophia, Catherine (in front), Irene, Minnie, Gertrude, two unidentified persons, and William, holding Cora.

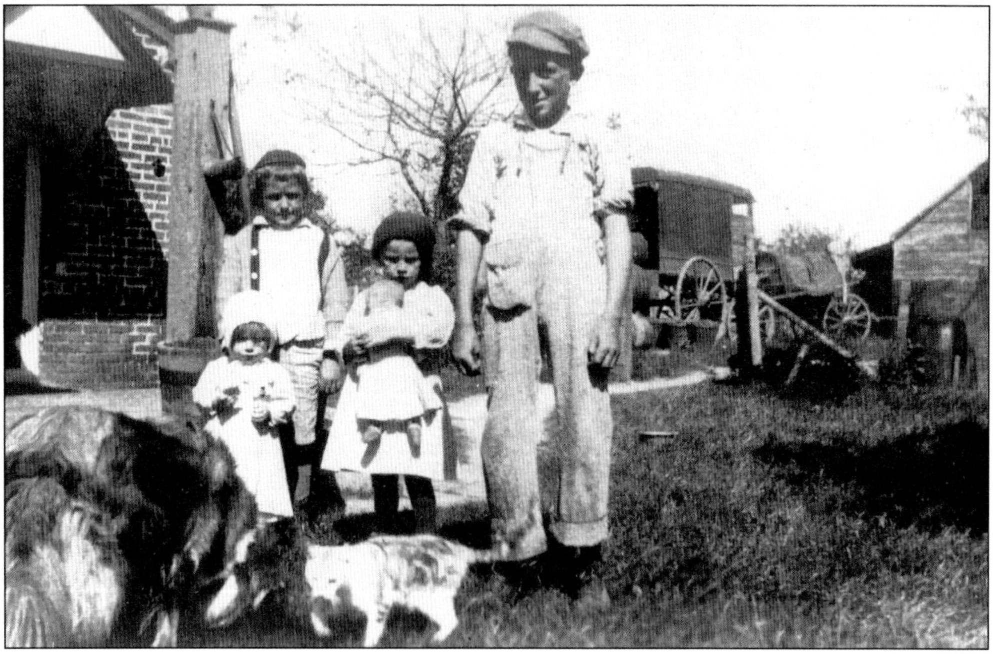

The old Somers property, which John George Krumm bought, stretched from Patcong Creek to the railroad tracks. In 1927, William Krumm donated land for the construction of part of Route 9. Some of John George's children are pictured in this earlier photograph.

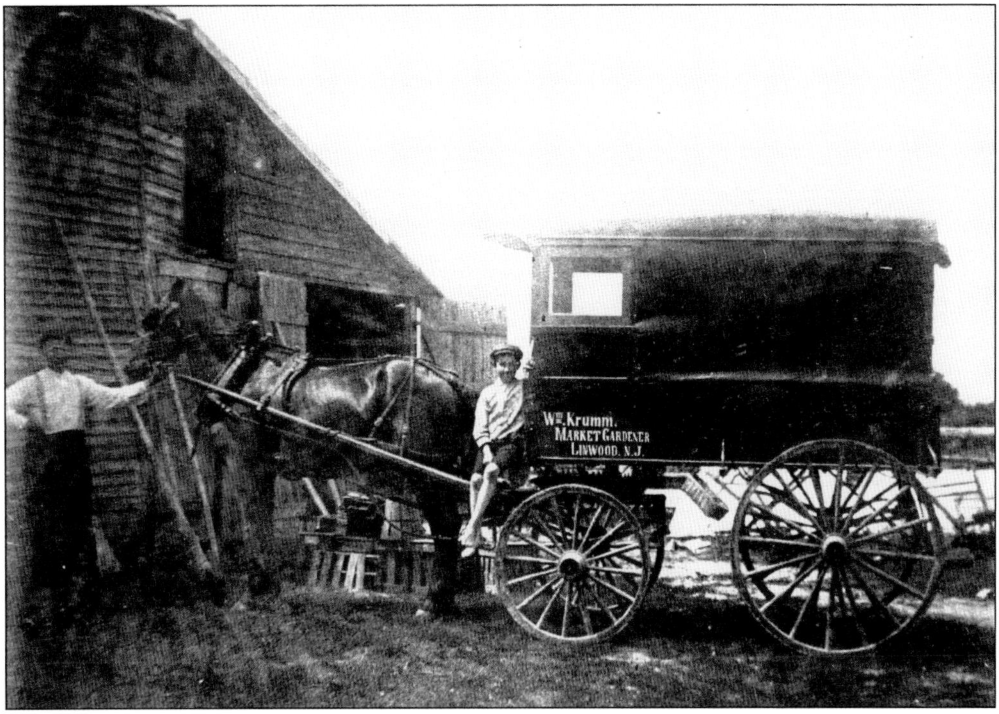

In 1912, John Krumm's son William (left) began to grow grapes and Seaview Winery was born. The company delivered wine to Atlantic City and sold it curbside from barrels carried in the back of a delivery wagon similar to the vegetable wagon above, but smaller. People brought jugs to the curb to be filled. The winery survived Prohibition by selling cooking wine and sherry, the only products permitted by the Volstead Act. The company's grape jelly was also a great favorite. The winery stopped retail production in 1975.

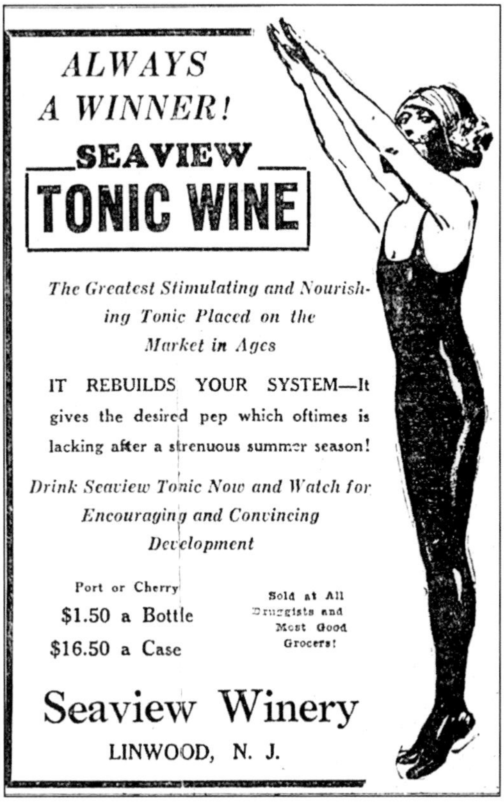

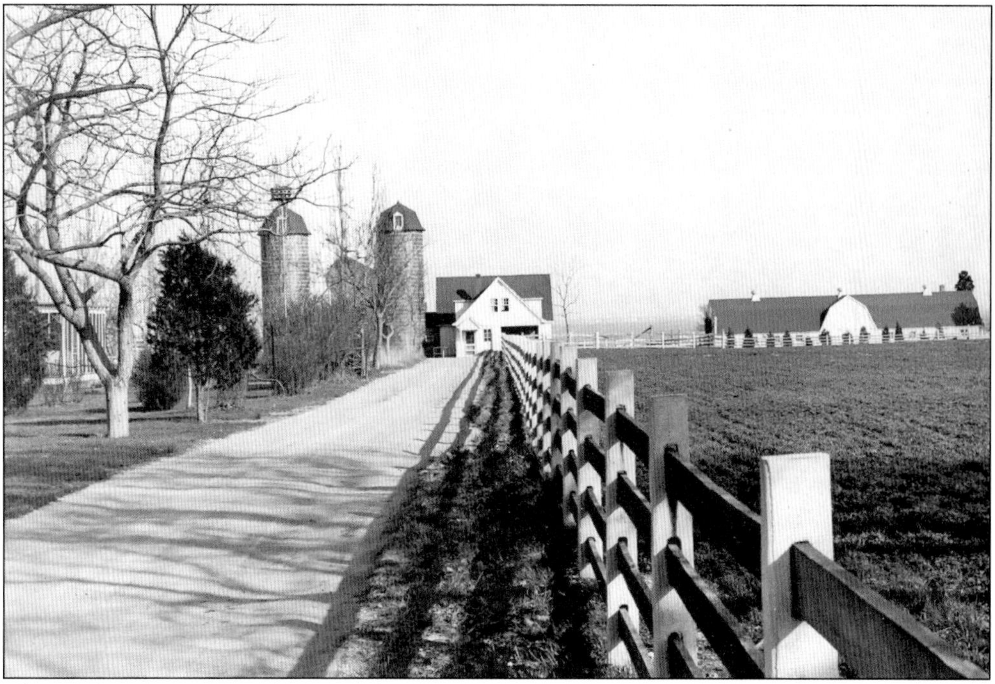

The Brighton Farms on Shore Road was known for milk production from its Guernsey herds. After a disastrous fire in the early 1950s, the farm went out of business. The farm lane to the barns is all that is left here and is now Country Club Drive.

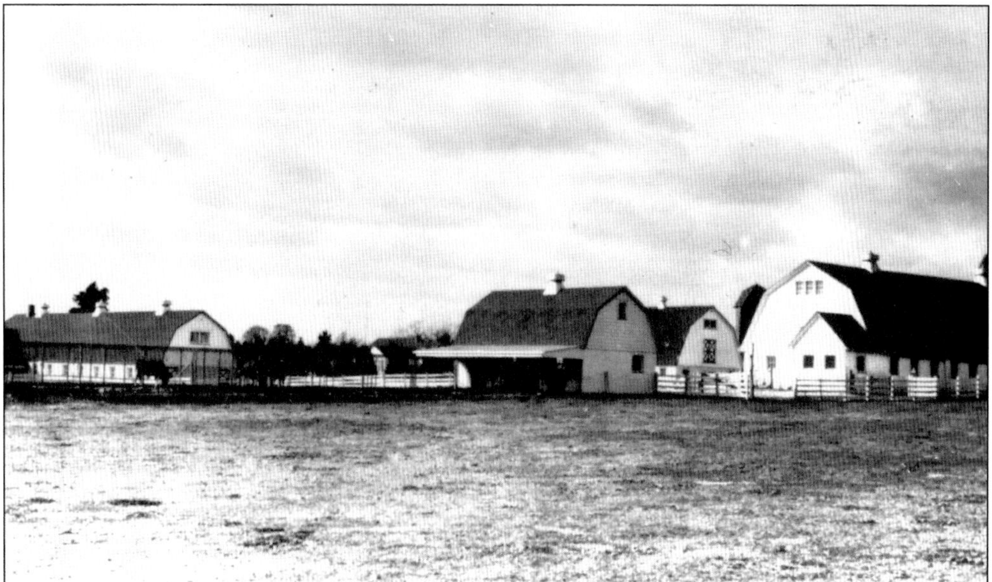

When the weather warmed up in the spring, the cows were let out to graze overnight. For the first several days after that, the milk had a grassy flavor. These fields were among the first properties sold for postwar housing.

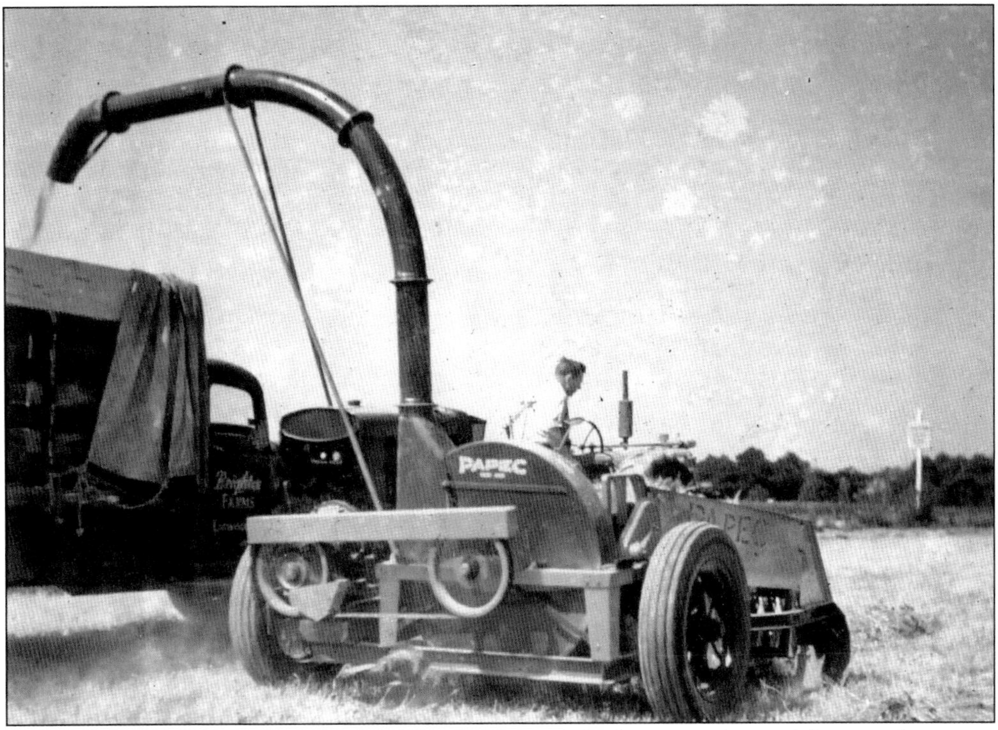

In the last years of operation, the Brighton Farms used the latest mechanical farm machinery to harvest the food raised for its cattle. Dick Adams is shown here chopping fodder for silage.

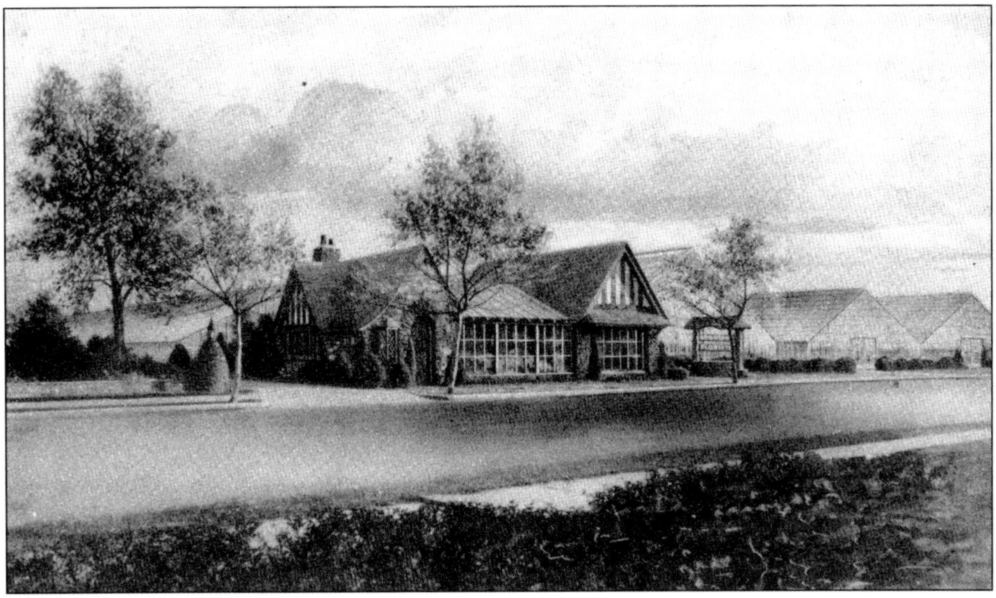

In 1934, George Off created the Brighton Florists, which began shipping orchids around the world.

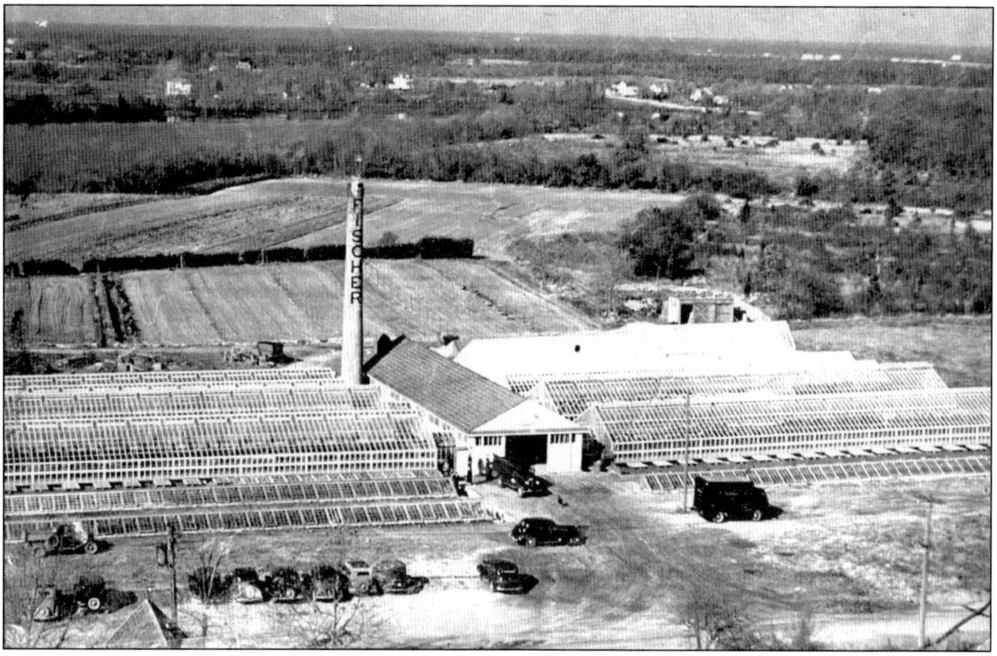

Fischer's Florist first began with a small shop in Atlantic City in 1876. In 1925, the company built a huge plant in Linwood and developed a worldwide reputation for its African Violets.

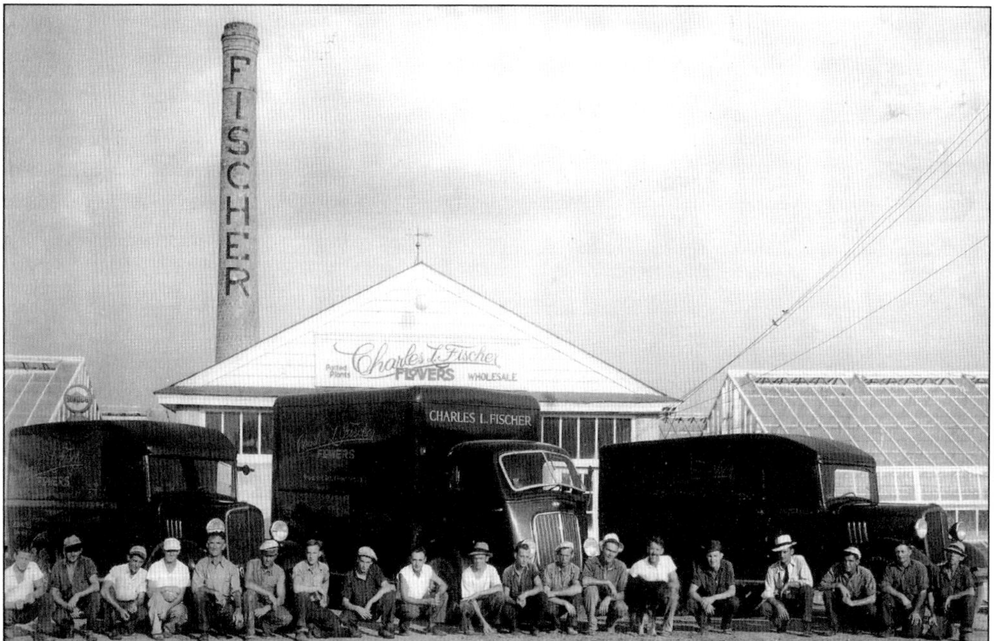

Workers are pictured here in a 1941 photograph. In 1988, Fischer's closed the greenhouses and the land was sold off for development.

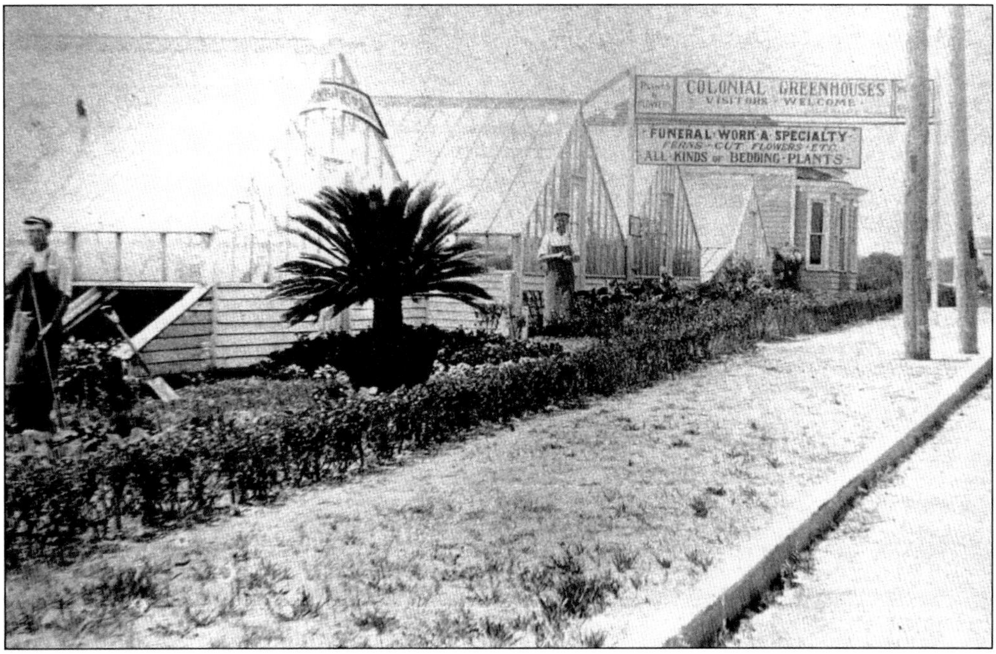

The Crane family, owners of the Colonial Hotel in Ocean City, opened the Colonial Florist on Shore Road at Ocean Heights Avenue *c.* 1900. In 1915, the Cranes sold the business to the Meskers, who kept it going for the next 65 years. In 1983, the Meskers sold the business to Fischer's Florist.

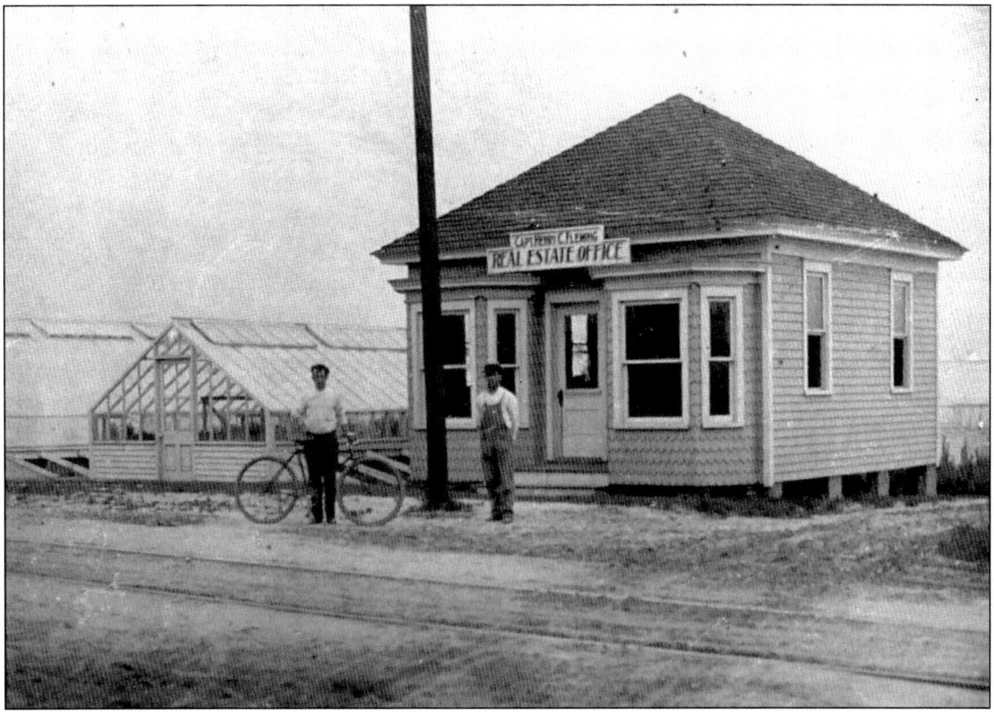

This is a very early photograph of the Colonial greenhouses and office. Shore Road appears to be a dirt road, but the tracks are visible. Shore Road was paved *c.* 1920.

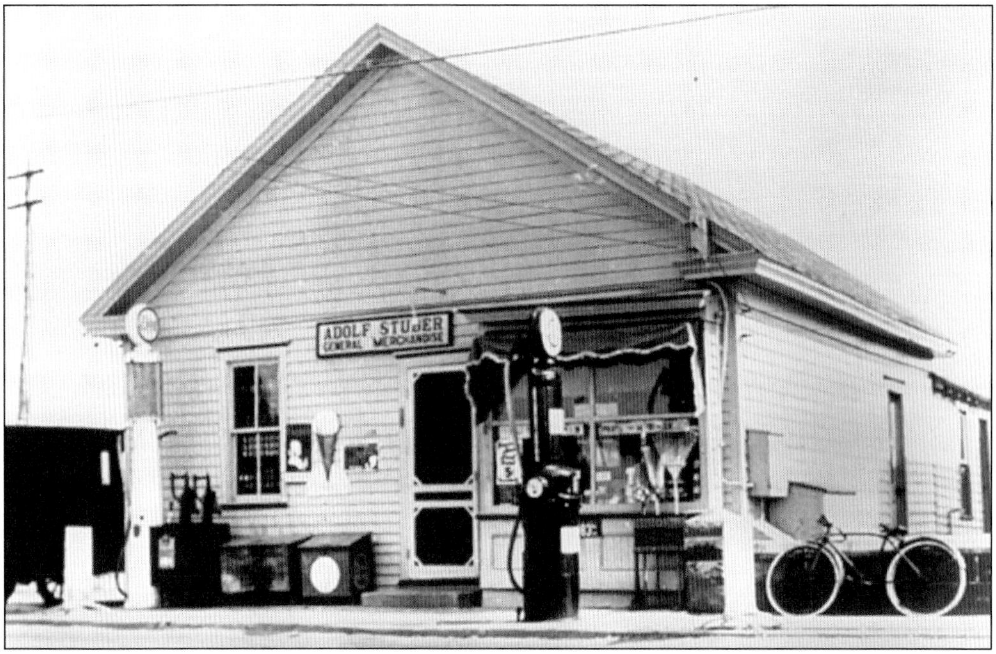

Adolph Stuber started out with a small bakery on Maple Avenue. In 1901, he opened a grocery store on Poplar Avenue at the railroad tracks. His daughter Elsie took over the store after his death in 1941. Elsie ran the store until she retired in 1958. Most of the corner stores, including the hardware store, also sold gasoline.

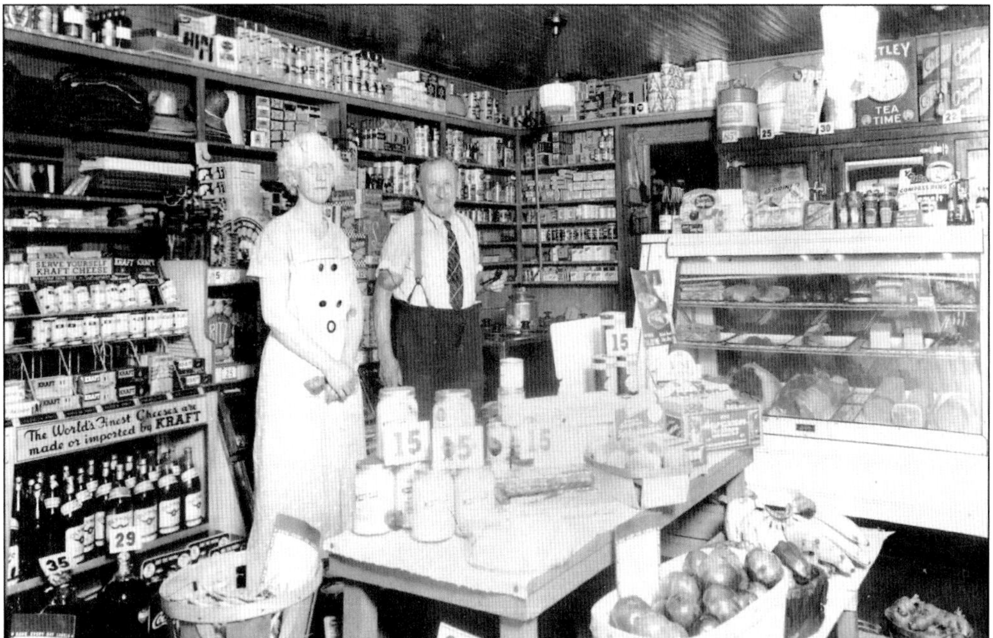

Elsie Stuber and her father, Adolph, are shown in this 1937 view of the interior of their store. Out of sight, behind where they stand, are Nabisco cookie tins from which customers could mix and match to purchase cookies by the pound or quarter pound in a brown paper bag.

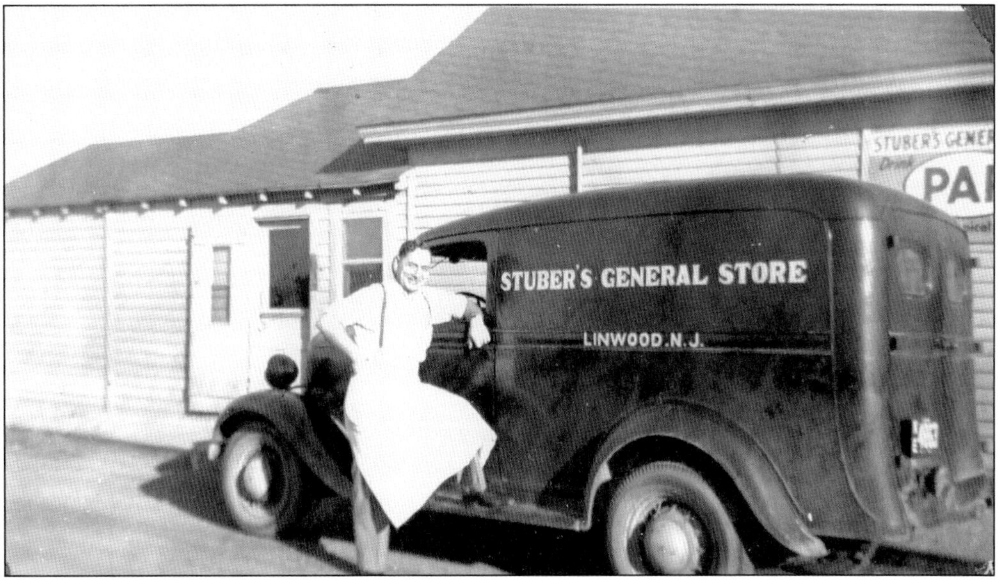

Jimmy Glenn delivered groceries for Stuber and often worked at the store. He is pictured c. 1941.

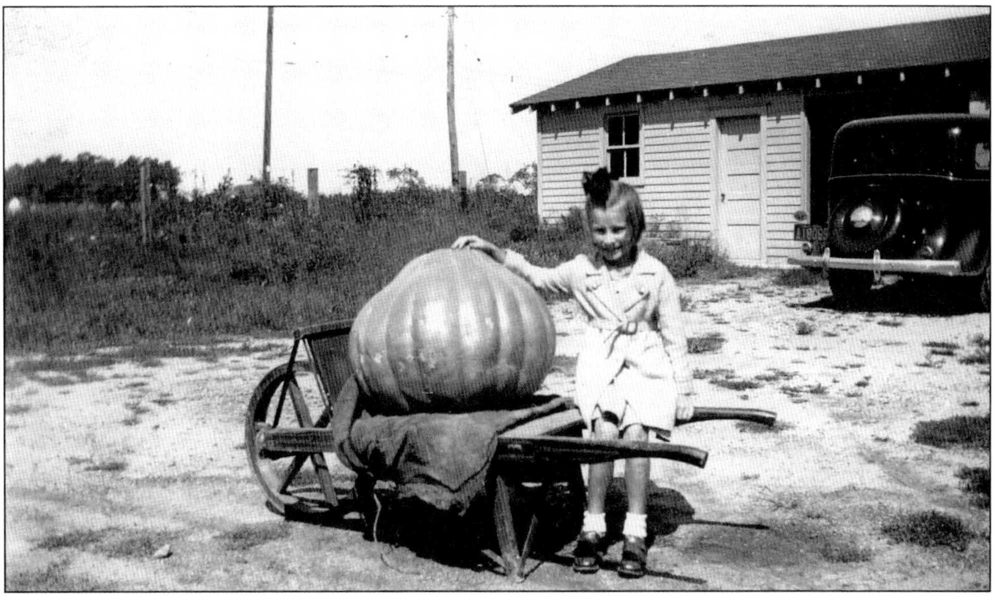

Betty Kears was Adolph Stuber's granddaughter. She poses with her prizewinning 117 1/2-pound pumpkin in front of her grandfather's new garage c. 1935.

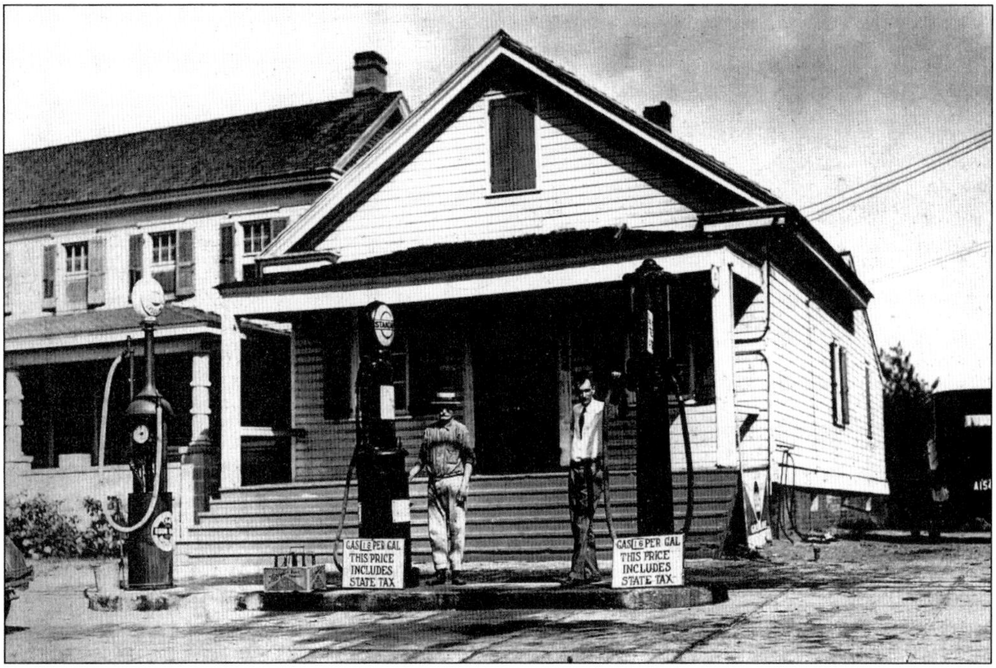

George Washington Hagerthey (left) came to town in 1884 and purchased a grocery store on Shore Road. Like most of the corner stores, Hagerthey's offered gasoline at reasonable prices. Legend has it that the southern end of Linwood was called Sea View because the only place where you could see the ocean was from the back porch of his store. His son Milton stands at the pumps (above right) and, at a later date, behind the counter (below).

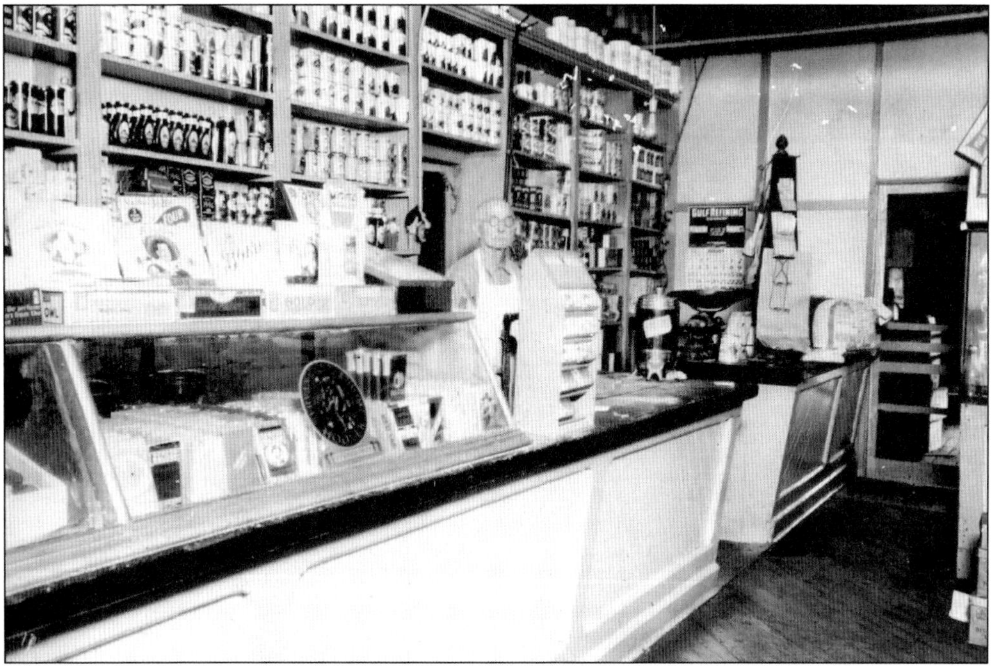

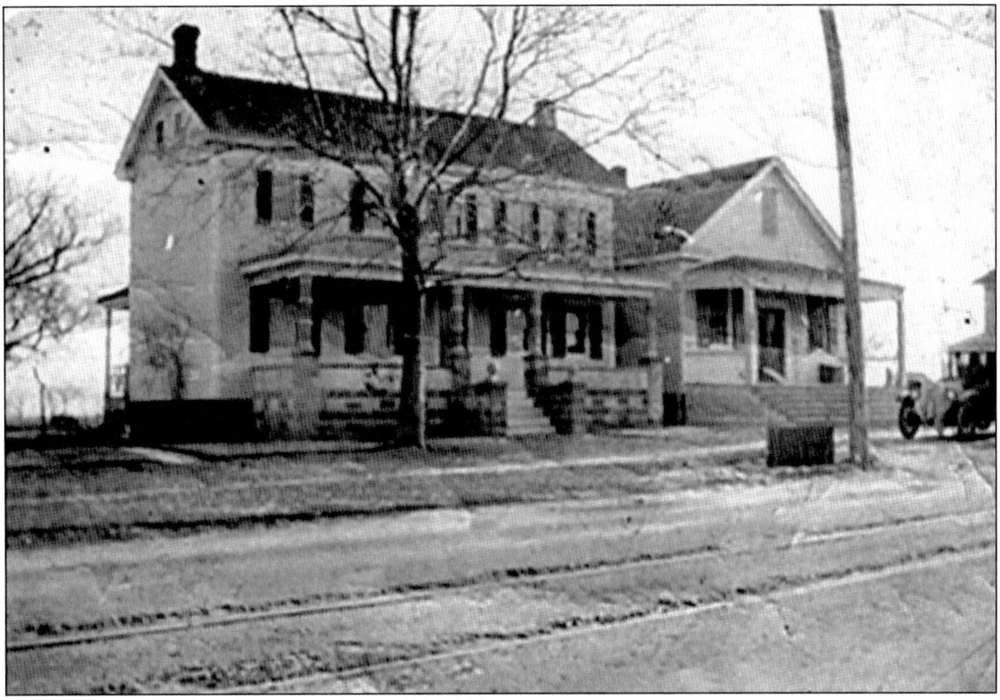

This early picture of the Hagerthey home and store on Shore Road shows the trolley tracks. It appears to have been taken before Hagerthey began selling gasoline at the store.

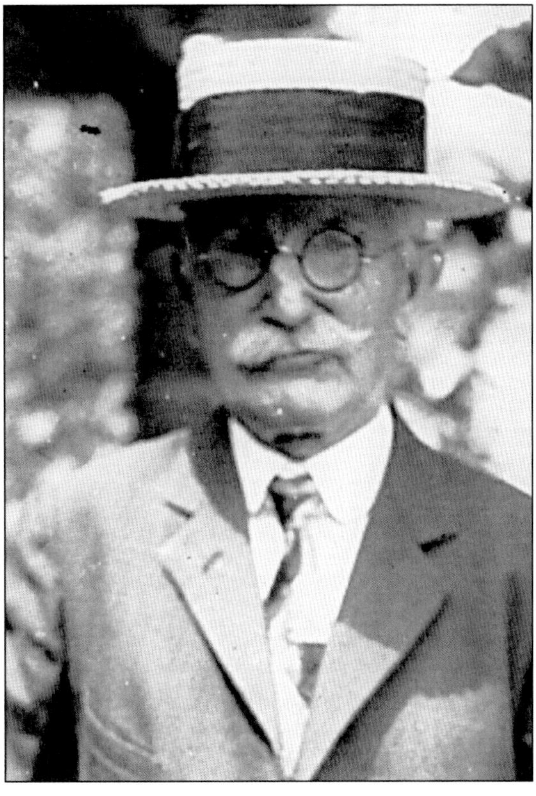

Hagerthey was an influential name in Linwood for over a century. In 1894–1895, George W. Hagerthey was Linwood's mayor. When he was the mayor, the population of Linwood was 400 and the borough had no bonded indebtedness. In a 1932 interview, he expressed concern about young people and their new freedoms. Hagerthey complained of "Too much golf, too much motoring, too many movies and too much dancing," and he added that "This also applies to many parents."

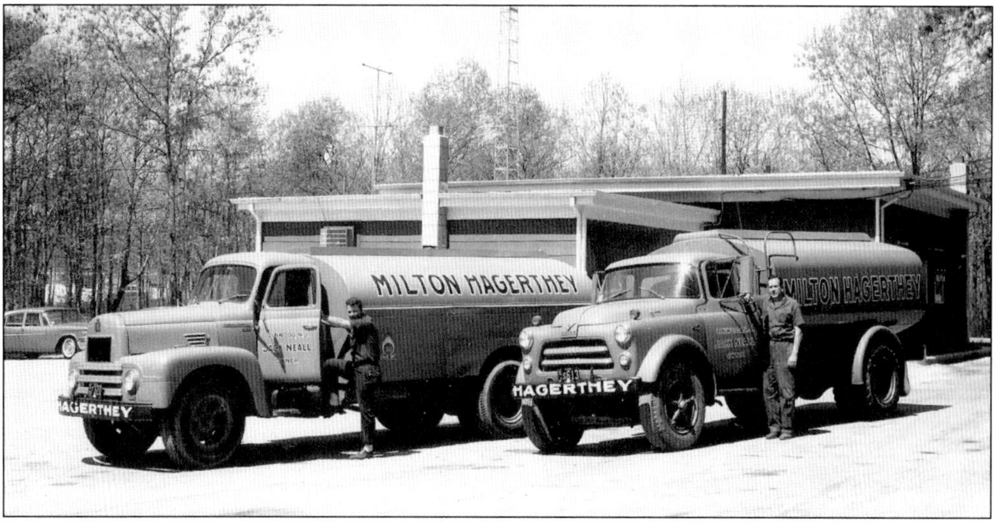

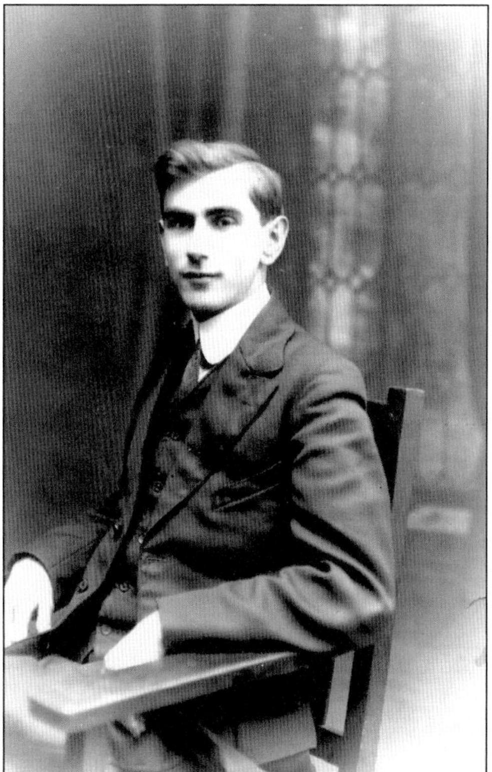

Eugene Hagerthey began delivering kerosene in 1917, and that was the beginning of a major oil business in Linwood. In 1929, Eugene moved to Chincoteague, Virginia, and his brother Milton (left), took over the company. Over the next 50 years Hagerthey Oil supplied fuel to families throughout South Jersey. Milton gave much credit for his success to his drivers. "I've as fine a bunch of men driving my trucks as you can find anywhere," he said. The photograph of two trucks and two men (above) was taken after Jack Naell took over the business.

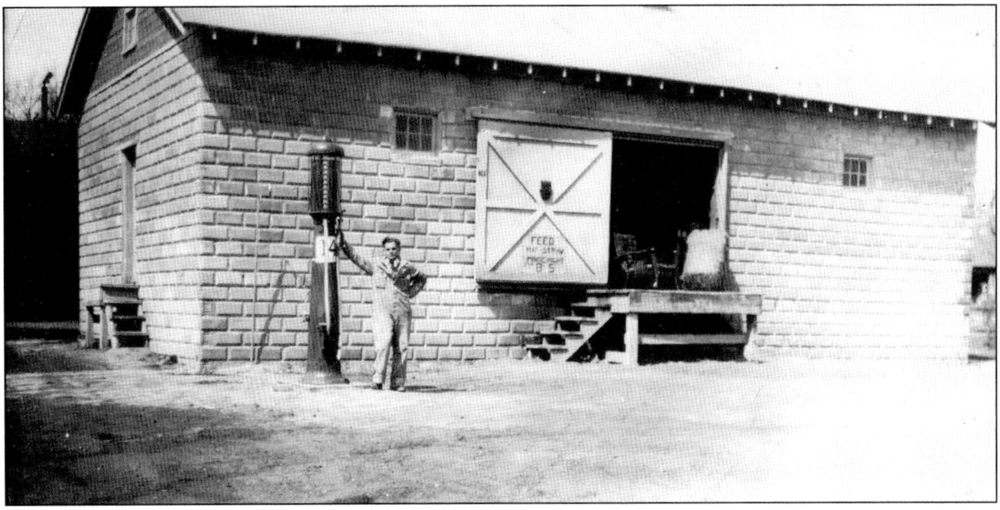

The Hagertheys also had a feed store located at the Maple Avenue train stop. Fertilizer, grain, and other farm supplies came in by rail, and farmers from around the county came here to pick up their supplies. Shown is young George Hagerthey. Eventually, the business was sold to Earl Anderson, but as farms began to disappear in the 1950s, the store was closed down.

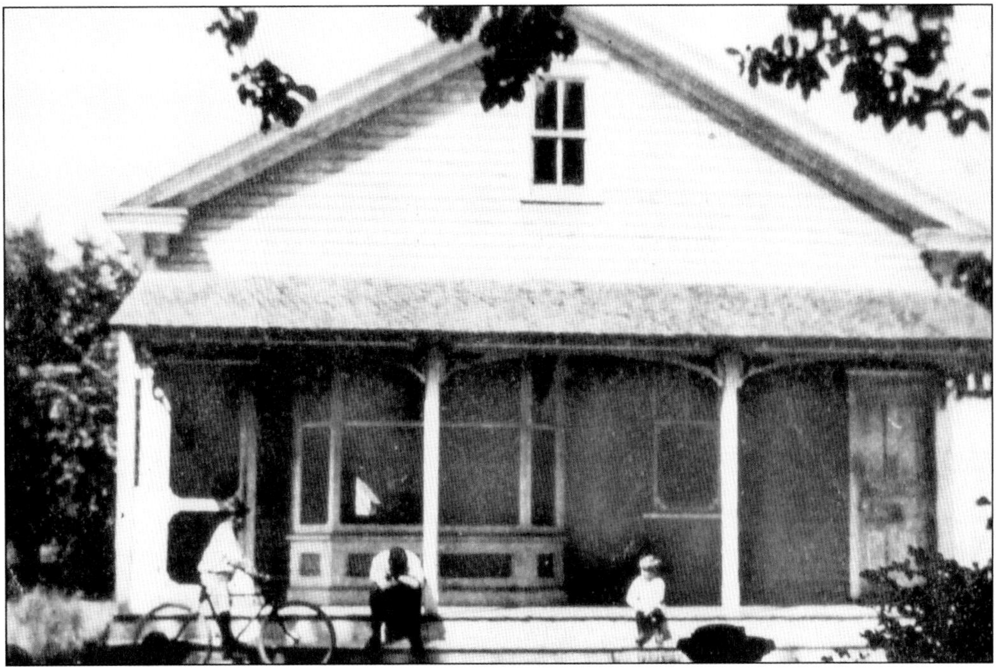

Walt Sanders' grocery store and barbershop was a few doors down the street from the feed store. Sanders was the postmaster here from 1898 to 1919.

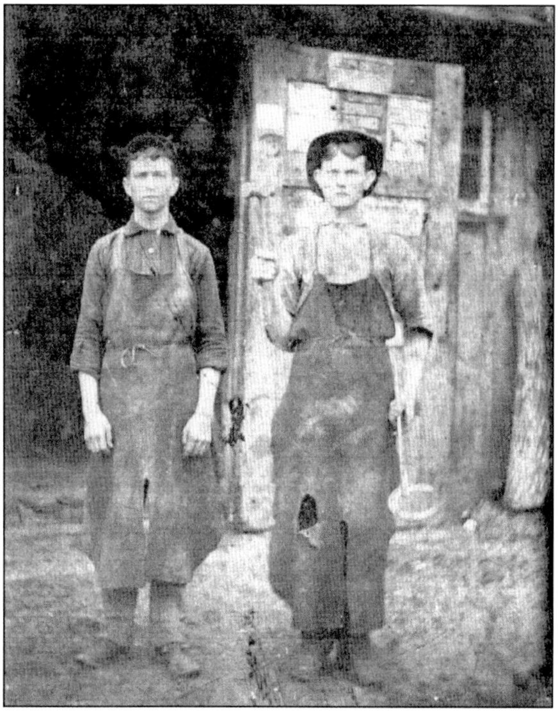

The 1872 Beers & Comstock Map of Leedsville identified Joseph Steelman as the blacksmith. Steelman's shop was on Maple Avenue next to his home. This *c.* 1870 tintype is most likely an image of that blacksmith shop. The question is, which man is Joseph Steelman?

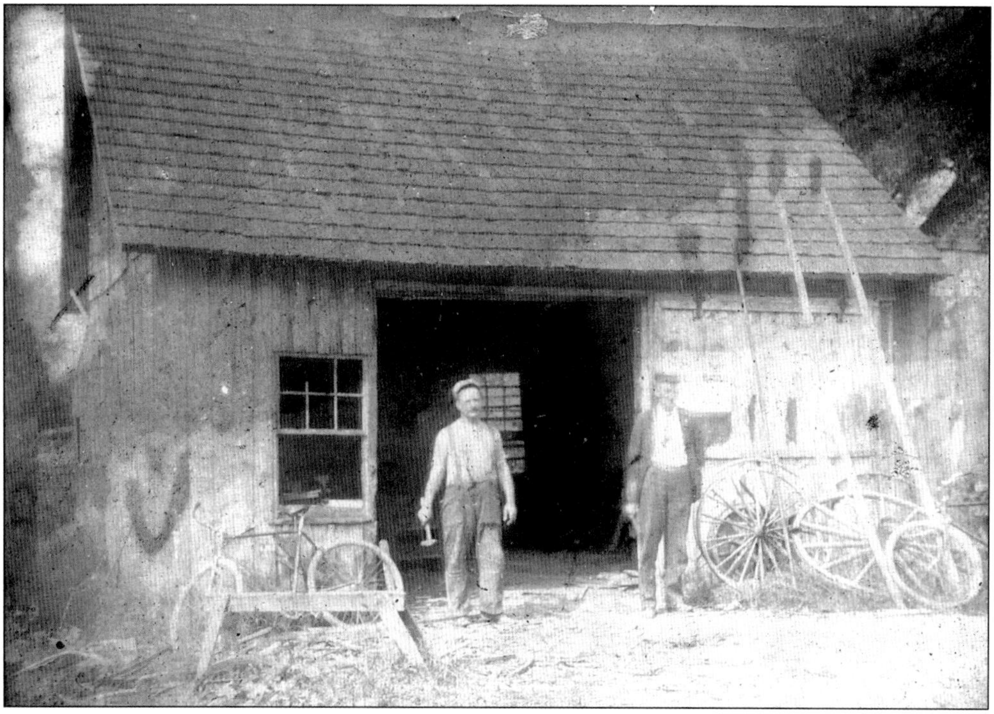

In 1902, Joseph Steelman retired and Harry Potter (left) came to take his place. The man shown with Potter is unidentified. Potter's blacksmith shop was behind his son's store near the railroad tracks. Another son, Mulford, had learned to be a blacksmith, but then the automobile came along. Mulford became one of the first automobile mechanics in town.

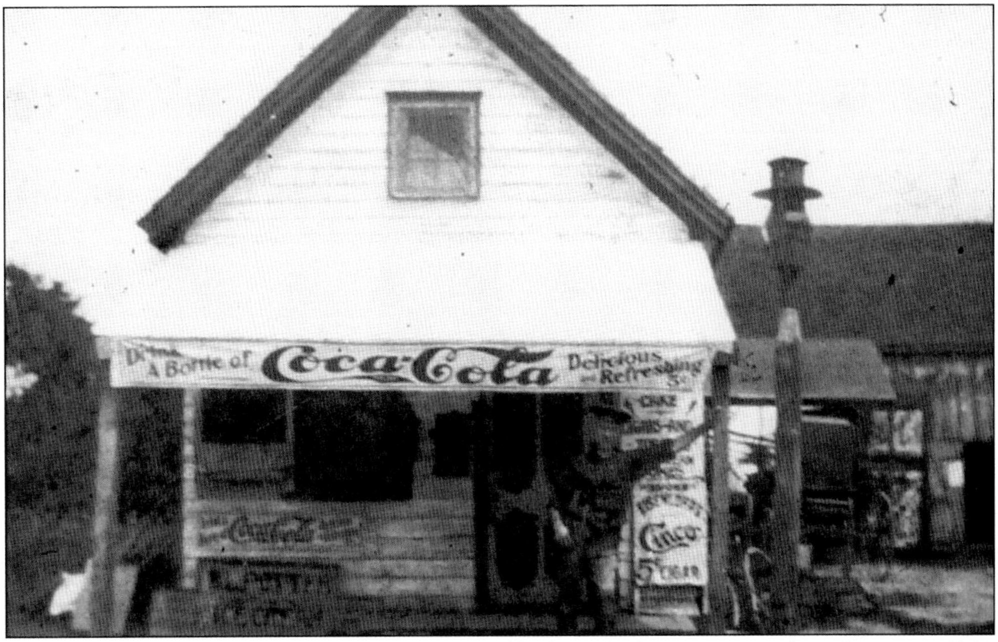

Warren Potter's little store next to his father's blacksmith shop is pictured in these rare 1901 photographs. The old Coca-cola sign adds interest (above). The people shown are unidentified. Members of the Potter family were all very active Linwood residents. Warren's brother Clarence was known for his oyster suppers. Clarence's wife, Sara, was a popular Sunday school teacher and sales representative for pay-by-the-week insurance policies.

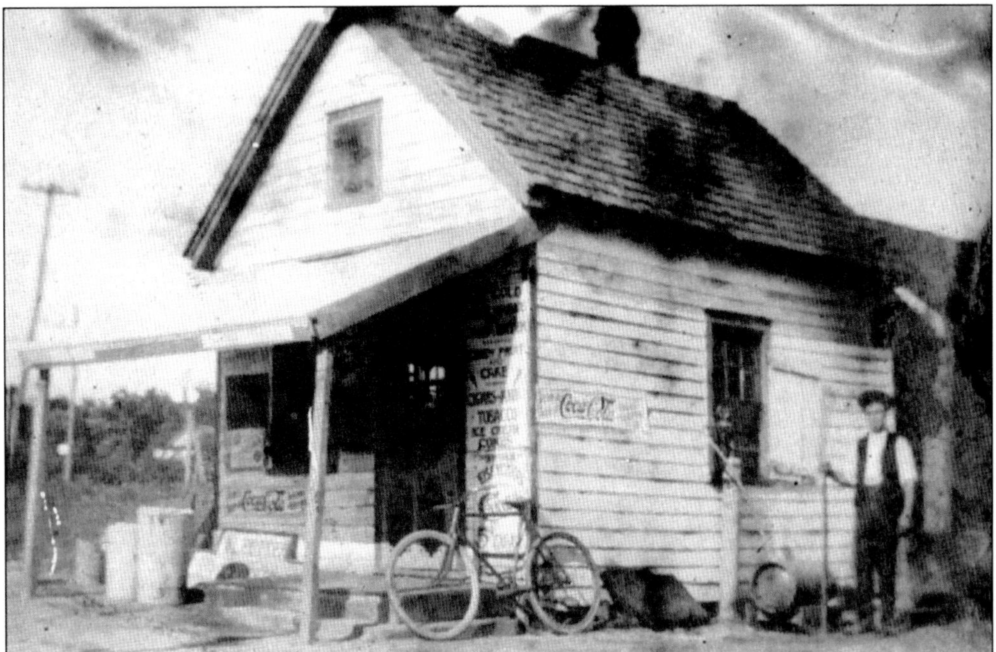

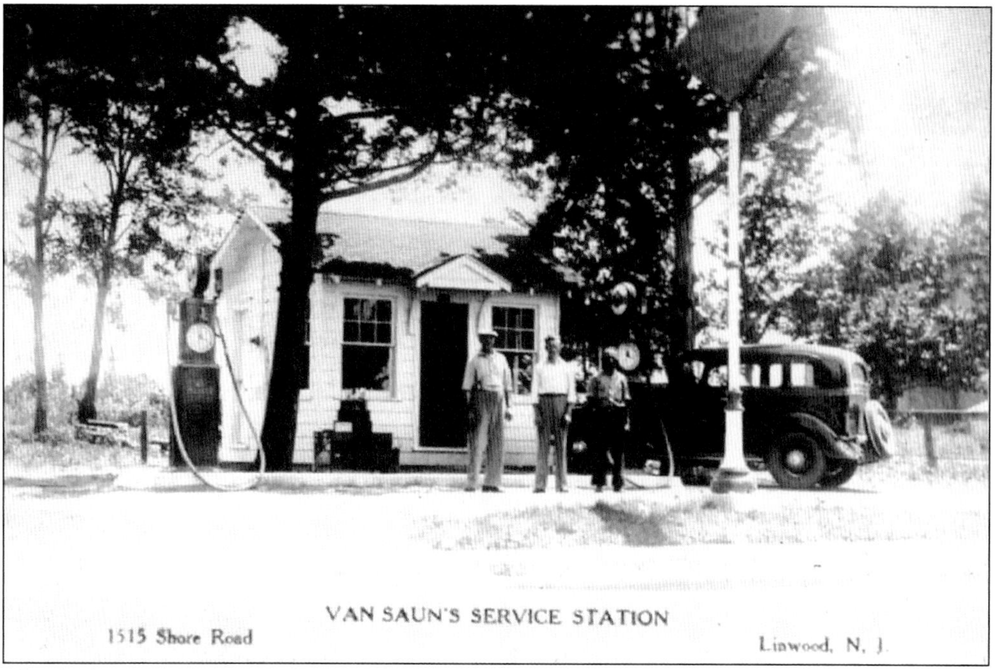

This little gas station was Alonzo VanSaun's first service station and battery shop. From left to right are Alonzo VanSaun, Bill Barrett, and Fitz Potter.

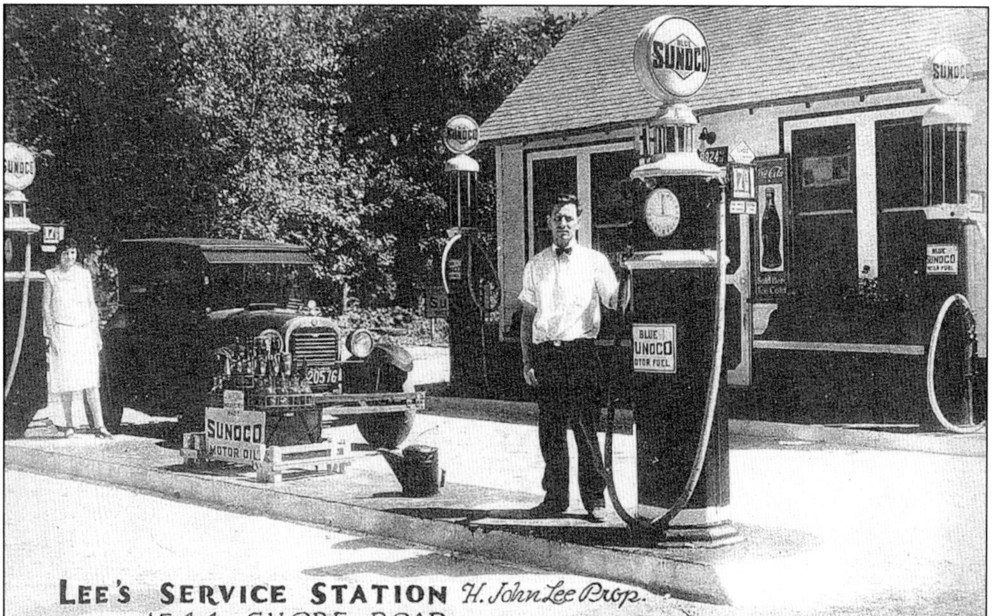

When Alonzo VanSaun opened his larger place across the street, his original shop became Lee's Service Station. The small building has seen much use over the years. In 1944, it was moved behind city hall for use as a police station. It was later used by the library as a workshop office.

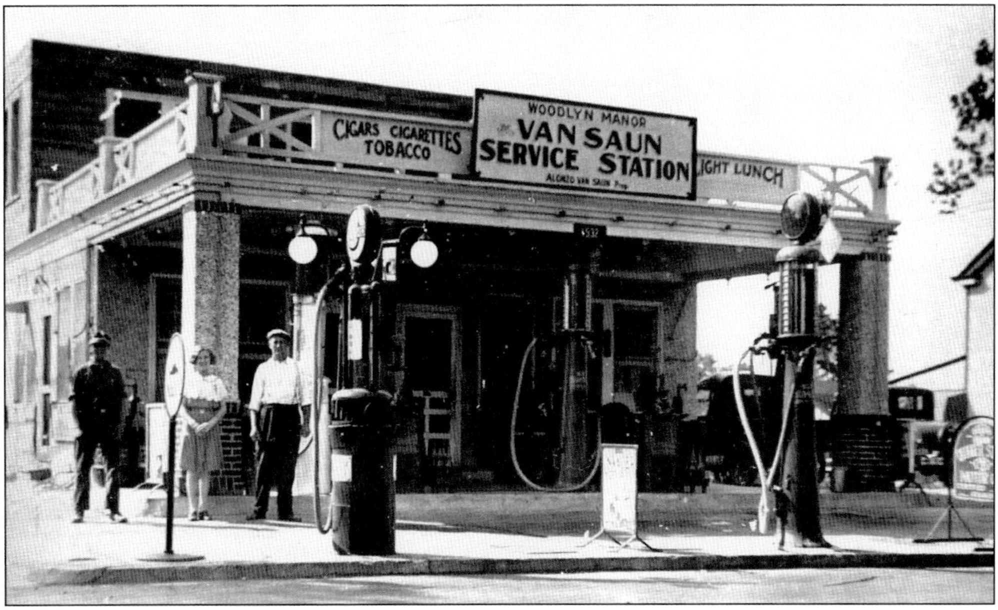

Pictured at VanSaun's new station across the street, from left to right, are an unidentified man Alice VanSaun, and Alonzo VanSaun. The building eventually became Boucher's grocery store, which children from Belhaven School visited on their way to and from school. In the 1970s, the Linwood Saw and Tool Shop opened here.

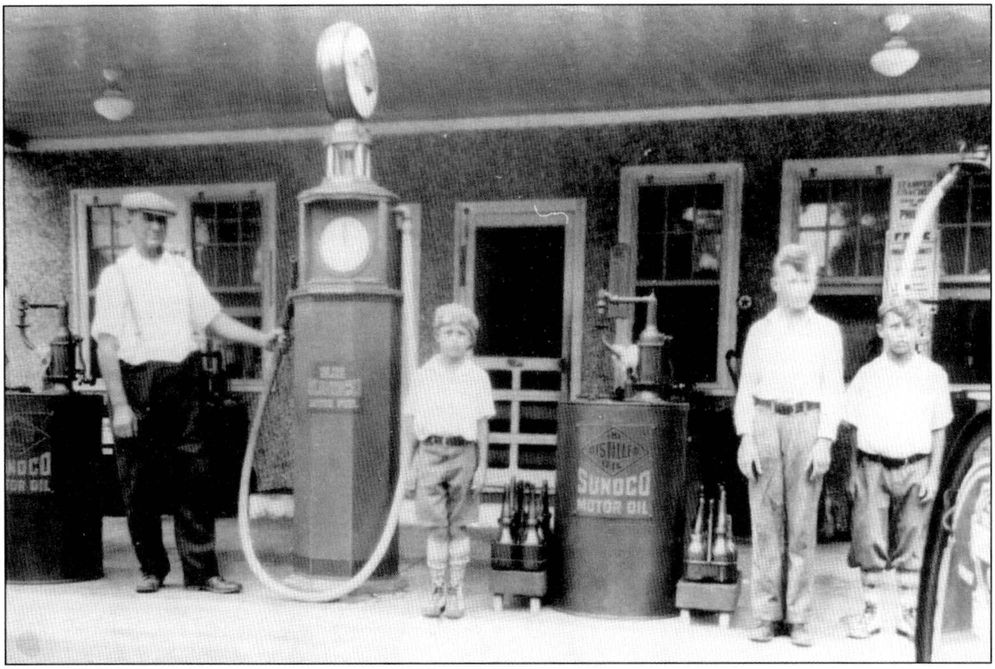

Shown in this c. 1927 photograph, from left to right, are Lonnie VanSaun, Tom Adams, Buddy Barrett, and Bob Adams.

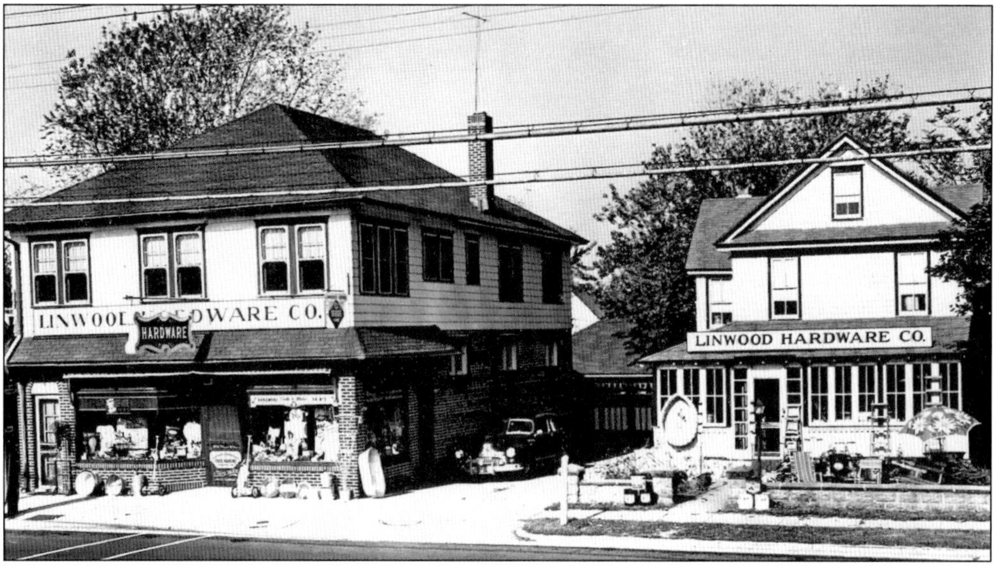

After leaving his job as a driver for baseball great Connie Mack, Roy Black opened a hardware store on Shore Road near Maple Avenue in 1928. The store was crammed full of merchandise (below) and, at one time, Black began selling groceries when the little Acme Store next door started selling buckets and shovels. The American Stores built a larger store in Somers Point and the little Acme closed, leaving the hardware business to Black. After the hardware store closed, the building was a delicatessen for a while before becoming the home of Schoppy Trophies.

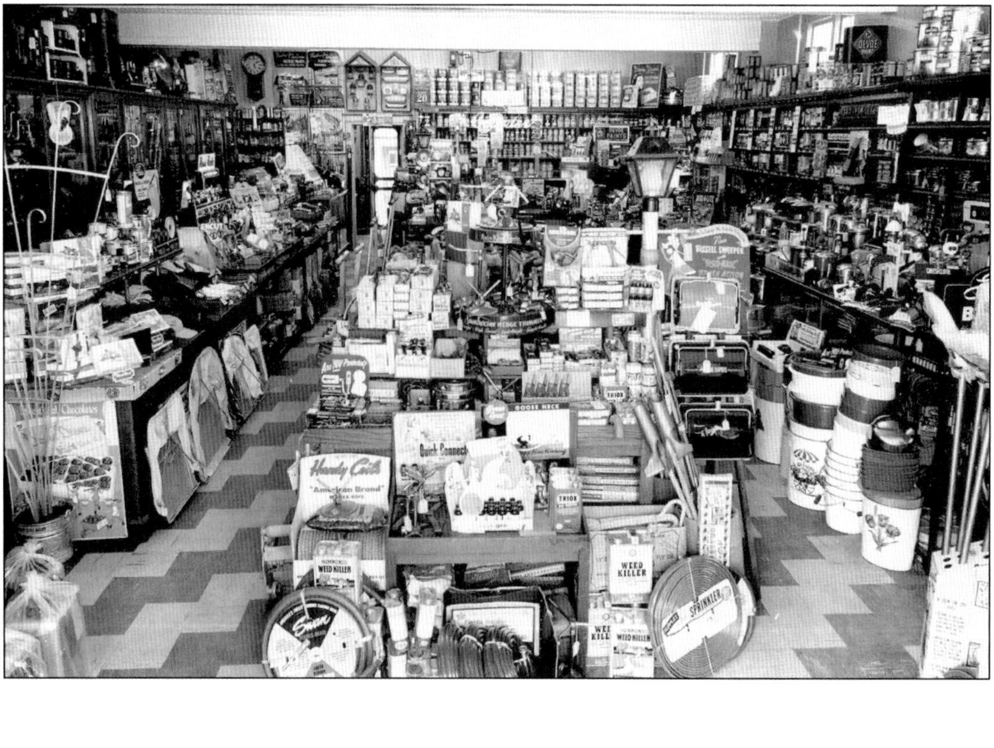

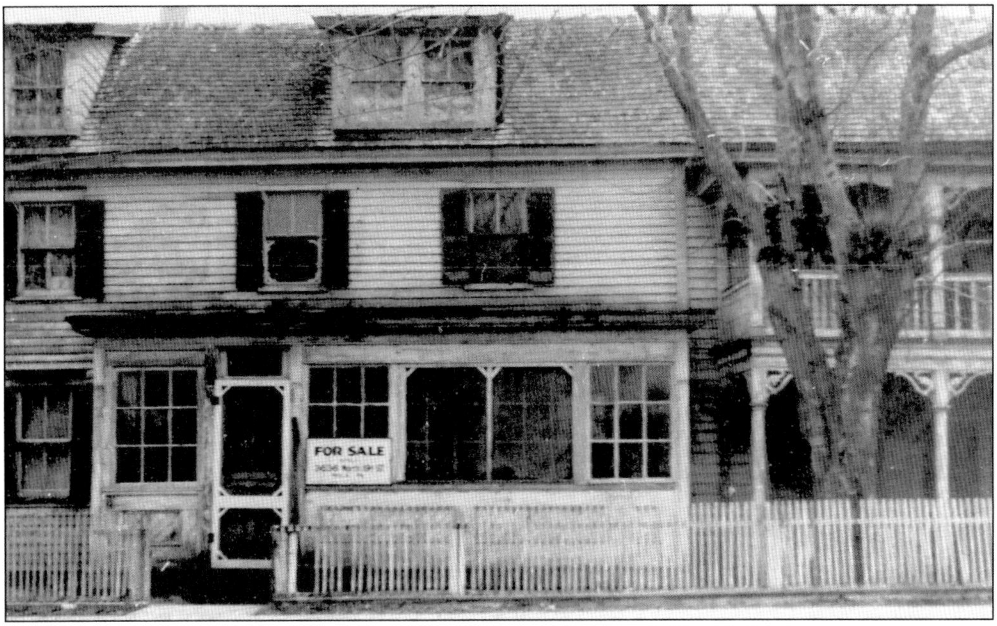

This home has often been called the oldest home in Linwood. David Somers, an early owner, operated a store here in 1850. In 1832, Somers was the schoolmaster at Cedar Grove School, near Garfield Avenue. Dr. Samuel C. Edmonds, a Leedsville doctor, lived here in 1881. Edmonds was reportedly the one who suggested Pearville when Leedsville was looking for a new name.

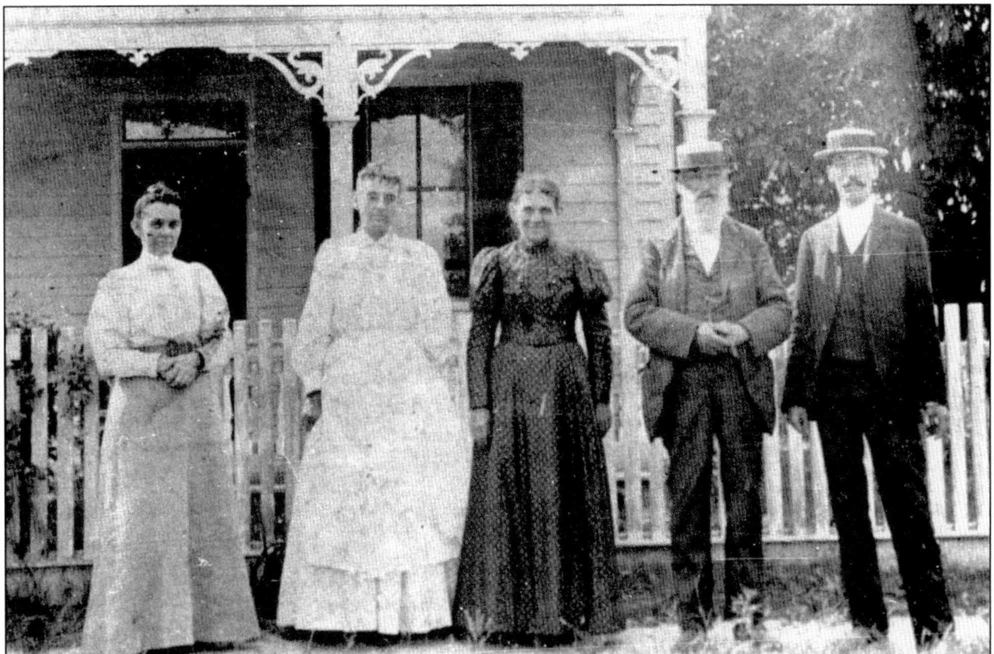

Five people pose in front of the Victorian section of Dr. Samuel Edmonds's home, a section that was later removed. It is very probable that one of the men is Dr. Edmonds. For a time in the mid-20th century, the home was a candy store. Foschi Studios opened here in 1983.

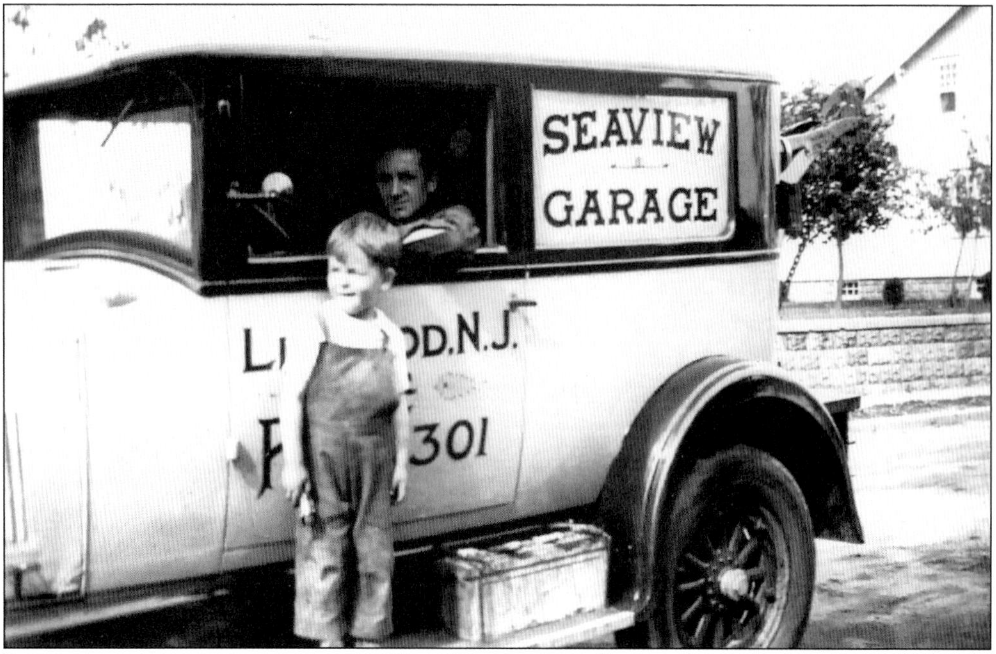

Carl Henning sits in one of his first trucks for the Seaview Garage in 1935. His son Carl Jr. stands on the running board. Henning took an old Studebaker and added a winch to the back to make his own tow truck. The business is operated today by his grandson. (Courtesy of Virginia Henning Clifford.)

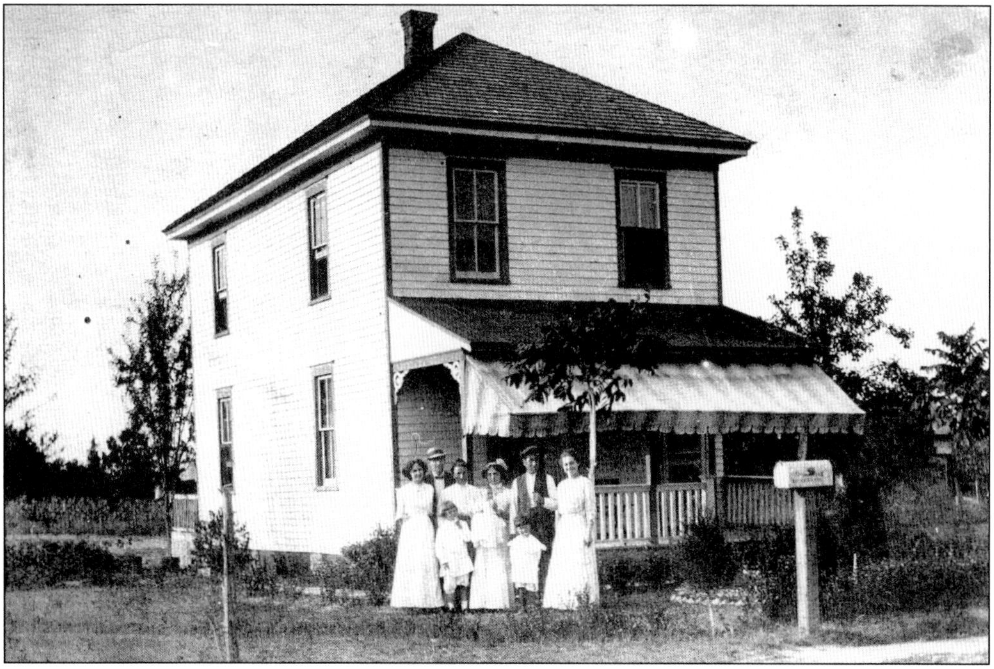

Carl Henning's parents, Harry and Eugenia Henning, bought their family home *c.* 1905. At that time, West Avenue was part of Bog Road, which later became Oak Avenue. Eugenia's sister Elizabeth Gamage and her family are pictured. (Courtesy of Virginia Henning Clifford.)

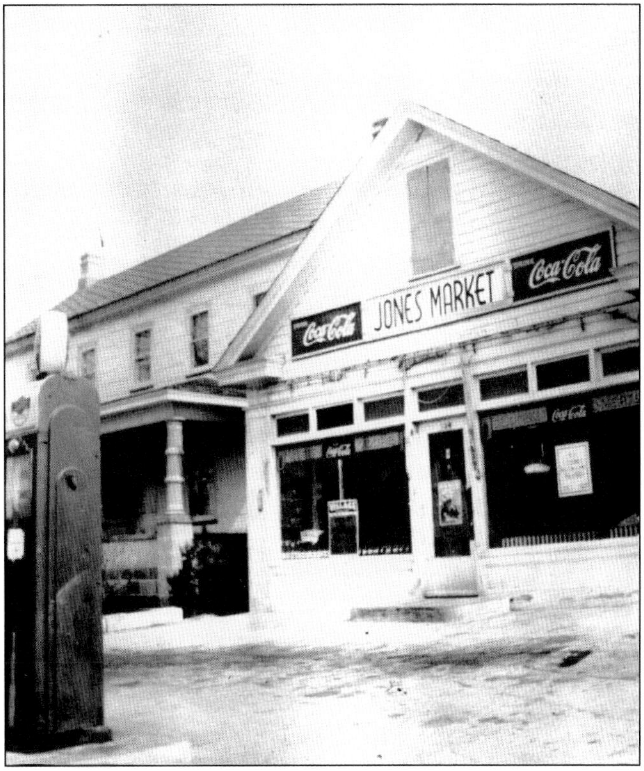

Jones Market operated in the old Hagerthey's Store building during the mid-1900s. The market got freshly butchered turkeys and chickens from a couple of turkey farms that were located close by. Thorne's turkey farm was across the street from Belhaven School, and students sometimes were taken there to visit at Thanksgiving time.

Jones Market

Linwood, N. J.

NOVEMBER 17 & 18 1950

Slices of Ham 95c lb

Rib Roast 68c lb

Felin's Sausage 55c lb

Order Fresh Killed
TURKEYS & ROASTERS NOW

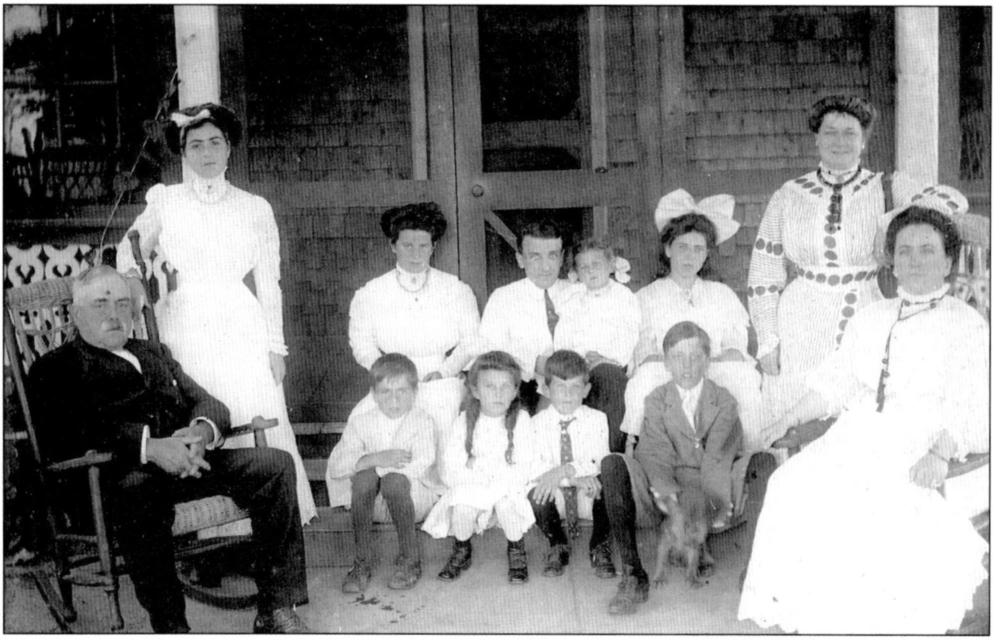

In 1904, Capt. James K. Carmack (left) owned a 22-acre farm across the street from Hagerthey's Store. With him on the porch of the main farmhouse of Hollywood Farm *c.* 1906 are family members. From left to right are the following: (front row) James E. Carmack, two unidentified children, Mark M. Carmack, and Carolyn Carmack; (back row) Ella Carmack, three unidentified people, Carolyn Carmack, and Cousin Cathy.

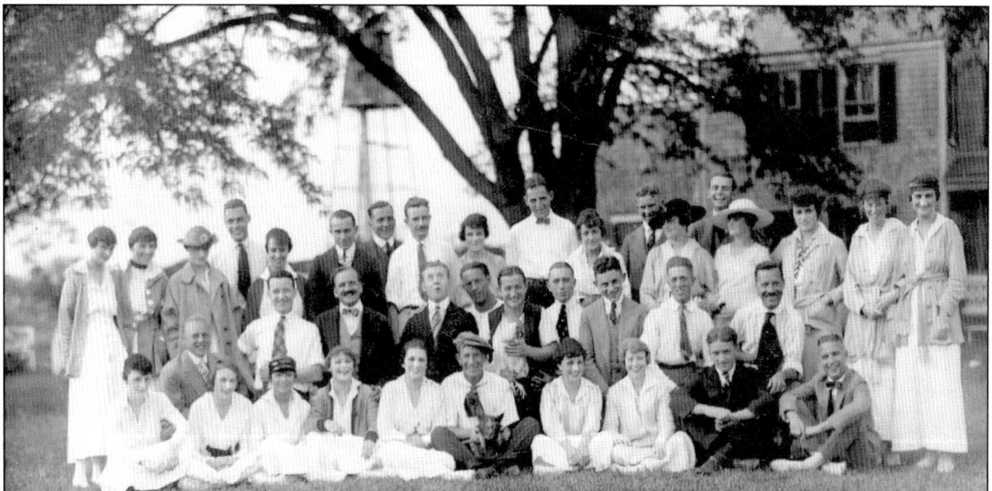

This large family group seems to be really enjoying the camaraderie of posing for this photograph in August 1915. The windmill in the background provided electricity to the farm.

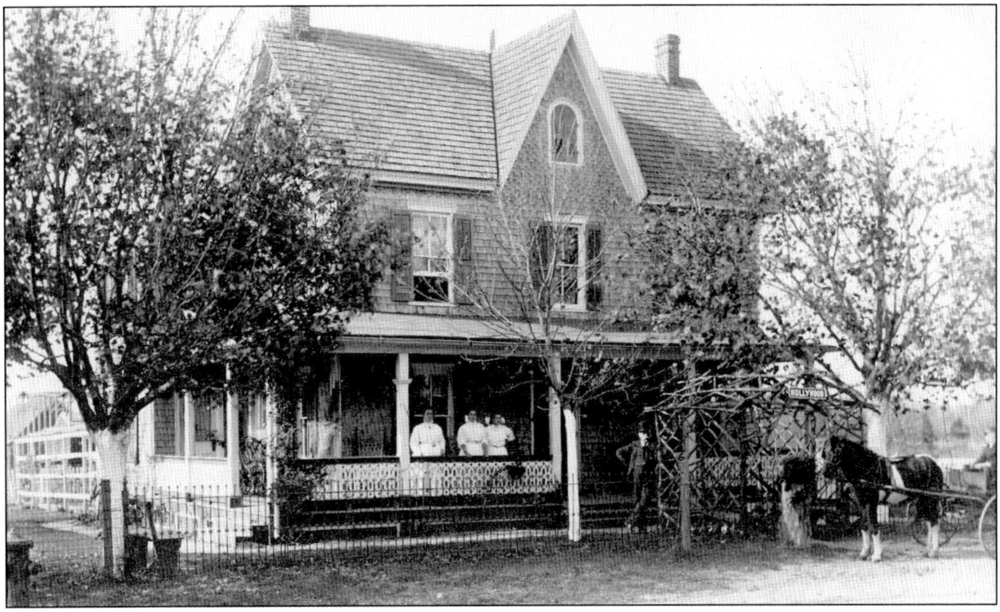

Capt. James K. Carmack's Hollywood Farm home shows the Victorian influence. This home and the Somers's house (below) are among Linwood's treasured old family homes along Shore Road.

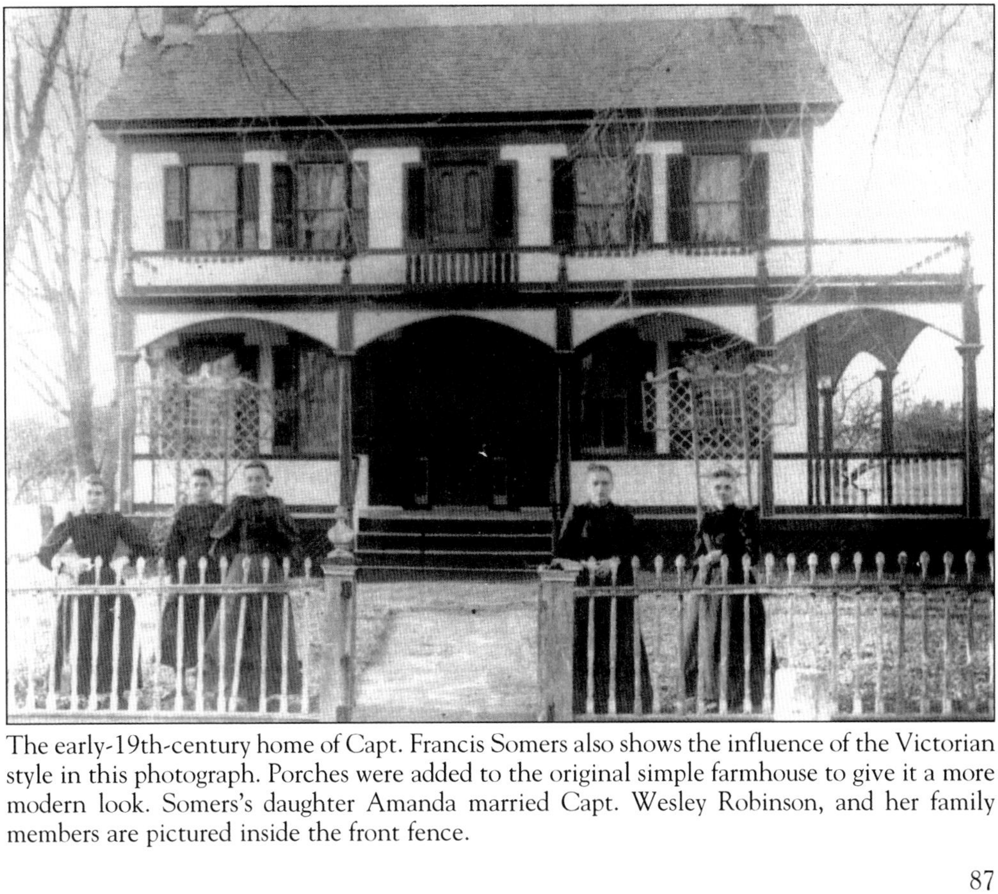

The early-19th-century home of Capt. Francis Somers also shows the influence of the Victorian style in this photograph. Porches were added to the original simple farmhouse to give it a more modern look. Somers's daughter Amanda married Capt. Wesley Robinson, and her family members are pictured inside the front fence.

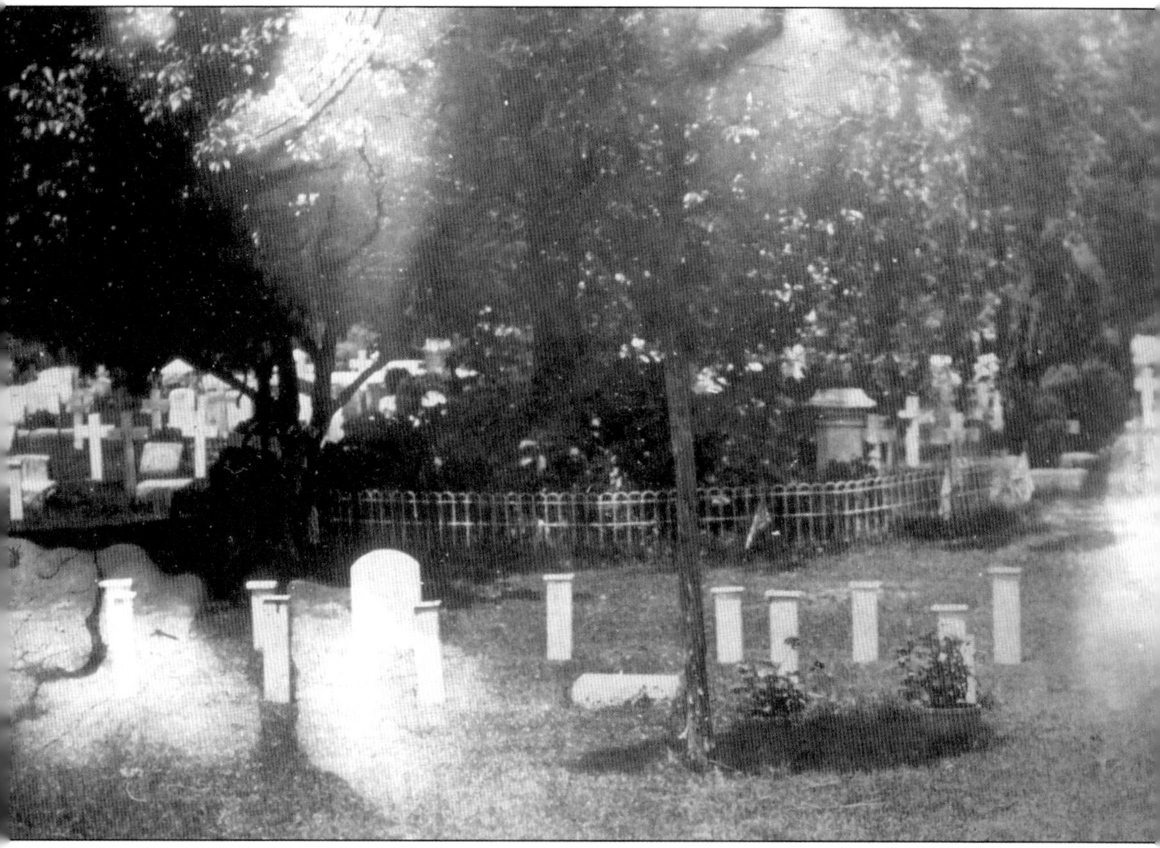

The Clara Glen Pet Cemetery, between Kirklin and Garfield Avenues, is one of the more intriguing Linwood properties. In 1920, animal lovers Glen and Clara White opened the cemetery on the old John Scull farm. Alex and Agnes Miller bought the property in 1955. In 1986, the cemetery was given to the historical society. Over 3,800 animals are buried at the site, including some famous pets and pets of famous owners. Billie Burke, J.P. Morgan, and Pearl Buck are some of the famous owners. Pete, from the Little Rascals, Rex the Wonder Dog, and a diving horse from the Steel Pier are some of the famous pets. In an unusual funeral procession in 1959, 20 limousines followed a hearse from Atlantic City to bury a dog called Night Life here. The dog, owned by bartender Spanky Davis, had been a favorite around the bar.

Four

THE TROLLEYS

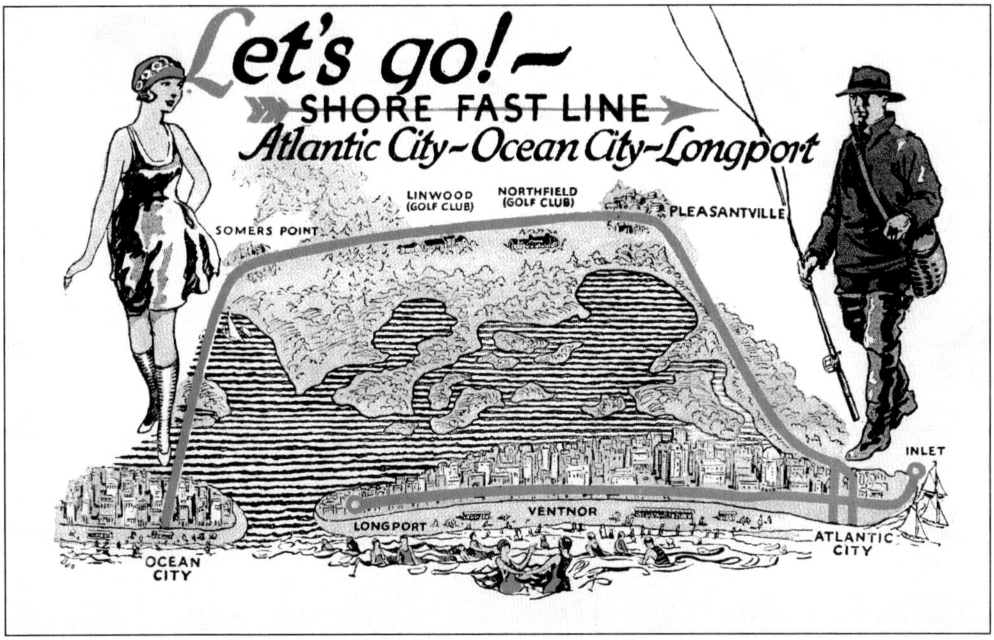

Two companies provided trolley service connecting the mainland communities to shops and entertainment centers in Atlantic City and Ocean City. The Atlantic & Suburban Trolley, which originated in 1902, had tracks down the middle of Shore Road and operated until 1929. The Shore Fast Line began operations in 1906, using the Pennsylvania Railroad tracks through the center of each town. By 1948, the Shore Fast Line cars and the track beds had begun to deteriorate. Buses offered cheaper service. The last Shore Fast Line trolley ran on January 17, 1948, ending an era. Those who remember riding the trolleys always speak nostalgically about them and get a wistful look in their eyes that says, "Why can't they bring them back?"

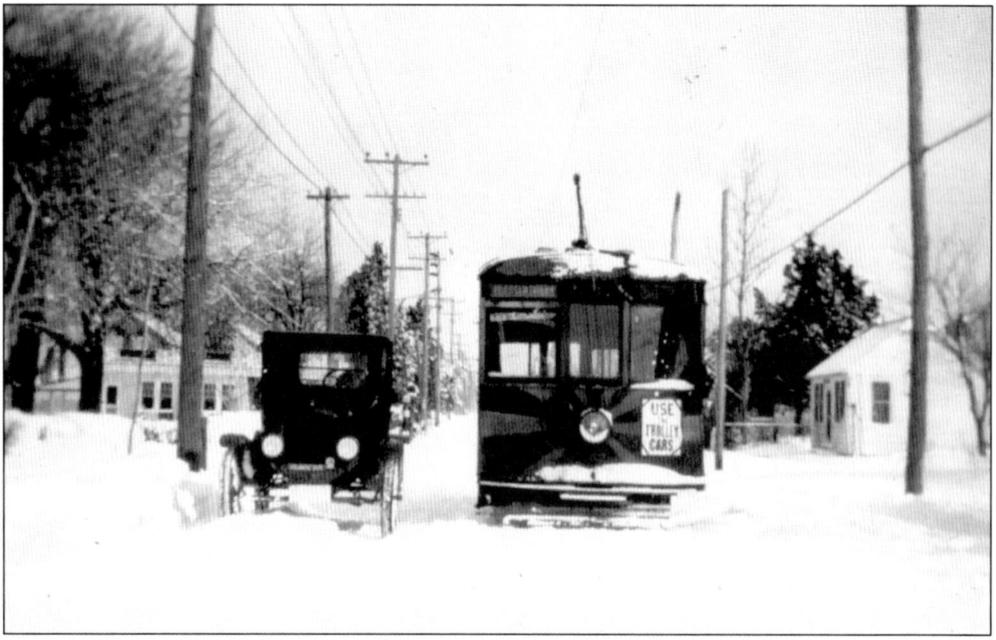

The Atlantic & Suburban trolley shown here is on Shore Road at Belhaven Avenue c. 1920. The small building on the right was a gas station and battery shop that was moved down behind city hall in 1944 for use as a police station. Resident Betty Martin remembered giving the conductor a container when he passed on the way to Somers Point. On his way back, he dropped off the container filled with ice cream.

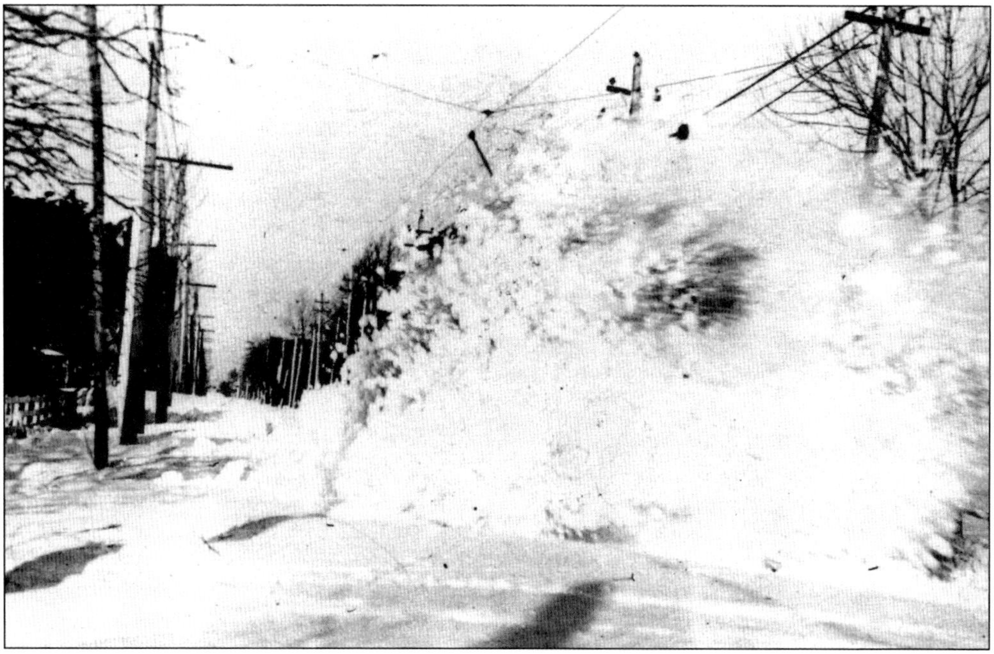

After a heavy snowstorm, attaching a snowplow to the front of the trolley was an efficient way to open the road.

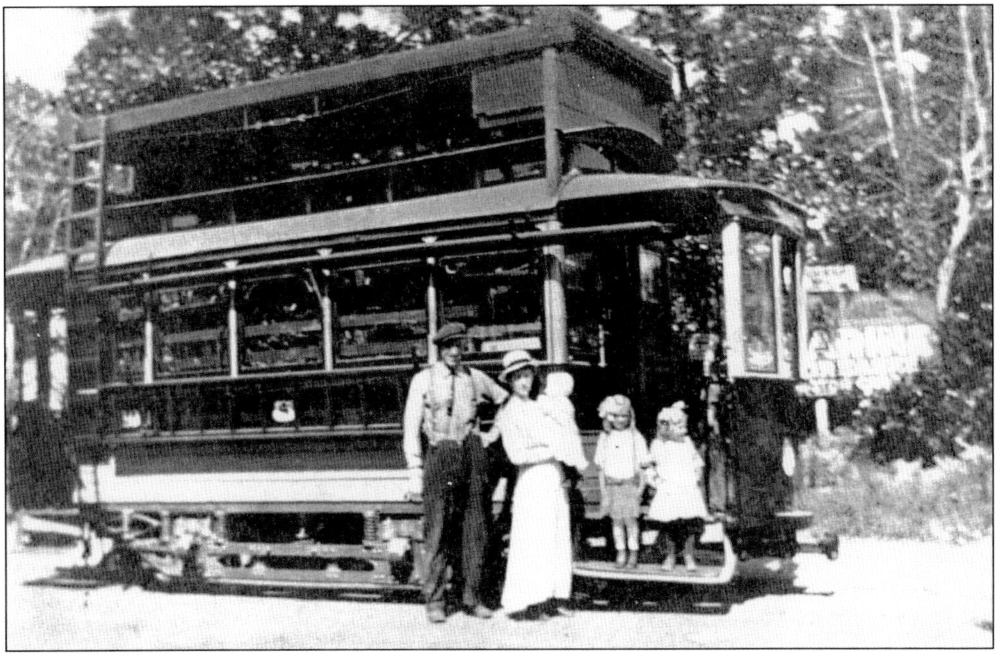

William Barrett (left) worked for the Atlantic & Suburban Trolley Company. Shown with him are his wife, Amanda Barrett, and daughters Dorothy, Phoebe, and Amanda. One of the company's utility cars made an interesting backdrop for this family picture taken in 1916. (Courtesy of Bill Barrett.)

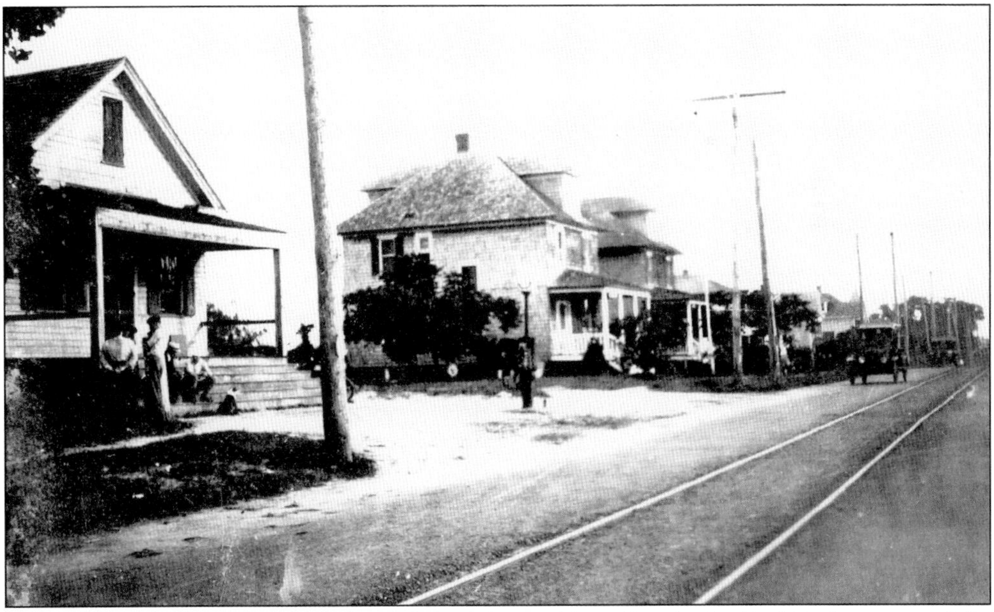

In 1935, an accident occurred along the tracks on Shore Road. Guilford Barker, wanted for bank robbery, thought G-men were chasing him and began to speed. He hit a telephone pole and was killed. Mary Haines, who lived in the house shown at the center of the picture, brought out a blanket to cover him up. It was a pretty exciting story at the time—Linwood's own Barker gang.

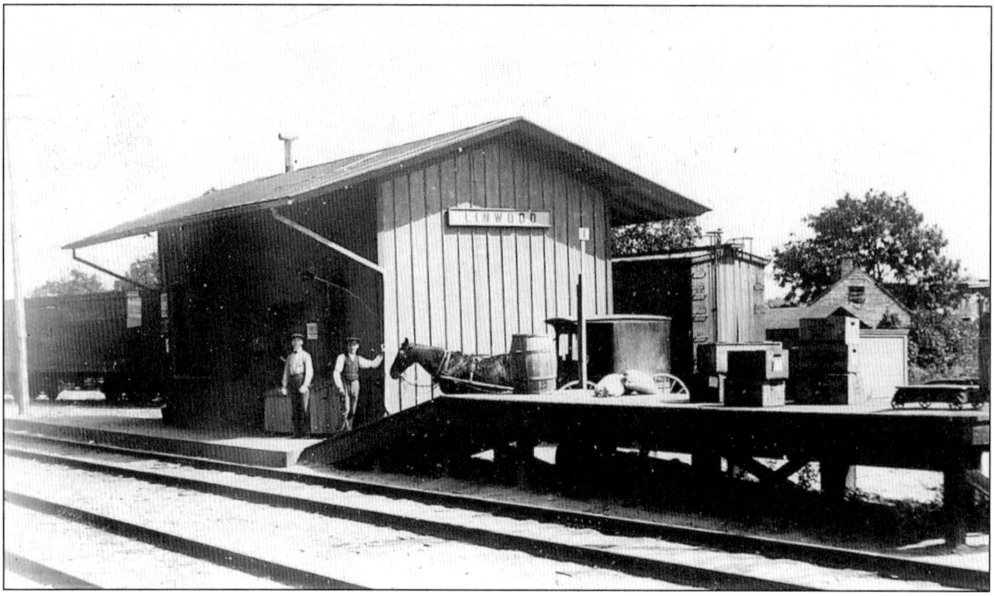

Linwood Station, shown in this 1909 postcard, was a busy place as most of the coal, mail, and other supplies were delivered by rail. Samuel Clark's coal yard was located next door, and the post office was just down the block. Henry Wolfbrandt and George Riggins were stationmasters.

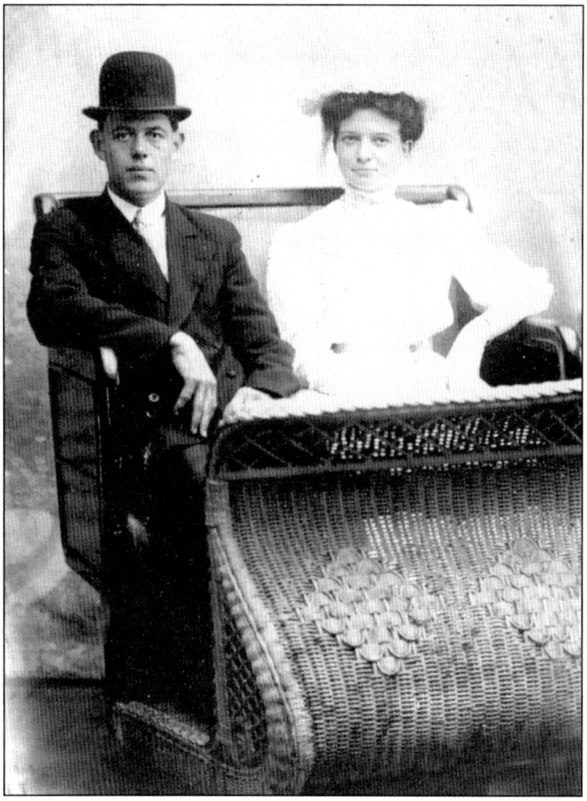

Henry Wolfbrandt was the stationmaster at Linwood Station from 1910 to 1919, when he went to Absecon Station. He and his wife, Clara, are pictured in a classic boardwalk photograph shortly after their wedding in 1910. Their daughter Elsie Wolfbrandt Thompson remembered sneaking out the back gate and through the neighbor's garden as a very small child to visit her father at the station. (Courtesy of Phyllis Wolfbrandt Marshall.)

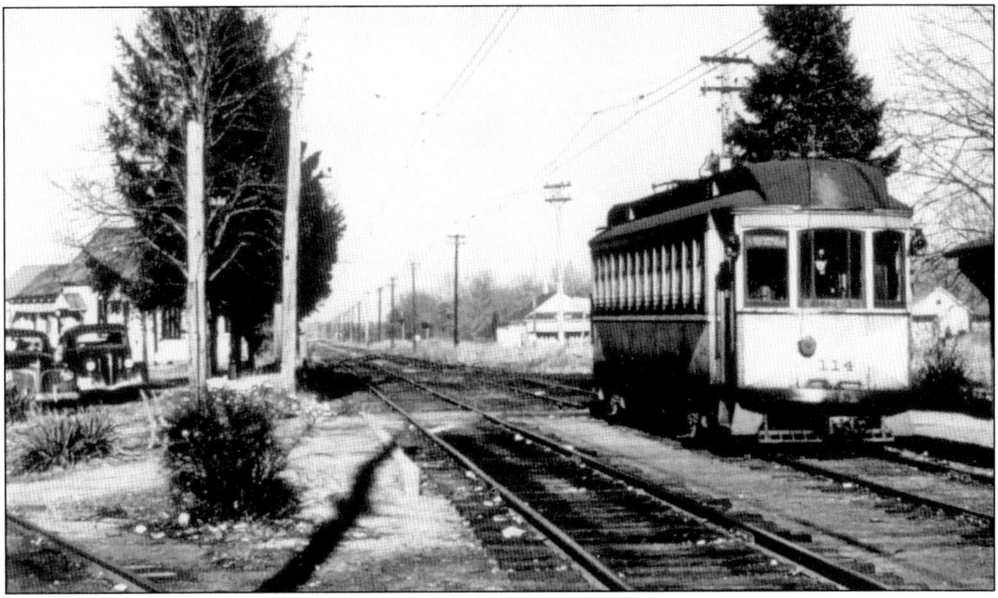

People from Bargaintown and nearby areas often came by horse and buggy to catch the trolley here at Maple Avenue. They stabled their horses in the barn (below) in back of Stuber's Store, which can be seen to the right of center in the background. In 1934, the barn was destroyed by fire. By then Adolph Stuber had a car and needed a garage more than a barn.

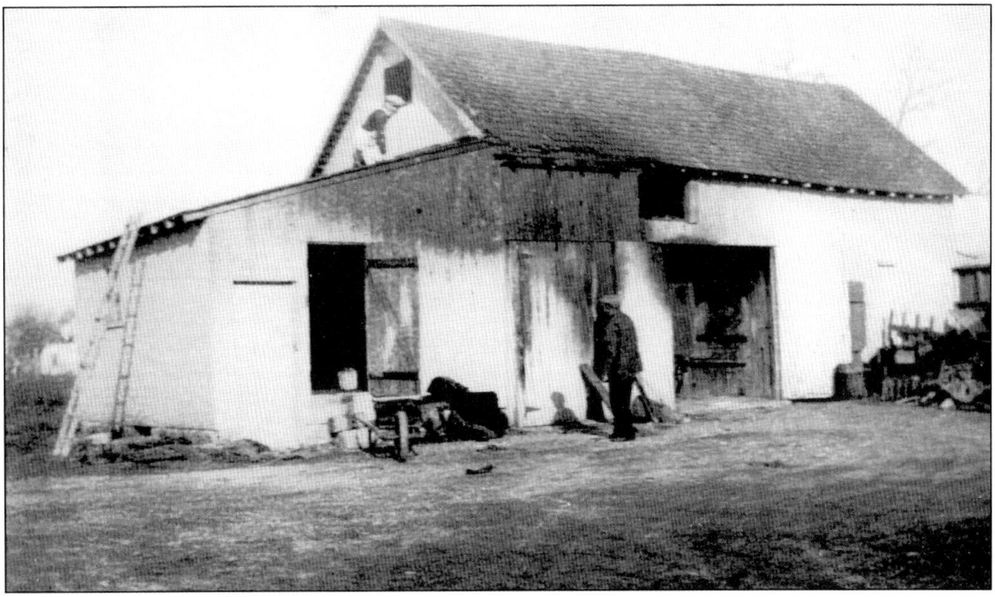

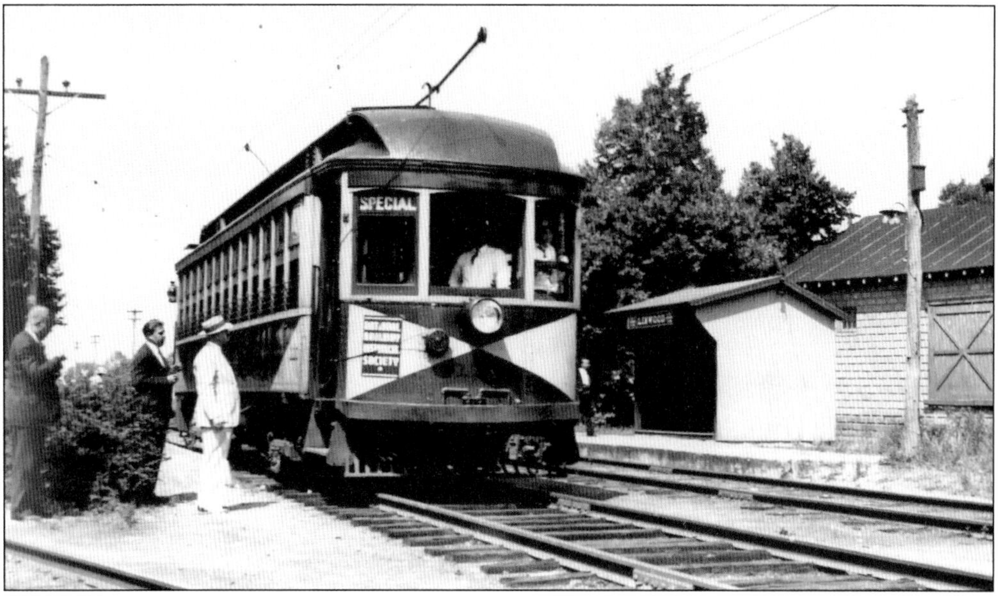

A trolley shed eventually replaced the train station. Hagerthey's Feed Store is shown on the right as these patrons prepare to board the trolley for Ocean City on July 21, 1940. Dot Buckley Gibson remembered one conductor who would slow down so they could jump off at their street, which was not an official trolley stop.

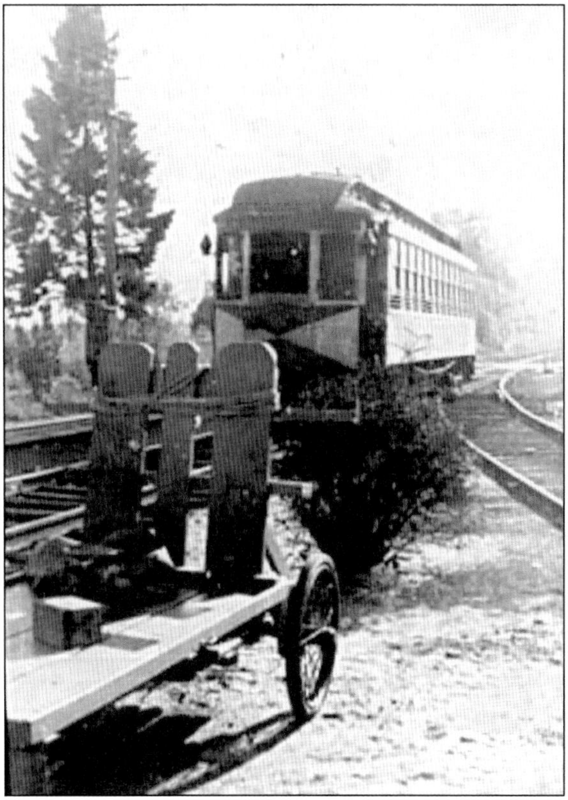

In 1925, there were six mail deliveries a day, three in and three out. Ernest Wright won the bid of $30 a month to move the mail on one of these mail carts. Wright paid his nephew, Arthur Risley, to come over from school on his lunch hour to haul the noon mail. Arthur missed eighth-grade English class often because he did not get back to school in time.

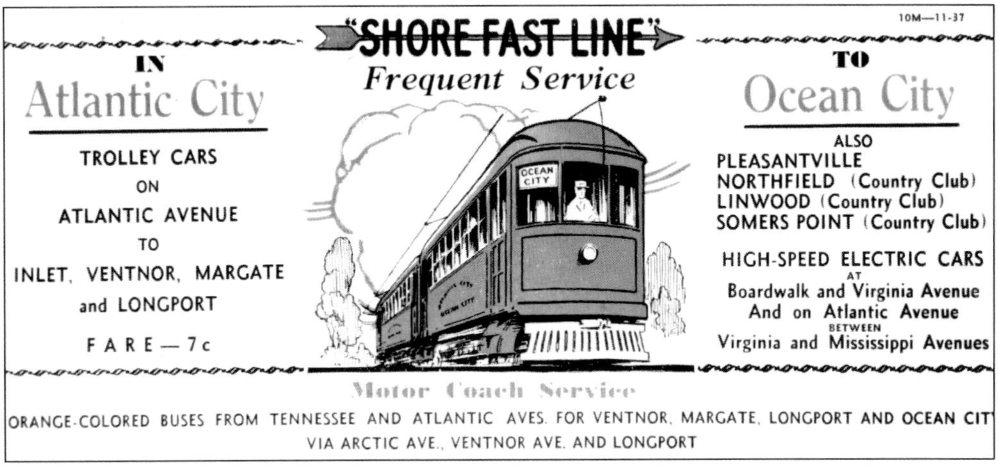

The trolley service was a safe way for young folks to enjoy the entertainment offered at the beach and boardwalks in Ocean City and Atlantic City, as well as the movies in Pleasantville. Students traveled by trolley to attend Pleasantville High School until the service ended in 1948. The trolley (below) winds its way between Patcong and Seaview Avenues. The old rail bed is now a bike path that links towns originally connected by the trolley route.

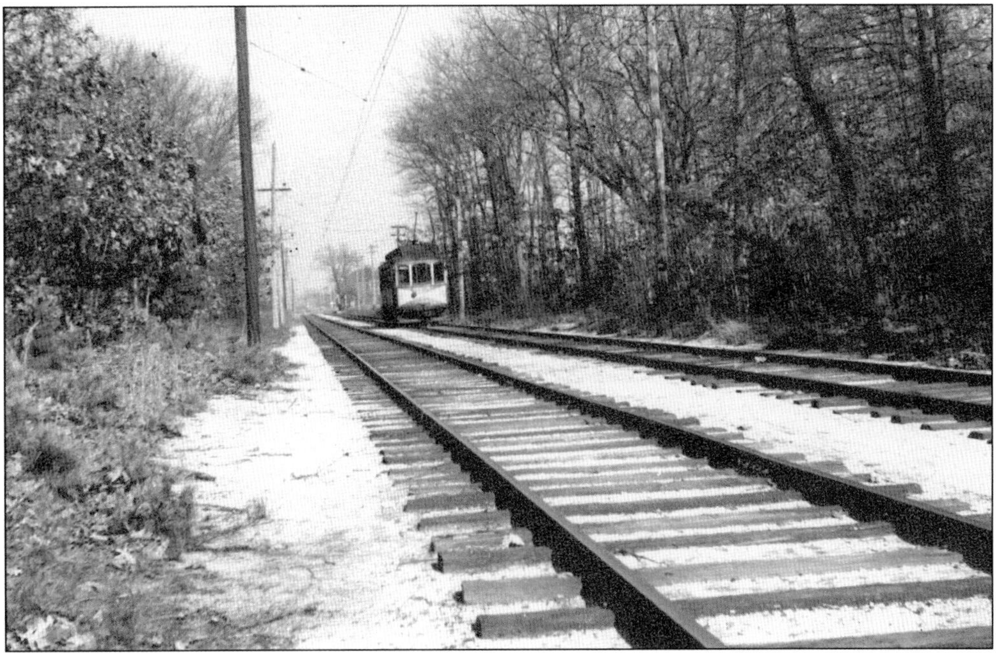

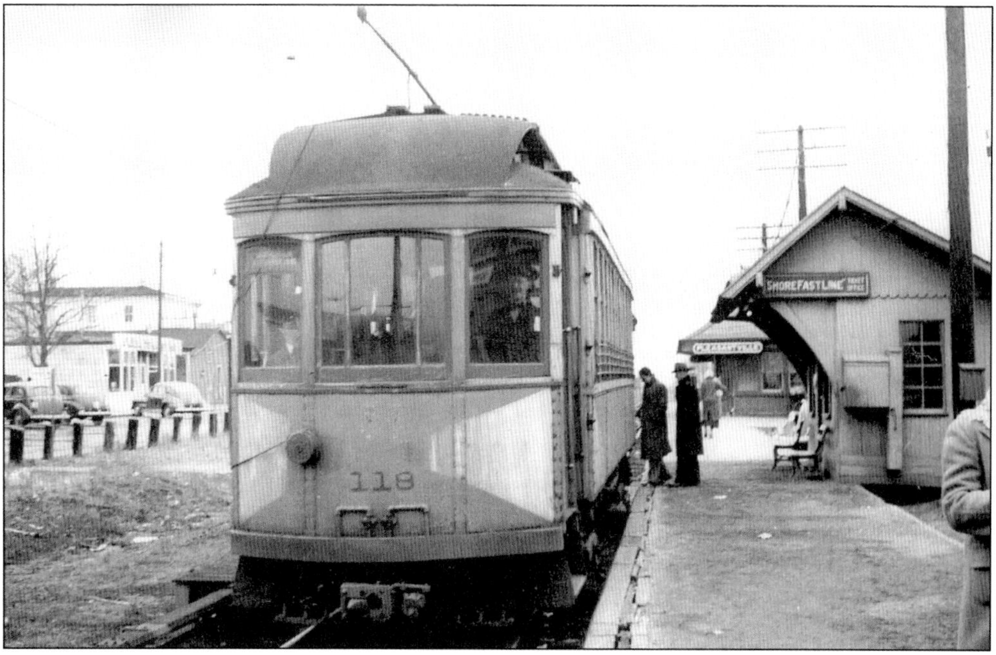

Pleasantville was the main shopping center for many of Linwood's families throughout the first 50 years of the 20th century. The supermarket was just across the tracks from the station. Students loved to catch the trolley to Pleasantville on Saturday afternoons to see the serials shown at the movie theaters. This was the main trolley stop in downtown Pleasantville. (Courtesy of Sarah Manning Adams.)

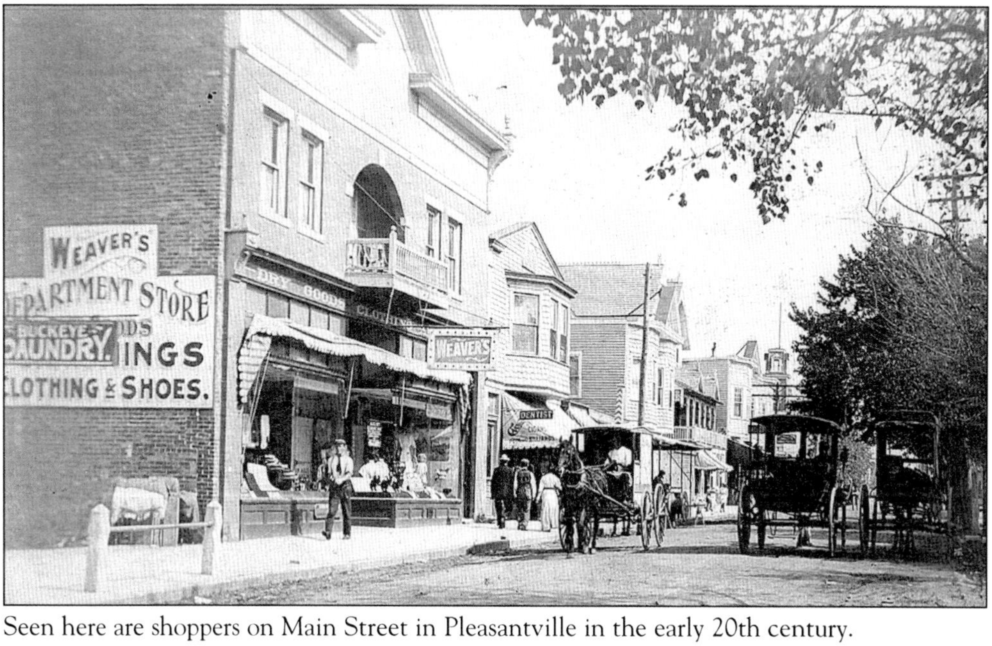

Seen here are shoppers on Main Street in Pleasantville in the early 20th century.

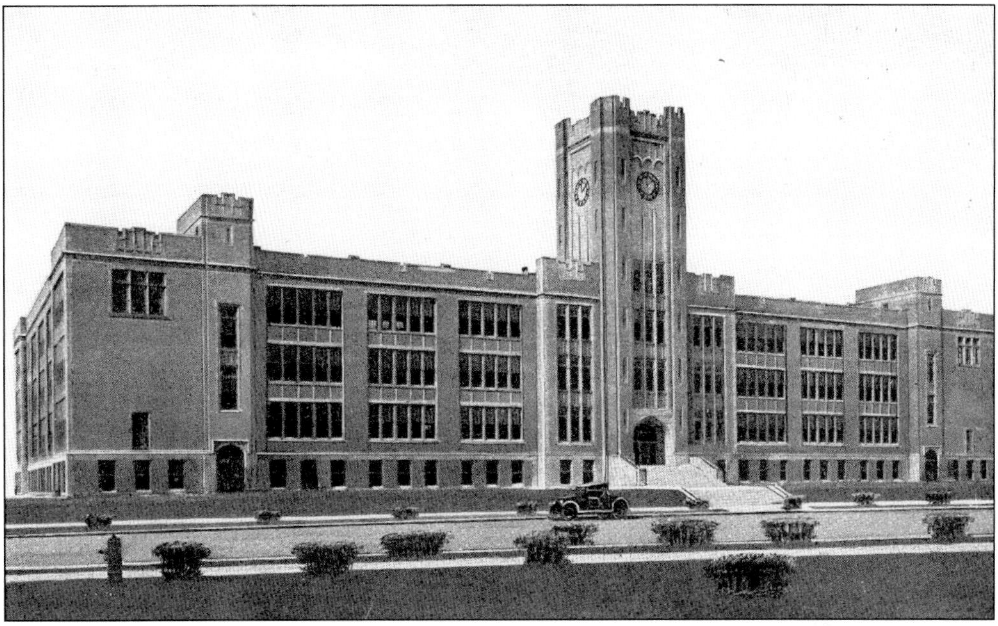

Until the opening of Mainland Regional High School in 1961, high school students from Linwood attended Atlantic City High School (above) until 1931, when they switched to Pleasantville High School (below). Until 1948, students traveled by trolley, using passes distributed monthly at Belhaven School. Those who lost their pass had to pay their own way.

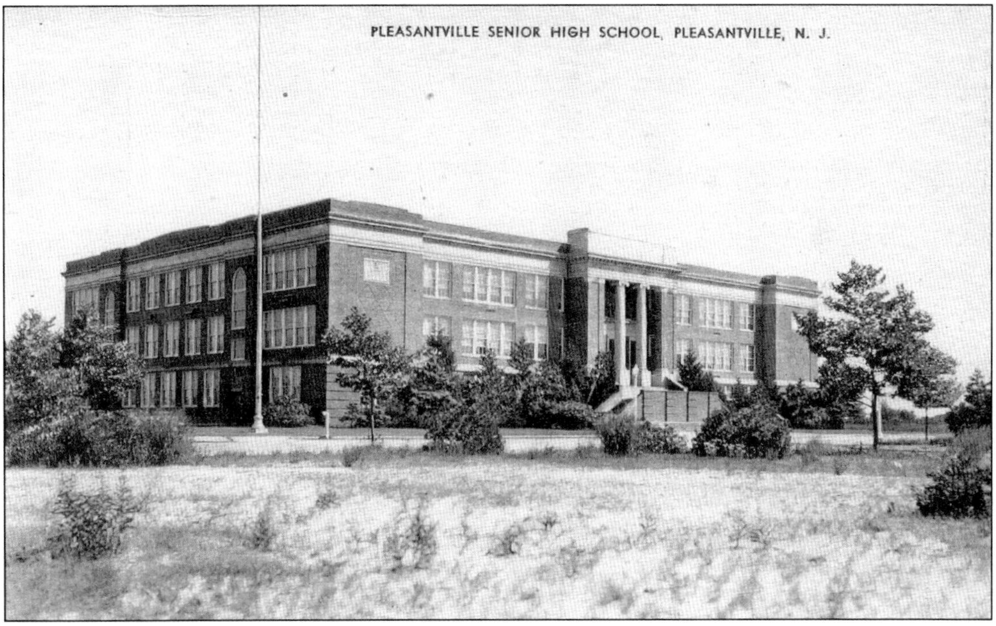

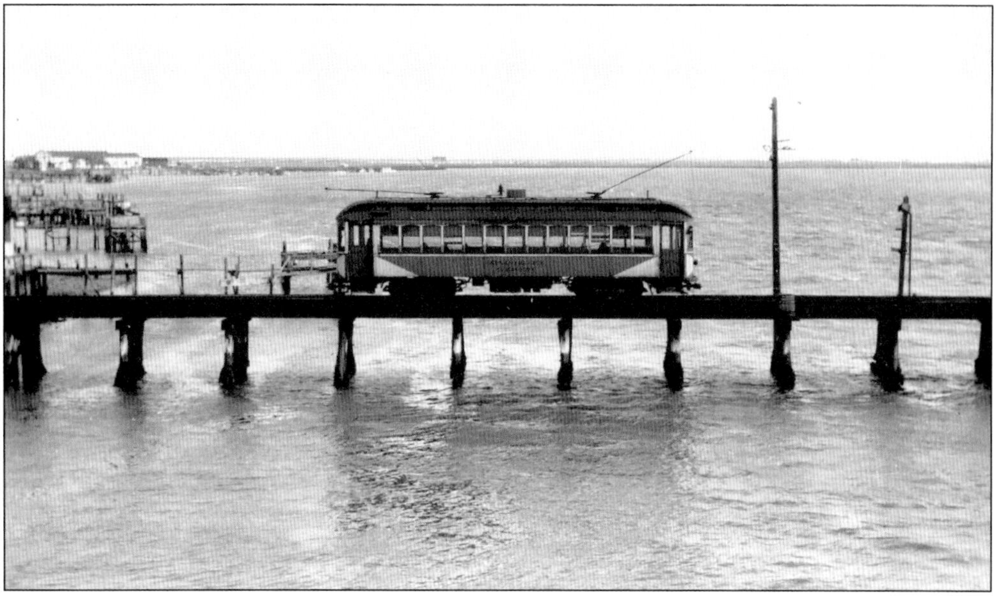

When this trolley (above) started out across the bay from Somers Point to Ocean City on October 11, 1947, the end was near. A fire destroyed part of the trestle into Ocean City and set the stage for a decision to switch to buses. Both the trolleys and the rail bed had deteriorated and were in desperate need of repair. Upgrading was just too expensive. A few months after the line closed in 1948, trolleys were photographed in the trolley graveyard (below).

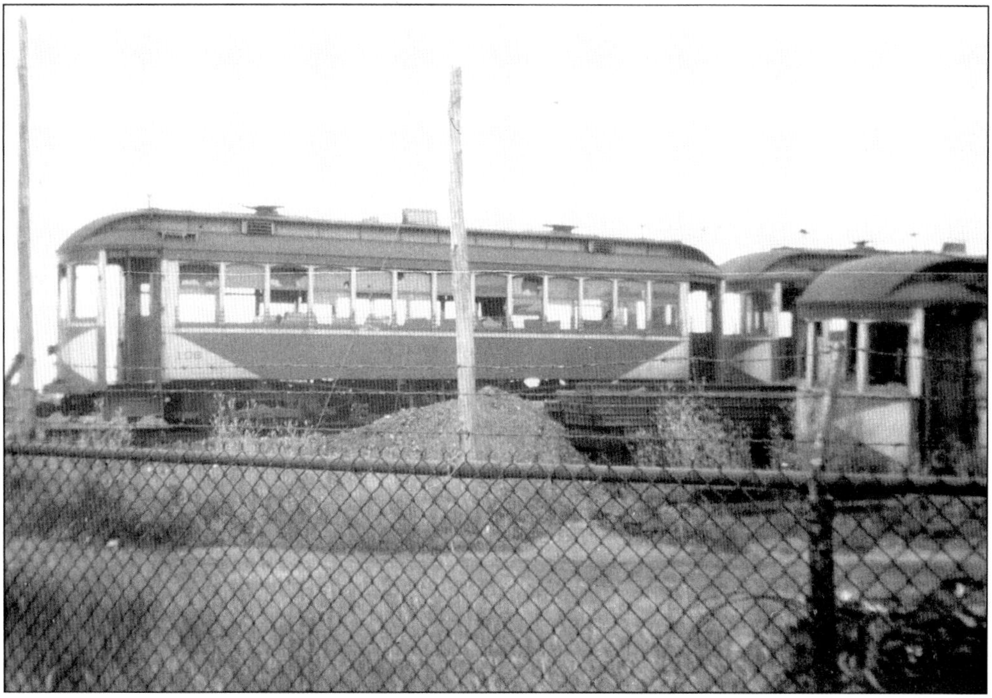

Five

Linwood City

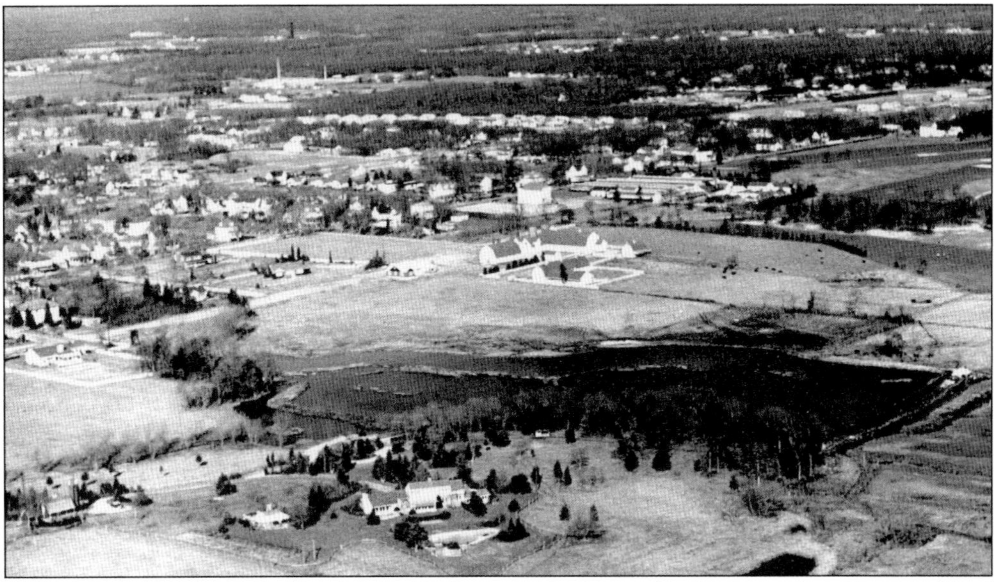

On April 27, 1931, under new state regulations, the borough of Linwood incorporated and became a city. The 1920s had been an optimistic time, with new homes constructed in Woodlynne Manor east of Shore Road and a new school called Crestlea Park that opened in the fall of 1927. Everything came to a halt during the Great Depression, and the new school was boarded up. Linwood residents rallied to the cause after the attack on Pearl Harbor in 1941, and everything else was put on hold for the duration. Industrial developments brought about by World War II created new jobs and new demands for housing that altered the landscape of Linwood forever. The Brighton Farm barns were still present in this 1954 photograph, but their days were numbered.

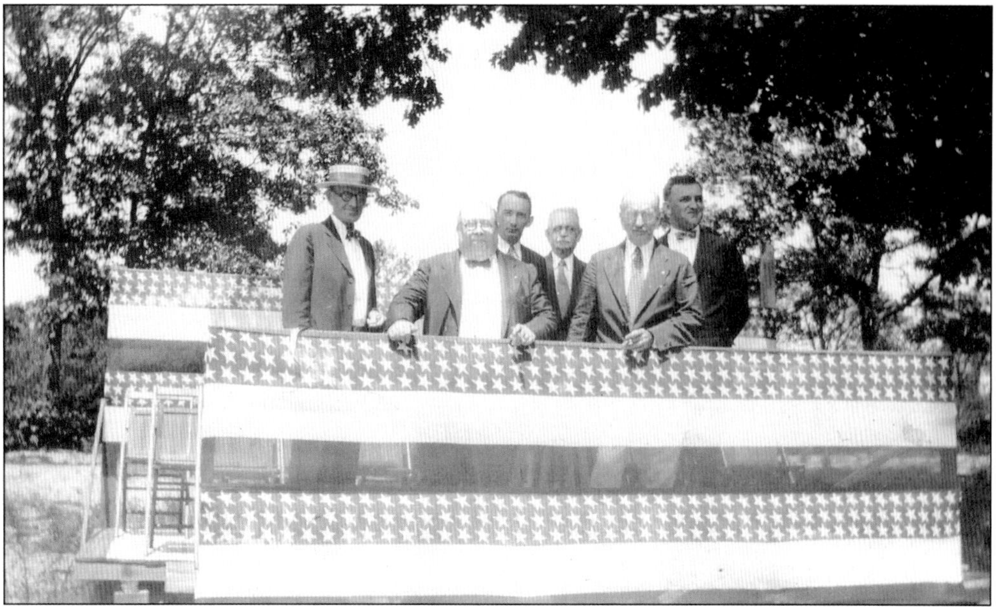

Prominent Linwood citizens appear at a patriotic rally *c.* 1931. From left to right are Winfred VanSant, Jacob Nagle, two unidentified people, Mayor Thomas Yates, and an unidentified man. Yates was the first mayor of the city of Linwood, but he resigned before the end of his term in an apparent dispute with city employees. He was succeeded in office by Winfred VanSant.

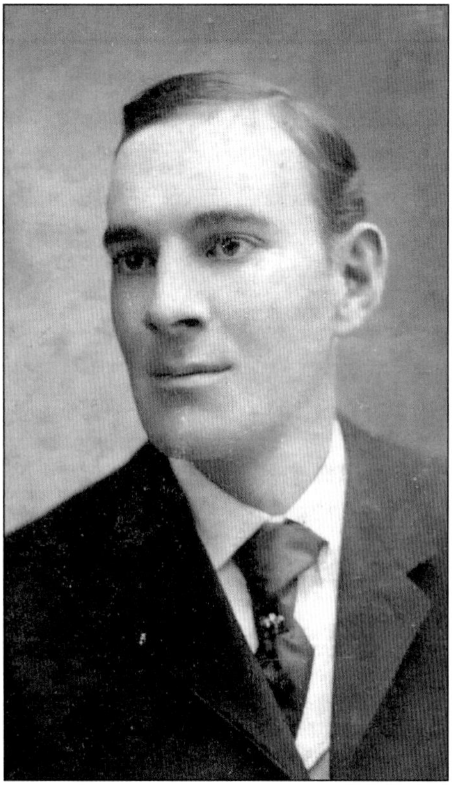

Winfred VanSant was born and raised in Linwood and graduated from the old Leedsville Poplar School in 1899. He served four terms as mayor of Linwood from 1934 to 1941. VanSant remained active in Linwood politics throughout his life. At his retirement the whole town turned out at a testimonial dinner in his honor. He served on the wartime defense council during World War II.

KEEP LINWOOD DRY

Our Town Voted Dry Long Before Prohibition

Lets Keep it Dry by voting ☒ NO on the Second Public Question.

If You Stay Home and Fail To Vote . . You are a Supporter of the Saloon.

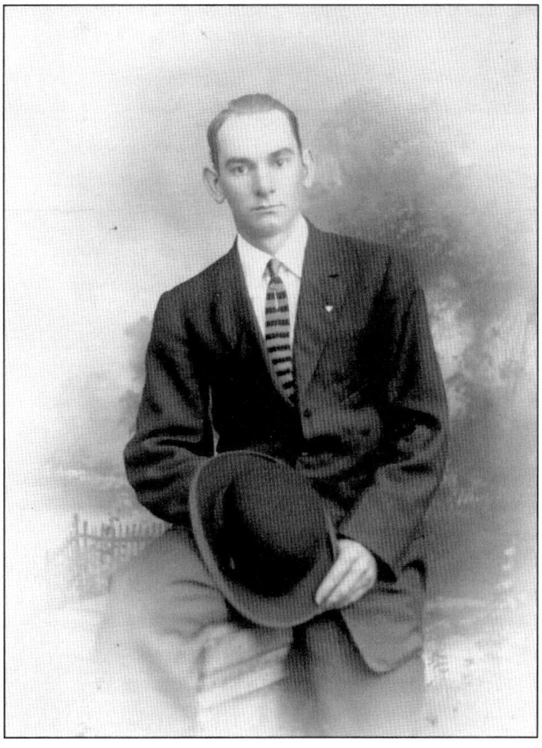

Walter VanSant (right) once said he felt that the most important accomplishment of his life was winning the vote to prohibit the sale of alcohol in Linwood. In 1935, a number of voters filed a petition requesting a referendum on the issue of prohibition. VanSant led a strong campaign to prevent liquor sales. The final vote of 287 for and 346 against allowing liquor sales made Linwood a dry town. William Krumm's Seaview Winery was exempted by the New Jersey Alcoholic Beverage Control, which permitted a limited winery license.

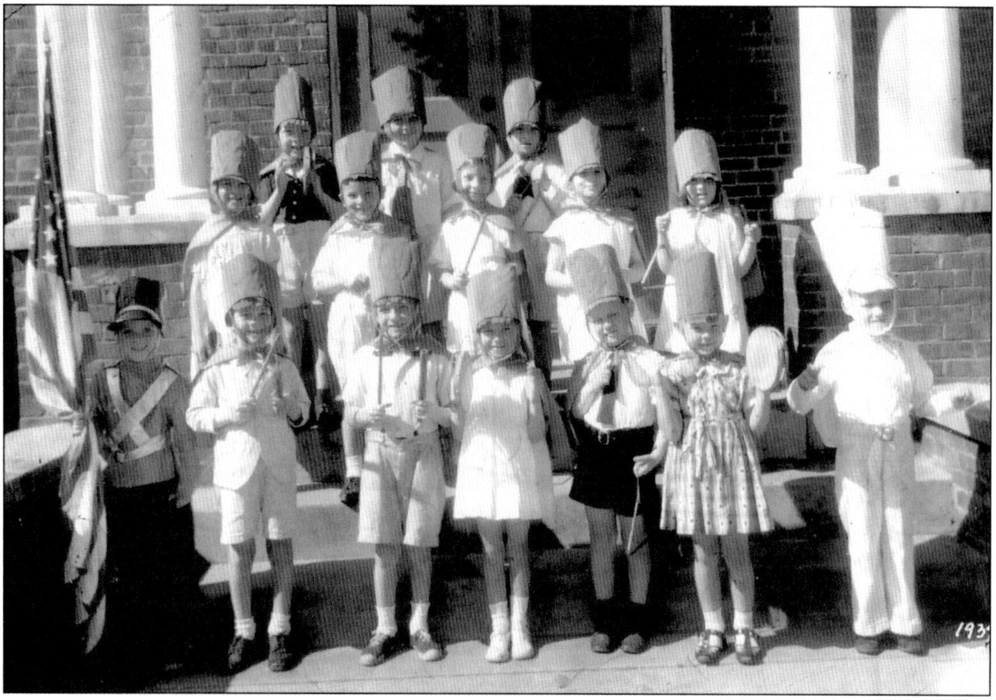

Members of the first-grade class enjoy showing off their musical ensemble in 1938. Participants included Bud Bell, Peggy Collins, Nancy Martin, Robert Miller, and Jerrie Gifford. (Courtesy of Jerrie Gifford Bruno.)

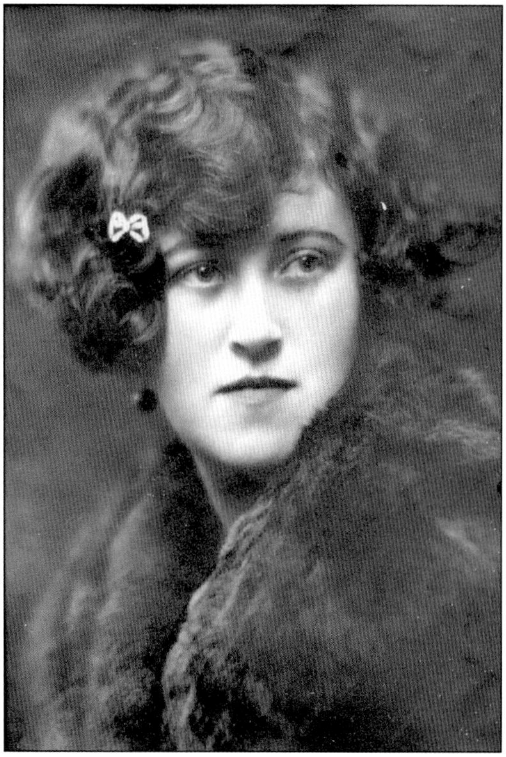

Altha Allen Kirk came to teach at the Belhaven School in 1923 and stayed for over three decades. Her students remembered her with great fondness as someone who cared deeply about them and gave them a strong start in their important primary grade school years. (Courtesy of James Kirk III.)

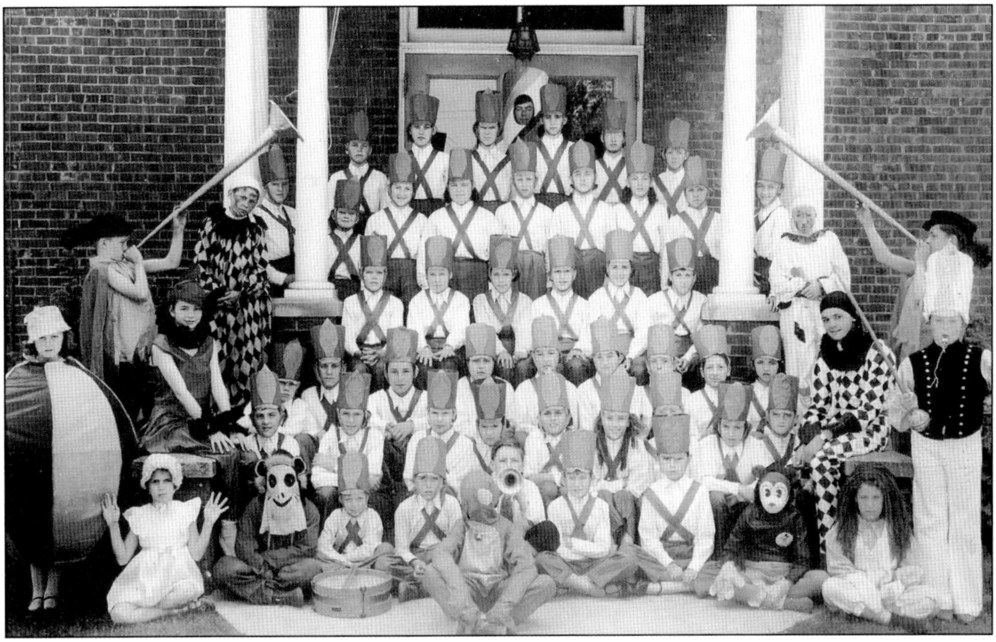

It looks like the whole school was involved in this Belhaven musical production of 1934. Just setting up this photograph must have taken hours.

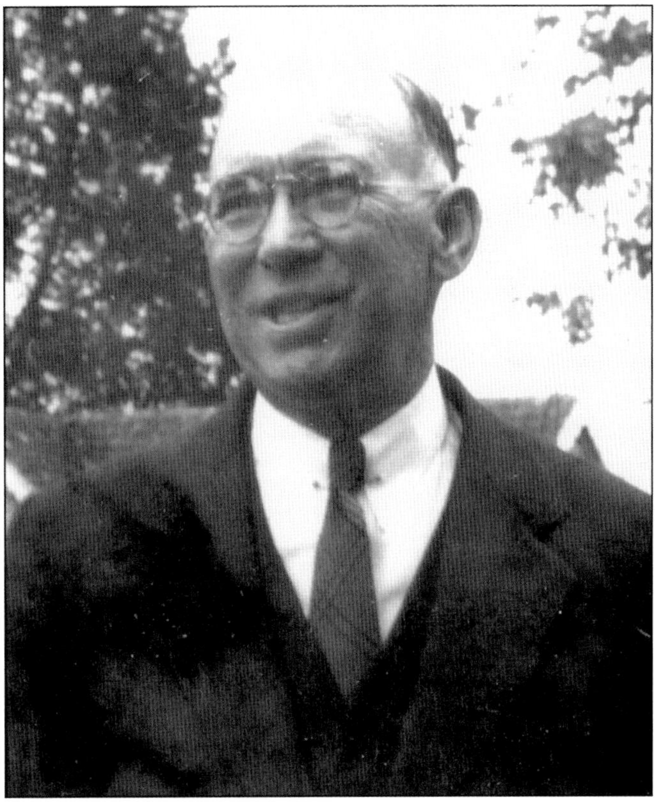

George L. Collins was a popular teacher and principal from *c.* 1923 to 1946. As principal, he tried to match the punishment to the crime and teach a lesson at the same time. When two boys were caught fighting on the playground, he pinned their collars together with a horse blanket safety pin and they spent the afternoon learning how to get along. (Courtesy of Jerrie Gifford Bruno.)

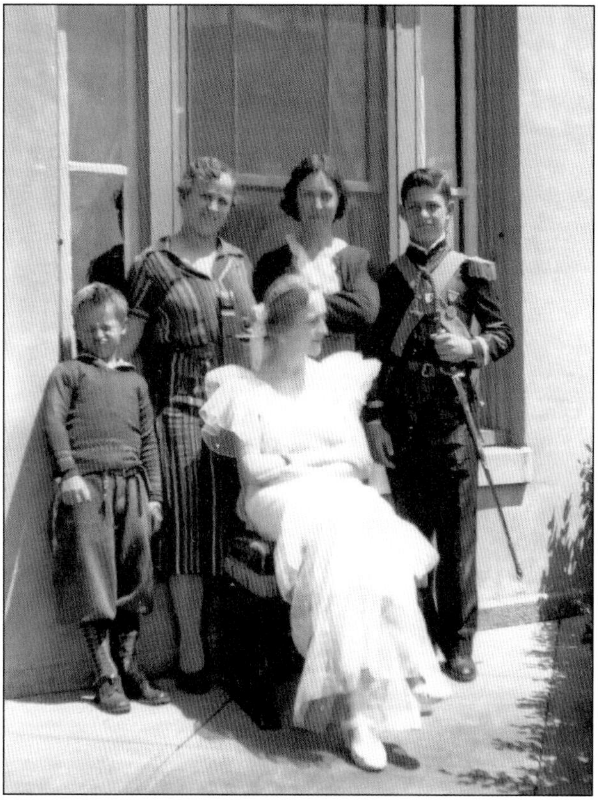

In 1933, Tom Adams (right) and Elsie Heeland (seated) appeared as the prince and princess in a school play. Before the performance, they visited Elsie's family. With them, from left to right, are Earl Heeland, Martha Heeland, and Virginia Adams.

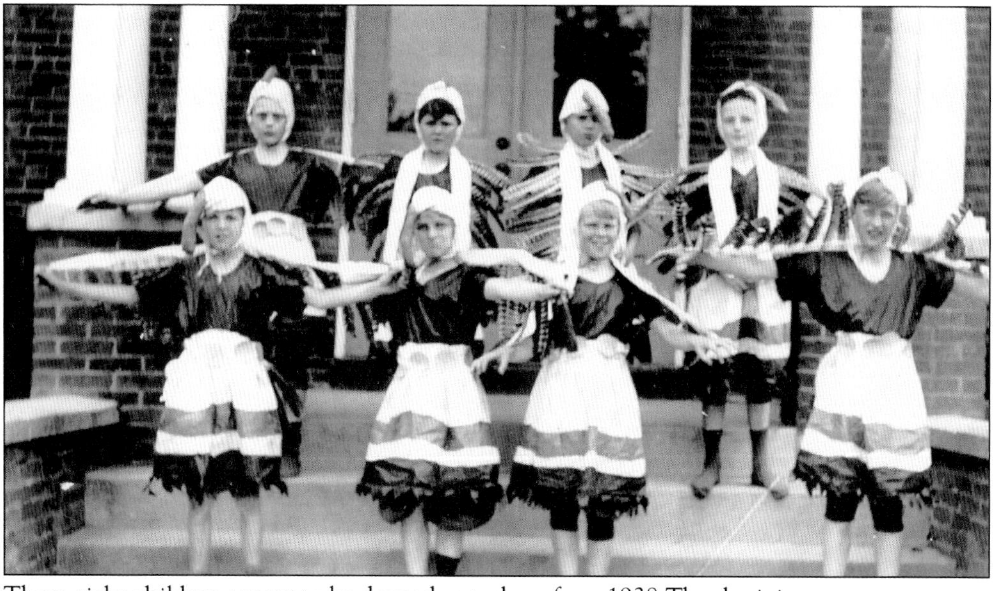

These eight children appear to be dressed as turkeys for a 1938 Thanksgiving program.

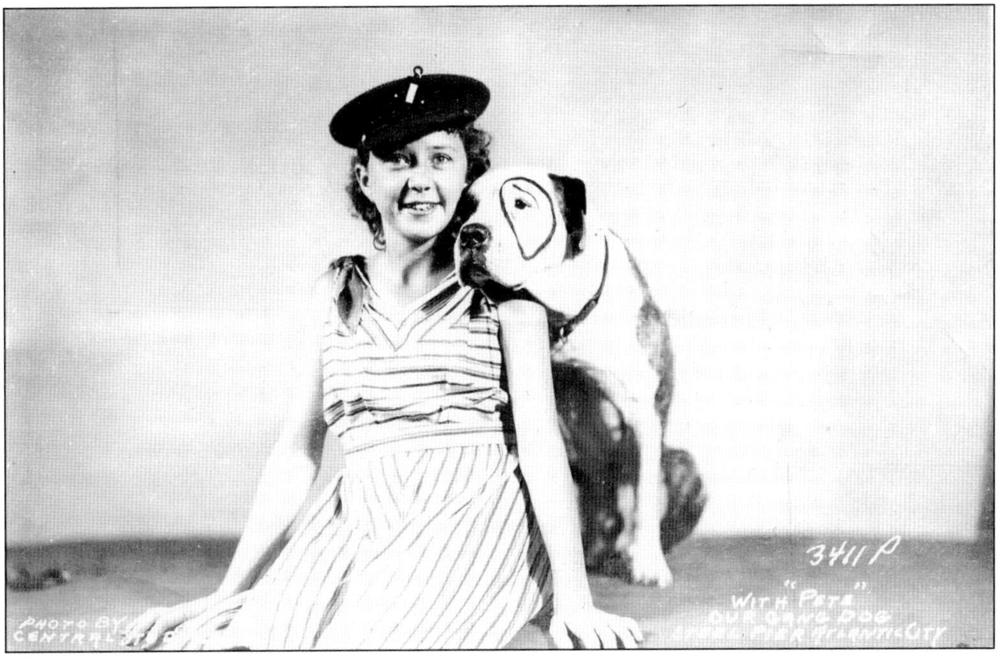

One of the delights of childhood in the prewar years was to go to Steel Pier in Atlantic City and have a picture taken with Pete, the dog from the Little Rascals. Adults knew that the dog was not always the same one, but that did not matter to children. Dolly Weatherby and Pete strike a charming pose. (Courtesy of Dolly Weatherby Street.)

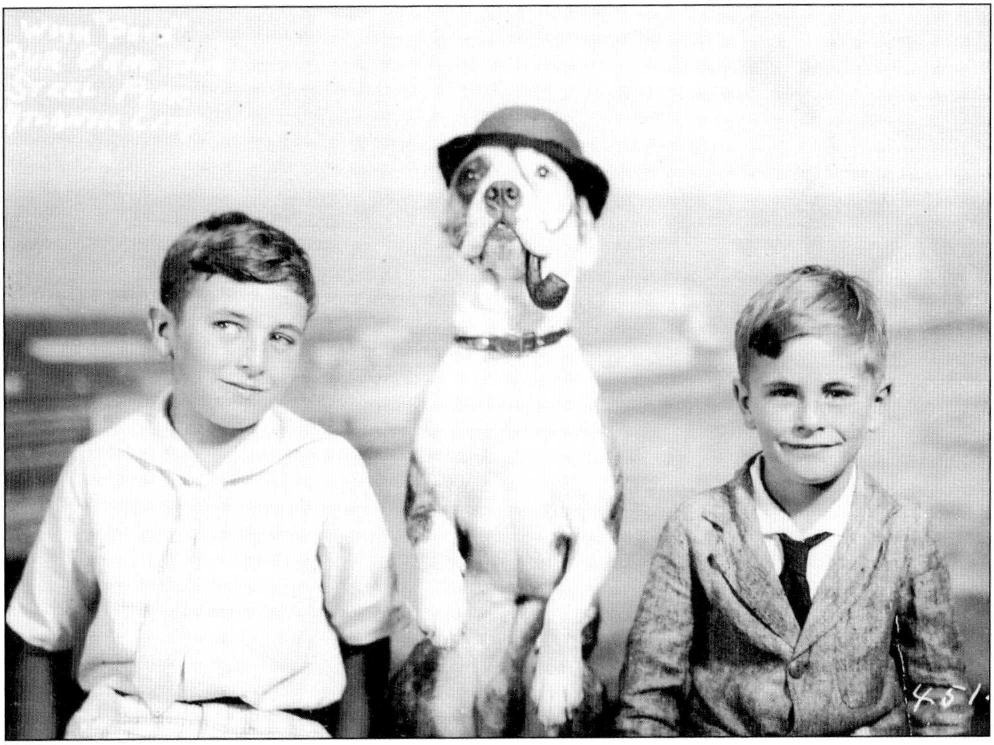

Walter and Eugene Ivins also enjoy their moment with Pete.

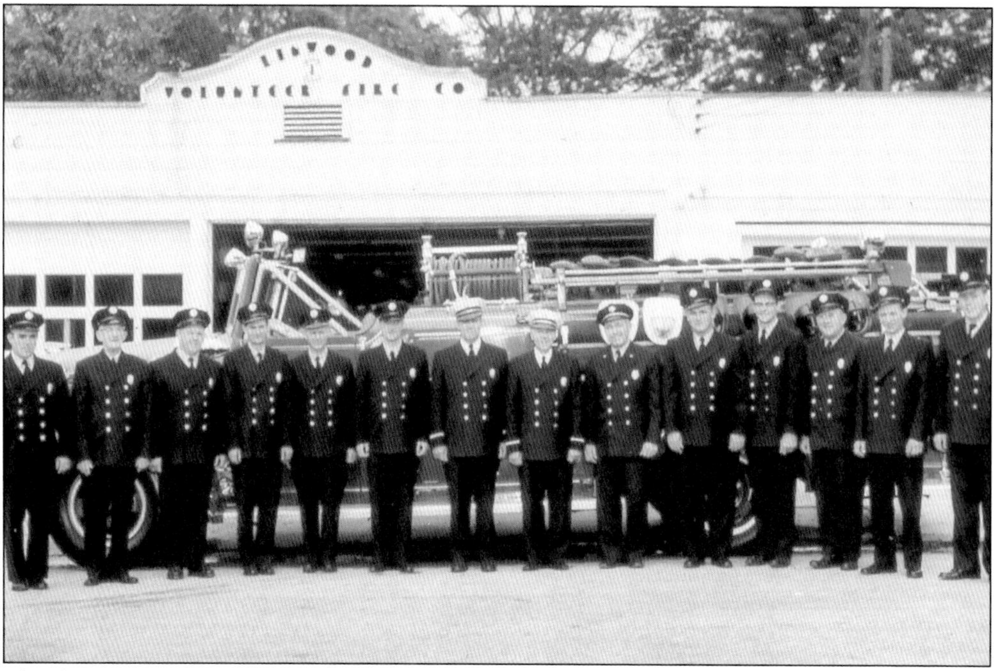

The fire company poses for a formal photograph sometime in 1956. From left to right are unidentified, George Dunbar, Walter Camp, Richard Bowen, two unidentified, Assistant Chief Tom Dix, Chief Stan Voss, Dudley Phillips, Wayne Blank, S. Bill Bartlett, Emory Lee, Robert Rinker, and unidentified. In 1976, the fire company built a new fire hall.

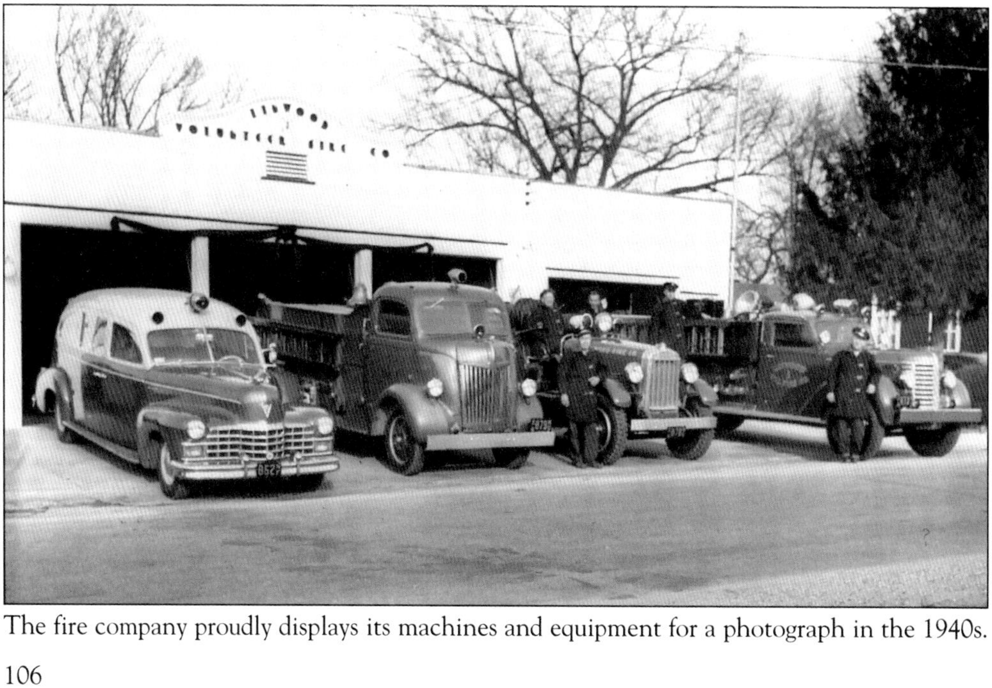

The fire company proudly displays its machines and equipment for a photograph in the 1940s.

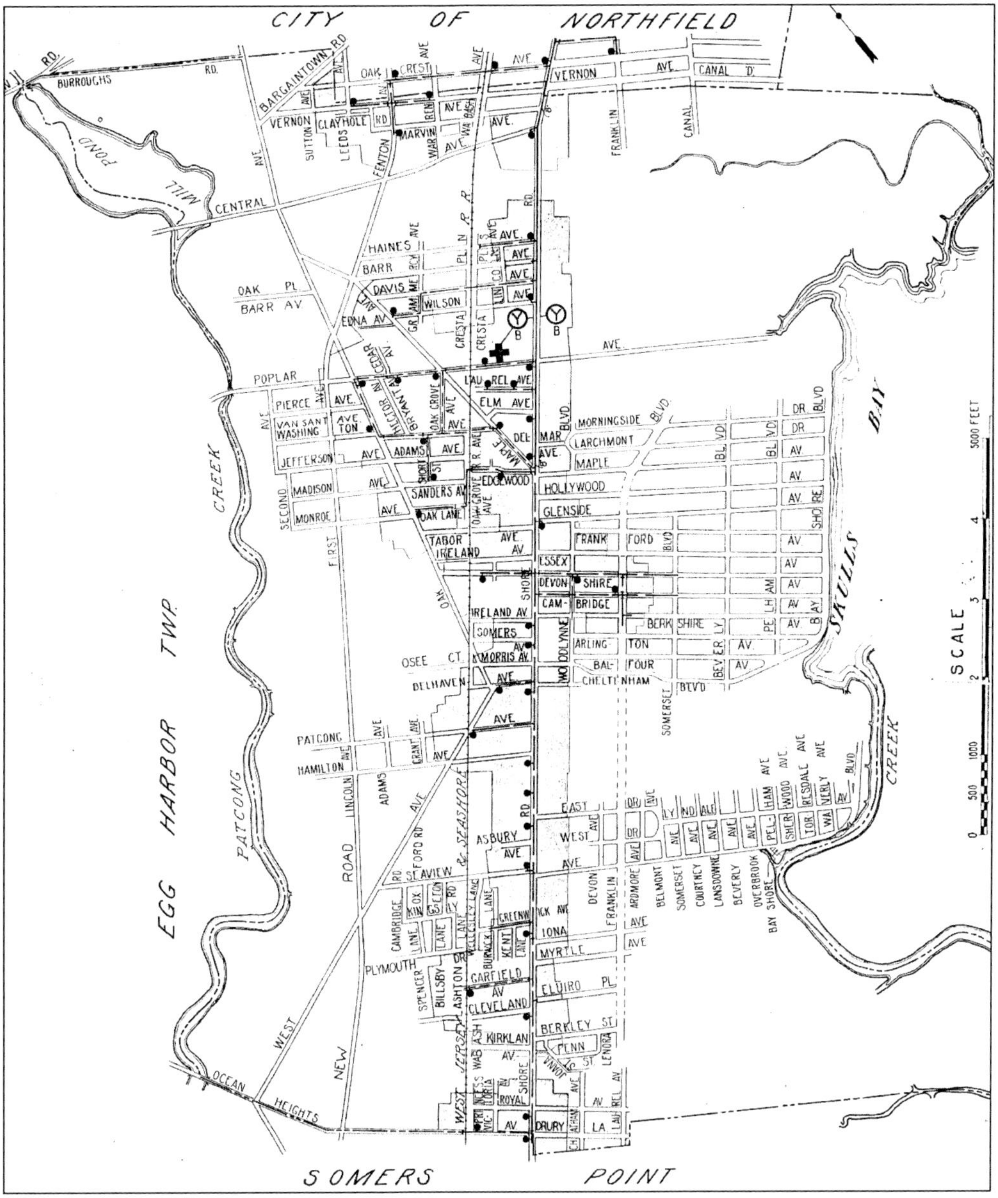

A 1937 fire survey report on Linwood accounted that "The population is 1514 from the 1930 census. The town is principally a residential community with no manufacturing. The area is about 4.25 square miles with main streets paved in good condition and other roads in gravel in fairly good condition. The fire station has electric lights, hot water, heat and two telephones. Chief drills are held twice monthly and the entire department responds to all alarms. Fire alarms are telephoned to the fire house and a coded signal is sounded on a siren on the city hall adjacent to the fire station. There is a uniformed marshal, special police officers and an automobile is provided."

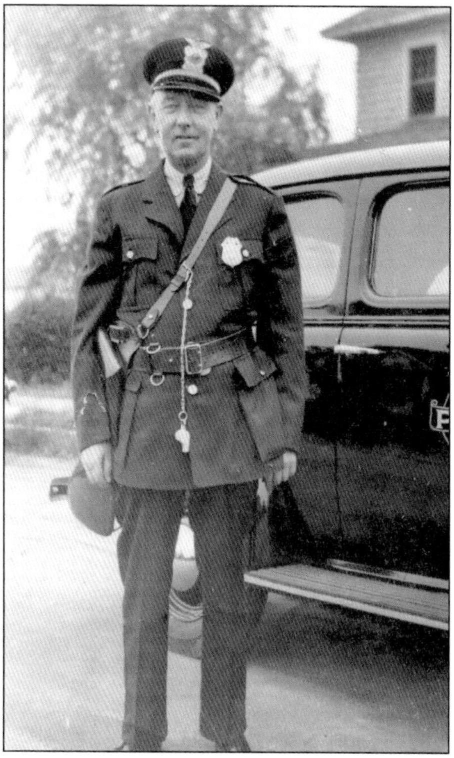

In 1928, the borough council voted against creating a police department, but by 1931, when the city was incorporated, the members had changed their minds. Jesse James was appointed as the town marshal. A few years later, the title was changed to chief of police. While they were waiting to set up a phone service, they installed a red light on the roof of city hall to summon the chief in an emergency. James kept a daily journal of each day's events.

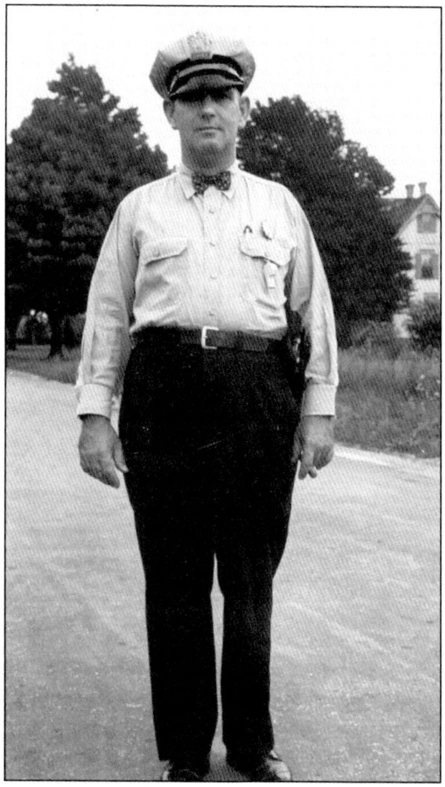

One of Jesse James's favorite stories to tell was based on an event that supposedly happened when he was off duty one day. Dressed in civilian clothes, he stopped a woman who was speeding down Shore Road. She asked him who he was, and when he told her he was Jesse James, she replied, "Well, I'm Betsey Ross," and drove away. James died in 1943, and Joseph Fabian (right) was appointed as his successor.

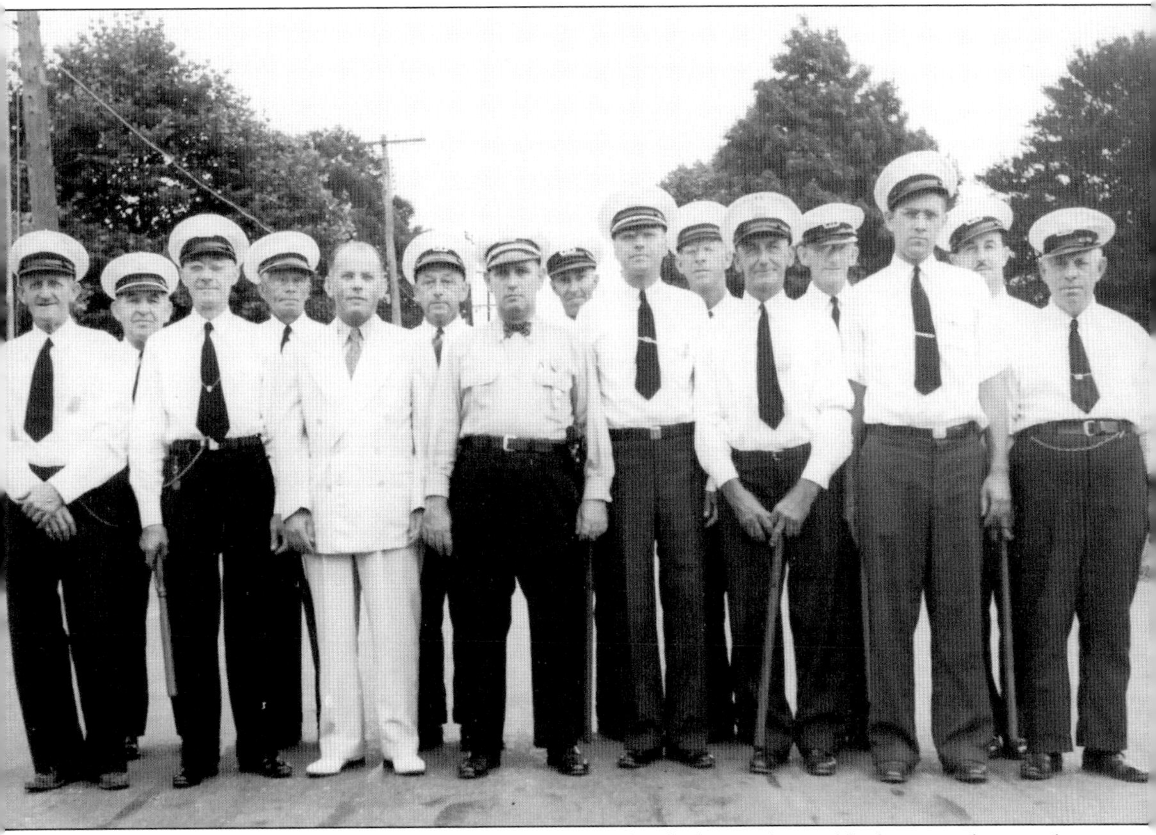

During World War II, auxiliary police were appointed to help out during blackouts and air-raid drills. They took time out for a photograph in 1945. From left to right are the following: (front row) Sgt. George Dunbar, Sgt. Lewis Shaw, Mayor Charles Buckley, Chief Joseph Fabian, Capt. Theo Giese, Sgt. Winfield Haines, Sgt. Thomas Dix Jr., and Howard Fluck; (back row) Charles St. Charles, Benjamin Sickman, James Price, Curtis Farish, Vincent Lake, Robert Young, and Lewis Kinzer.

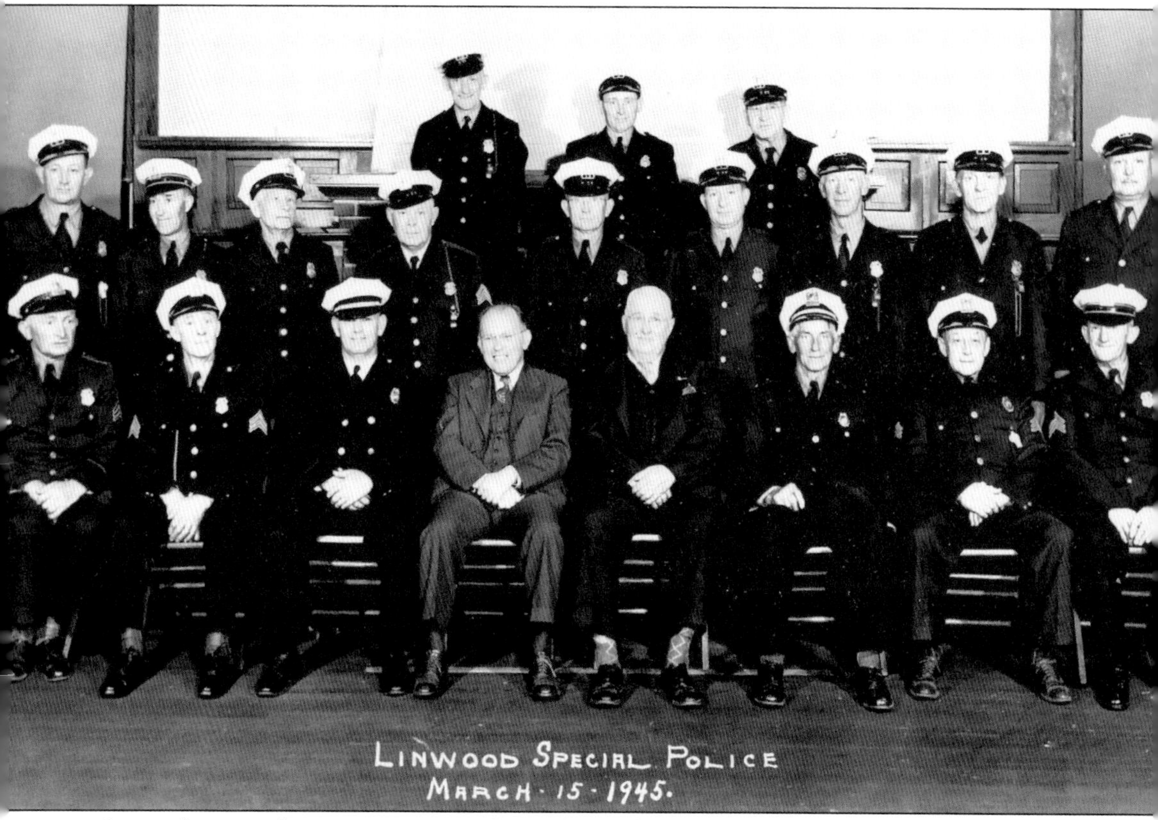

In another pose for posterity in March 1945, members of the special police force are recorded with city officials. In 1942, Winfred VanSant was defense council chairman. He reported that the telephone company was installing two telephones on August 19 for use of the defense council. The telephones were for emergency use only. Another 15 telephones were being installed throughout the city for use by air raid wardens. From left to right the following: (front row) Mark Kears, Lew Shaw, Joe Fabian, Mayor Charles Buckley, City Clerk Harry Pennel, Winfield Haines, Jim Price, and George Dunbar; (middle row) Ray Kearsley, Curt Farish, Ben Sickman, Howard Fluck, four unidentified men, and Ralph Hunt; (back row) unidentified, Jim Hutchins, and unidentified.

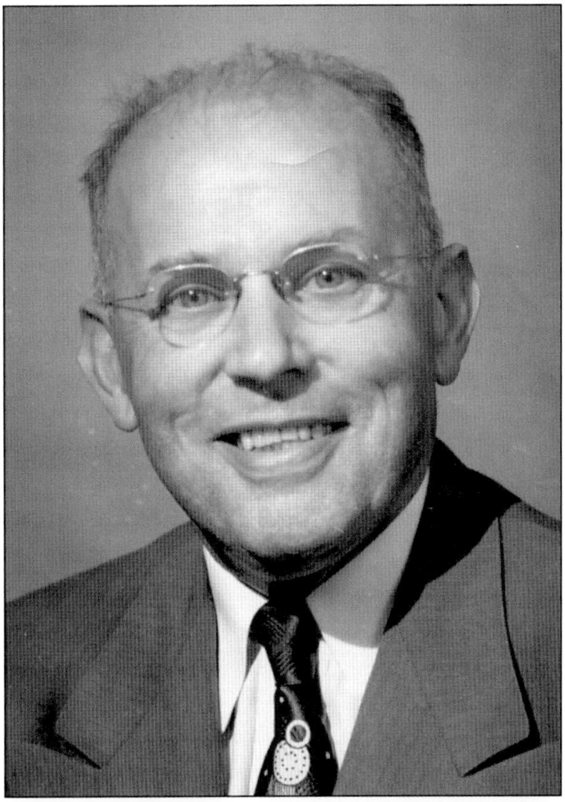

Charles Buckley served four terms as Linwood's mayor from 1942 to 1949. He married Marion Aydelotte (below). Buckley was an instrumental figure in the creation of the recreation field in 1947 and is credited with suggesting that the field be called the All Wars Memorial Park. He was a very popular figure, and at his retirement grateful citizens presented him with a testimonial certificate signed by most of Linwood's adult residents.

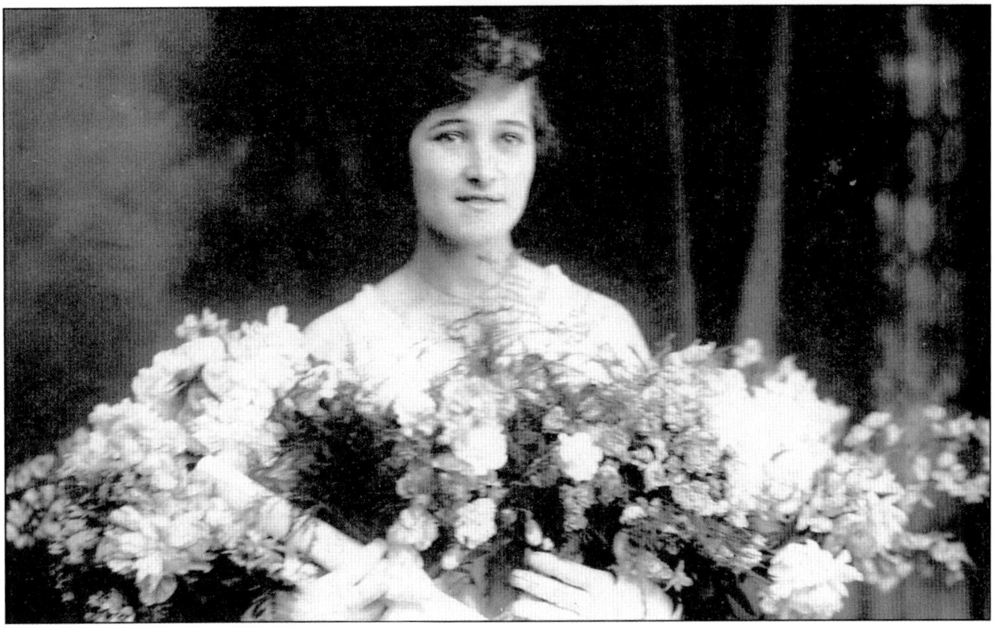

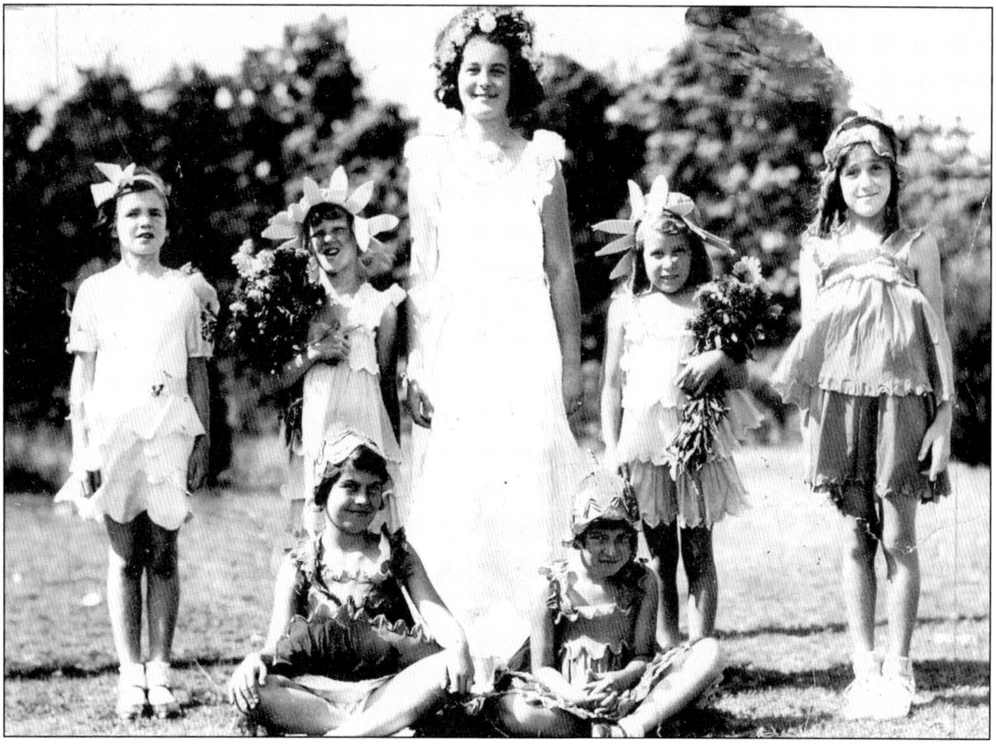

Shown are the queen and her attendants in the *c.* 1931 Mother's League Central Church Baby Parade. From left to right are the following: (front row) Florence Probst and Phyllis Wolfbrandt; (back row) unidentified, J. Ruth Buckley, Doris Hopper, Betty Buckley, and Marie Schug.

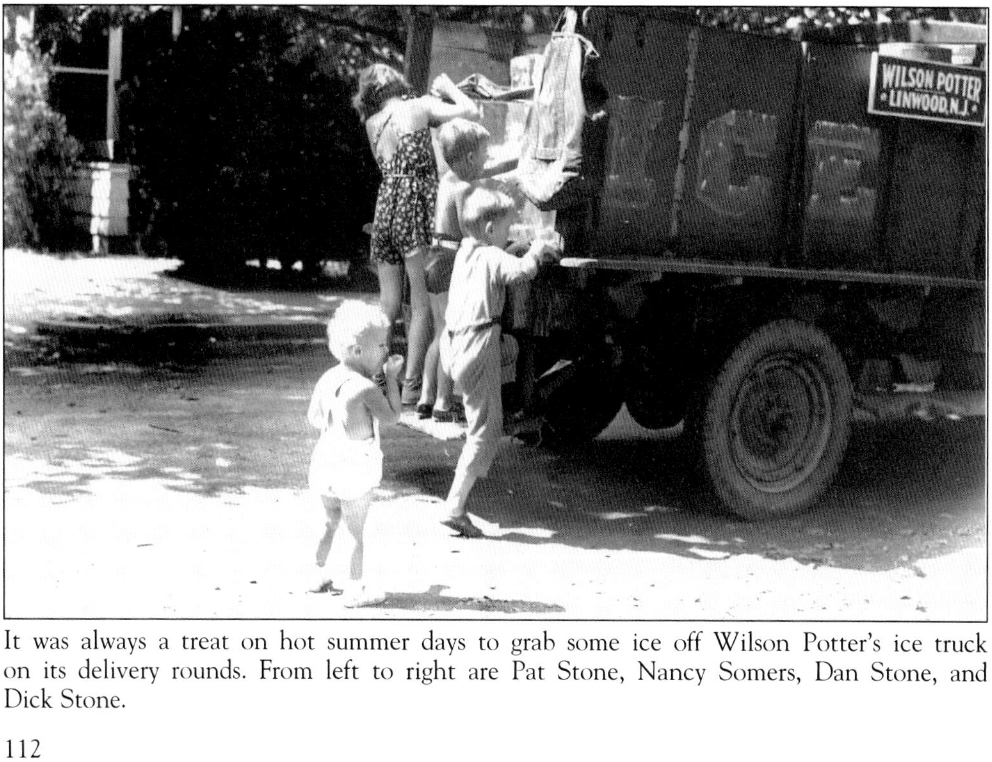

It was always a treat on hot summer days to grab some ice off Wilson Potter's ice truck on its delivery rounds. From left to right are Pat Stone, Nancy Somers, Dan Stone, and Dick Stone.

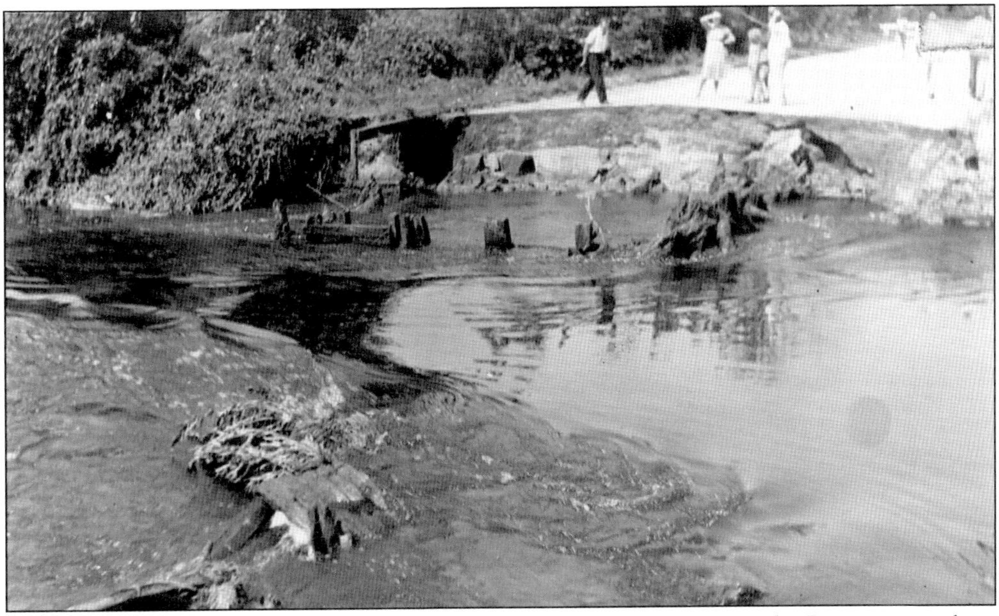

In the summer of 1933, a major washout occurred on Central Avenue at the Bargaintown dam. People came from all over town to see it. It was the second of three such washouts to occur in the 20th century. Others were in 1908 and 1997.

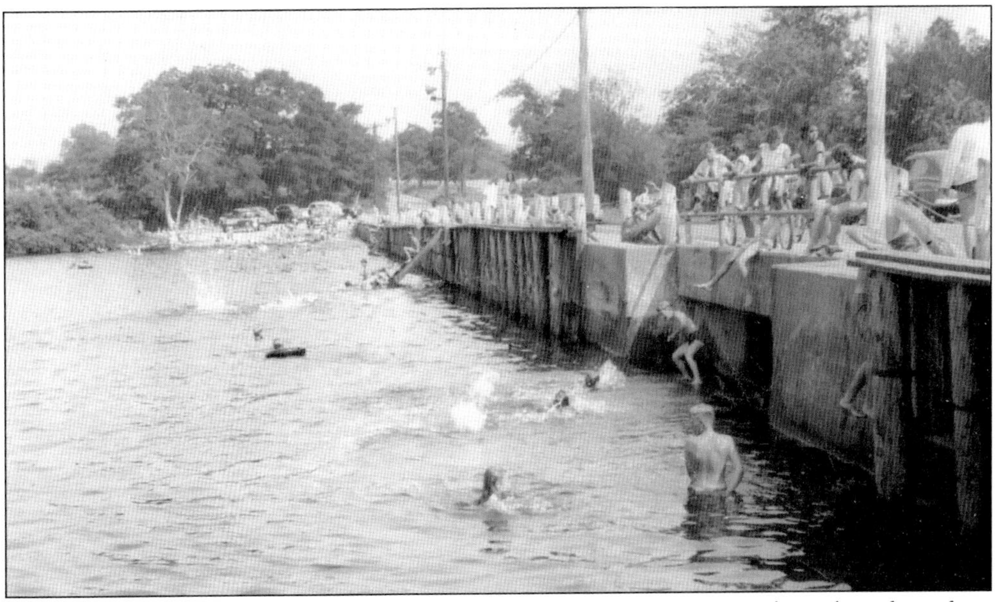

The pond was a favorite swimming hole for decades. The water was the color of tea from the cedar stumps left in Patcong Creek. By summer's end, all of the bathing suits had the tea-dyed look.

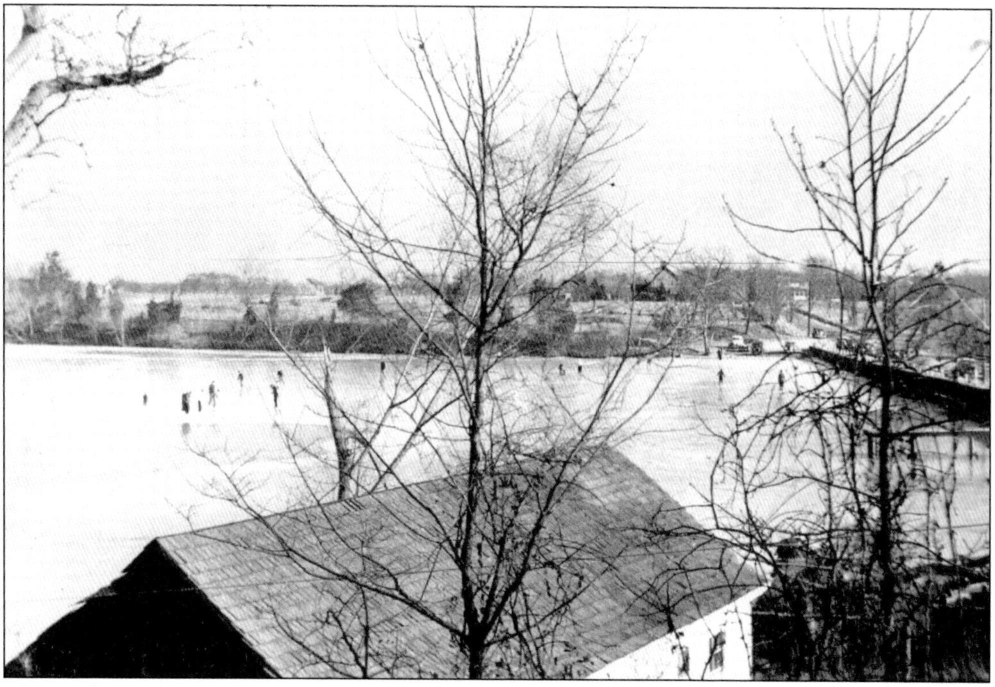

The Mill Pond continued to be a recreational center into the mid-1900s, as these pictures indicate. The upper photograph was taken during the early 1940s, and the lower one is from the 1950s. Both pictures were taken by Win Boileau.

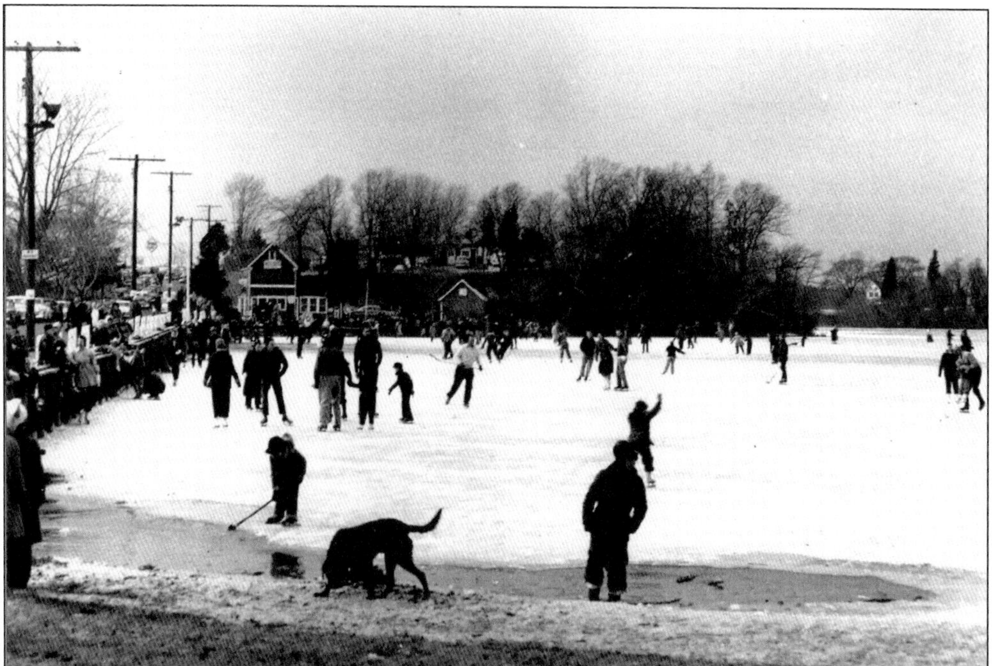

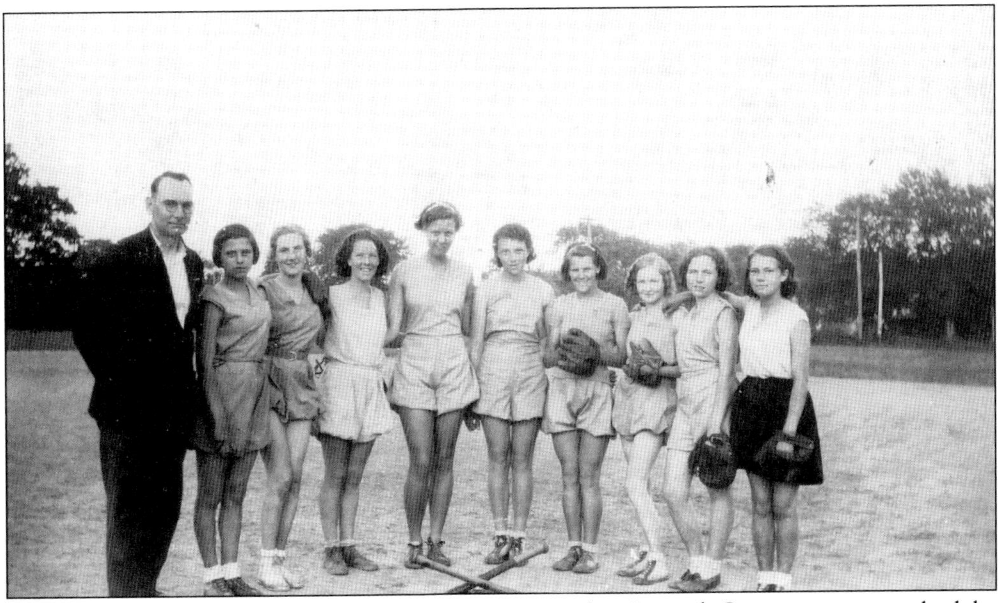

Linwood had a girls baseball team in the 1930s. The Central Comets were coached by Walter VanSant (left). With him, from left to right, are Betty Wright, Martha Wenlock, Myrtle Rose, Caroline James, Jeanne Buckley, Hazel Rose, Elizabeth Thorne, Dorothy Phillips, and Loretta Brown.

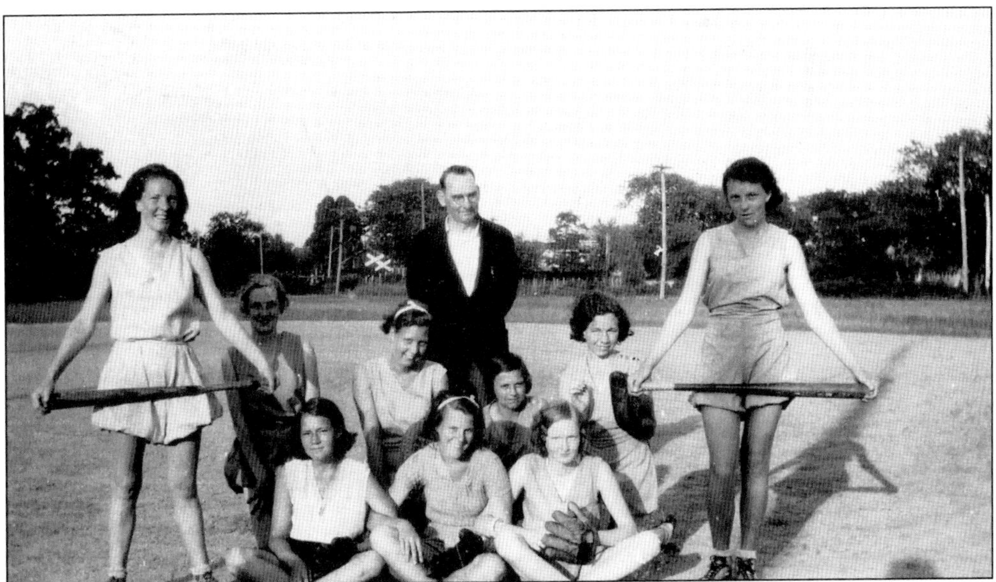

A newspaper article stated that the team had scheduled a game with one of the boy's baseball teams, but nothing could be found about the outcome of that game.

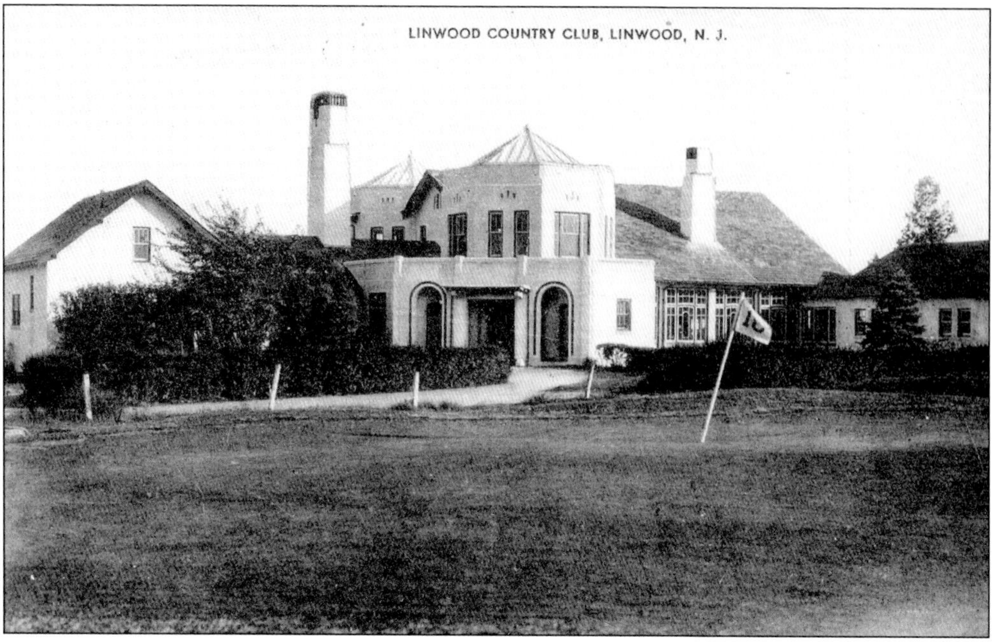

The Linwood Country Club opened in 1921. Men who helped to construct the links told stories about finding Indian grave sites during the work. This is not surprising since the club was built near the Poplar Avenue landing area where Indians came to spend summers long before Europeans settled here.

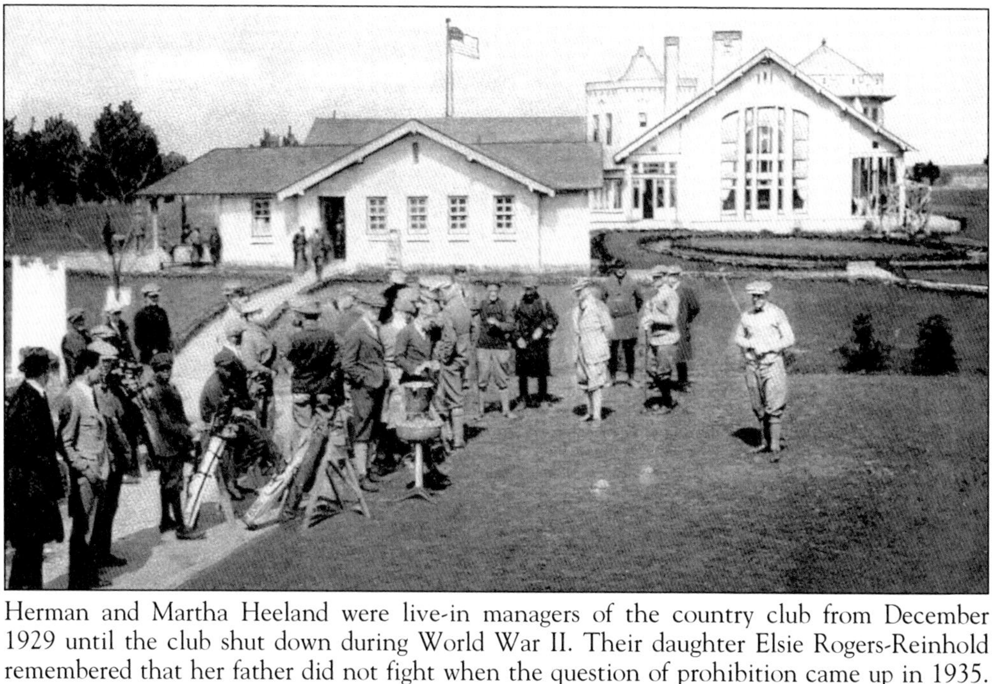

Herman and Martha Heeland were live-in managers of the country club from December 1929 until the club shut down during World War II. Their daughter Elsie Rogers-Reinhold remembered that her father did not fight when the question of prohibition came up in 1935. The club's license was a permit issued by the state Alcoholic Beverage Control Commission and not the local government.

Don't Miss the

Annual Old-Time
COUNTRY FAIR

CENTRAL HALL

Shore Road & Central Avenue

Linwood, N. J.

SEPTEMBER 17, 18, 1943

BOOTHS

Home Made Candies — Toy Shop

Cakes & Pies — Flower Mart

Fancy Goods — Home Made Products

Handkerchiefs — Kitchen Booth

Hot Dogs — Ice Cream

ATTRACTIONS

Straw Rides — Knocking Down Bottles

The Orchard — Rebecca at the Well

The Nut Girls — Side Show

Fair Opens: Fri. from 5 to 11 P. M. Sat. from 2 to 11 P. M.

SUPPER SERVED EVERY NIGHT FROM 5 TO 7 P. M.

Free Prizes — **Plenty of Parking Space**

One of the great events of the year was Ye Old Country Fair, sponsored each September by the Central Methodist Episcopal Church. Everyone in town turned out for the fun and great food. The hayrides were a particular favorite.

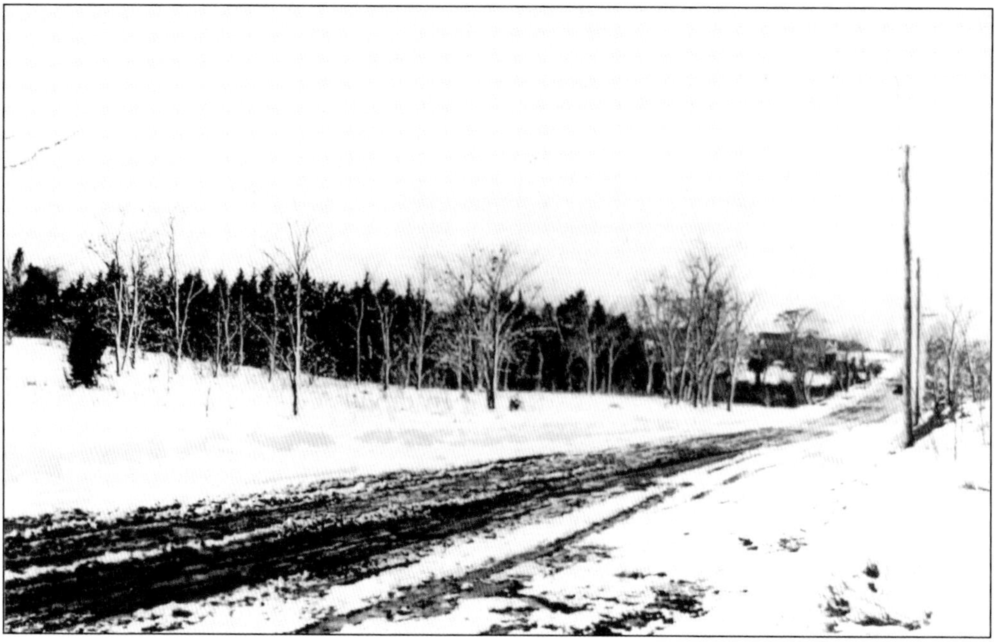

This picture is the first of several old photographs of streets around town. In 1920, this view of a snow-covered Central Avenue heading west shows little development. The land on the left was still used for farming then.

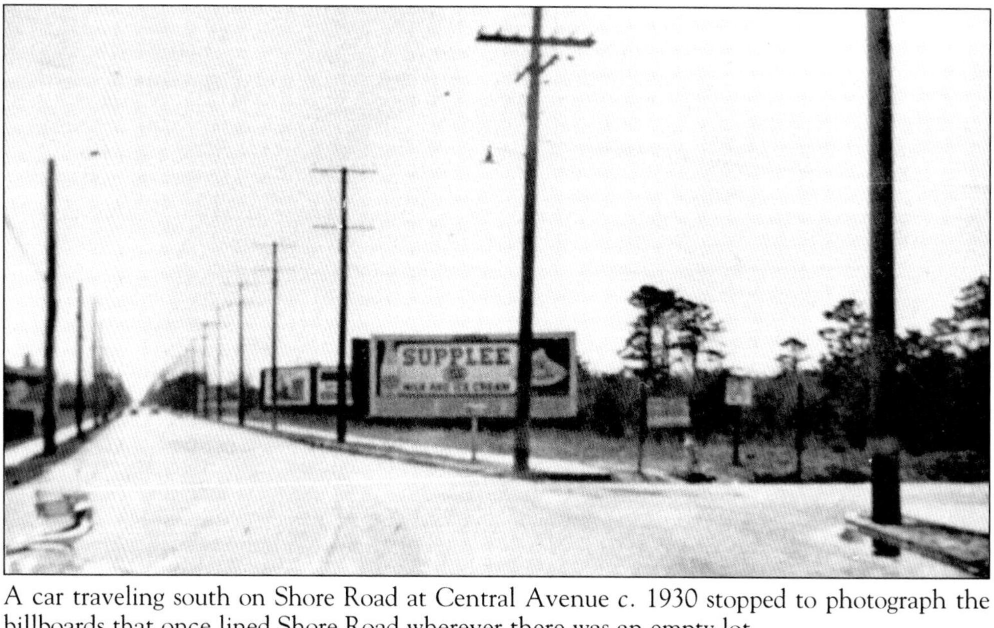

A car traveling south on Shore Road at Central Avenue *c.* 1930 stopped to photograph the billboards that once lined Shore Road wherever there was an empty lot.

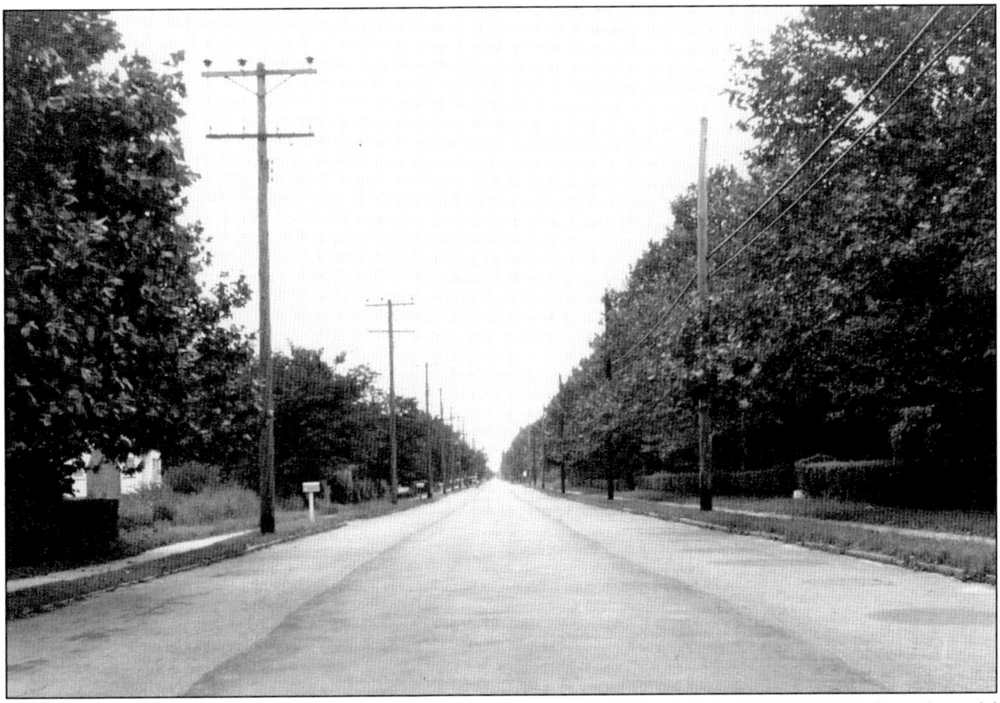

Win Boileau photographed the newly paved Shore Road in the 1700 block after the old Atlantic & Suburban trolley tracks were removed in 1943.

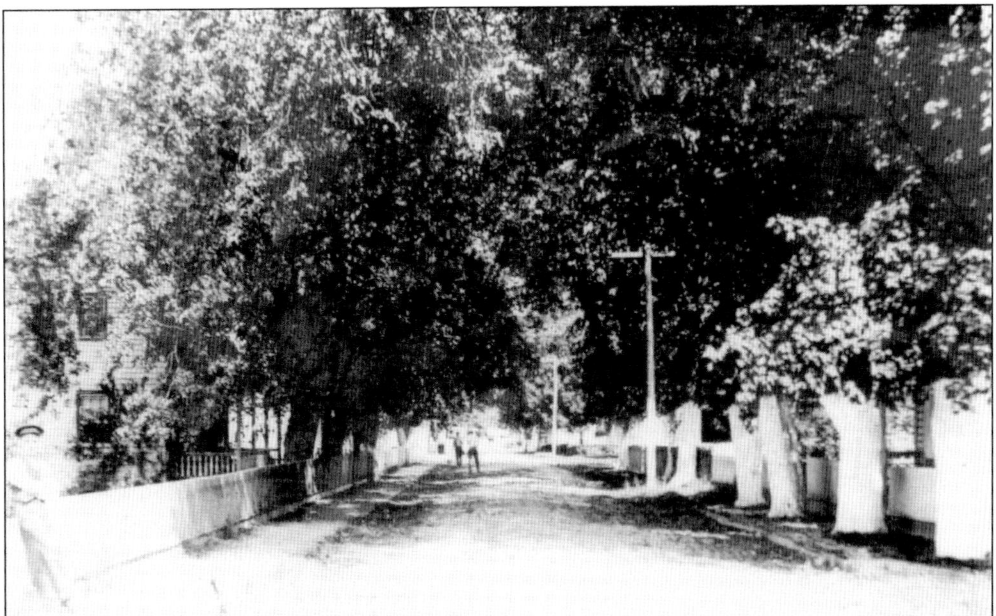

Maple Avenue appears as a quiet, restful street in this old Max Kirsch postcard. In the early 1930s, it became the first side street to be paved in Linwood. On Friday nights the city would block it off so that young people could use it for roller-skating.

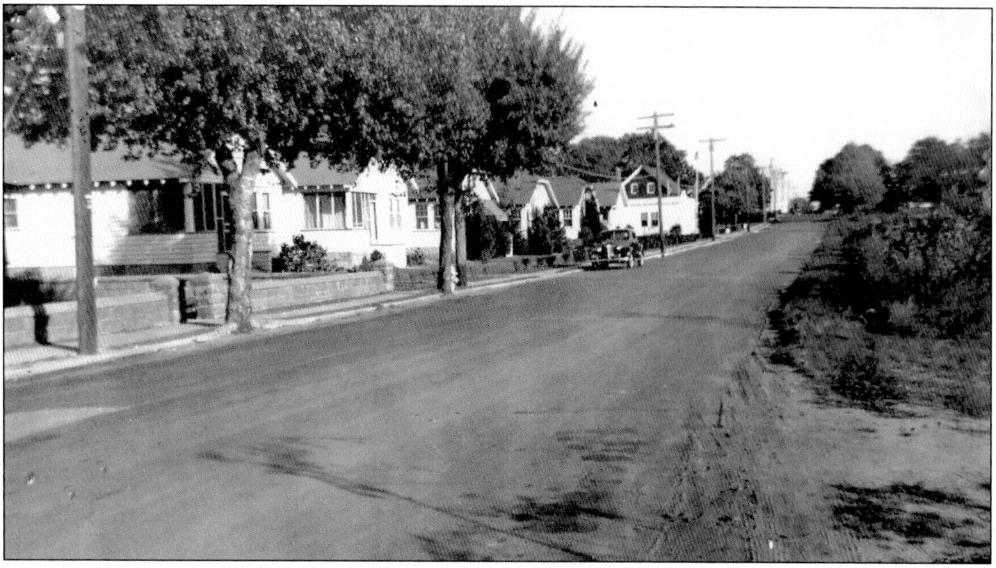

A 1941 view of Poplar Avenue shows houses on one side and empty lots on the other. In 1910, there was a baseball field on the corner at the lower right of the picture. The firehouse and city hall can be seen in the distance.

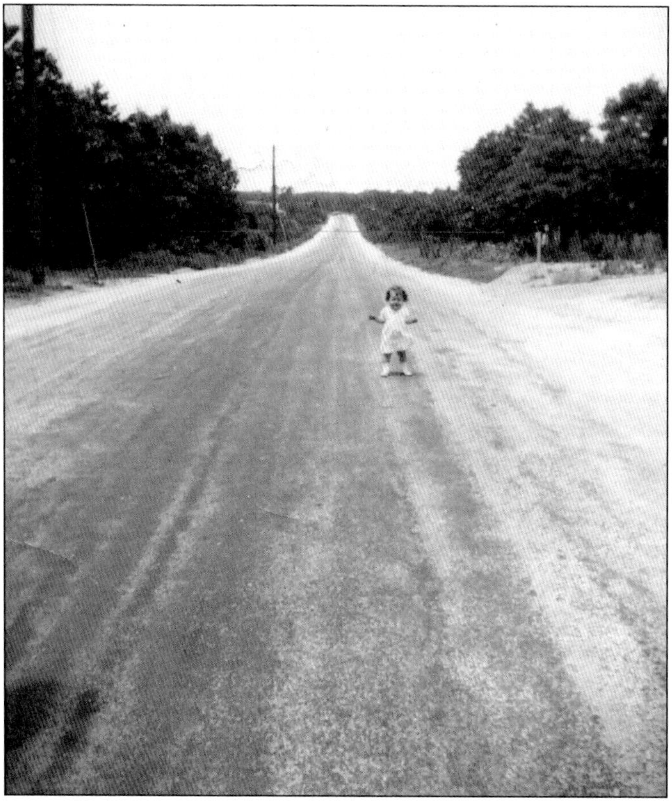

Patcong Avenue c. 1940 seems quiet enough and empty enough to allow a small child to play in the street.

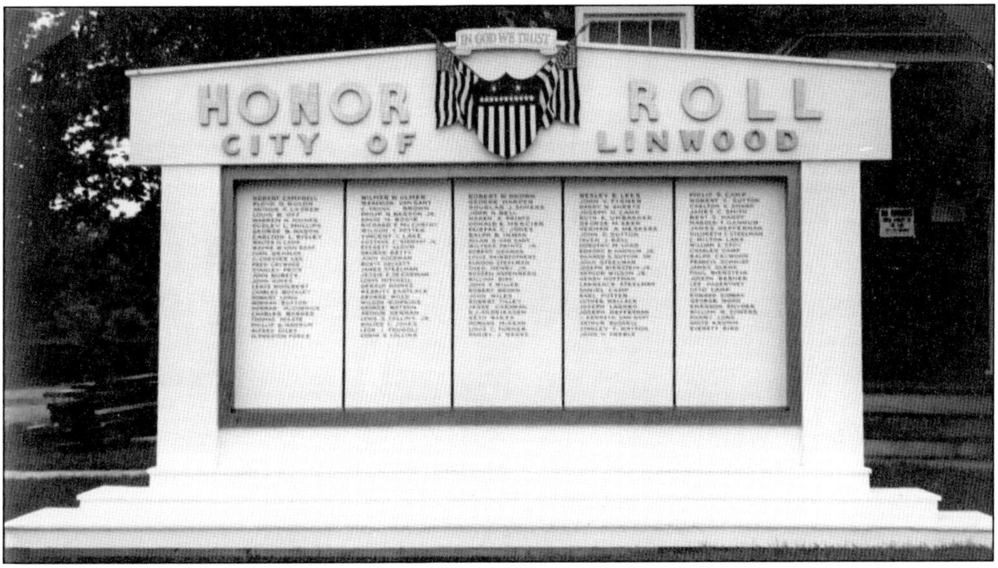

Linwood citizens joined with others across the nation in defense of their country after the bombing of Pearl Harbor. On Memorial Day 1943, an honor roll board was dedicated on the lawn at city hall, listing 131 names of those who were in the service at that point. Other names were added as the World War II went on. Three Linwood men were lost in the war: Leon Frugoli, Jimmy Lee, and Louis Fairbrothers. Frugoli died in action in France, as indicated on the plaque (below). Lee died on the destroyer USS *Monaghan*, which went down in Typhoon Cobra on December 18, 1944, with only six crew members surviving.

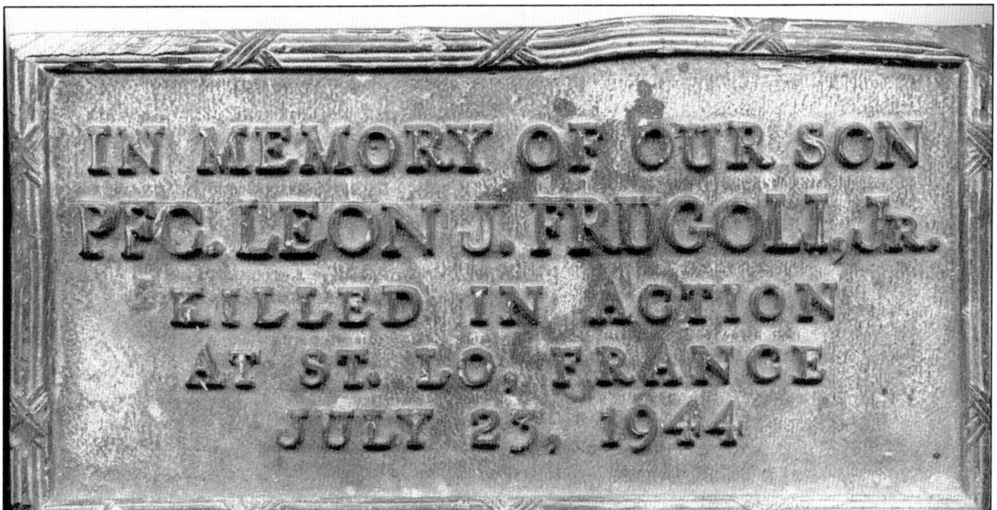

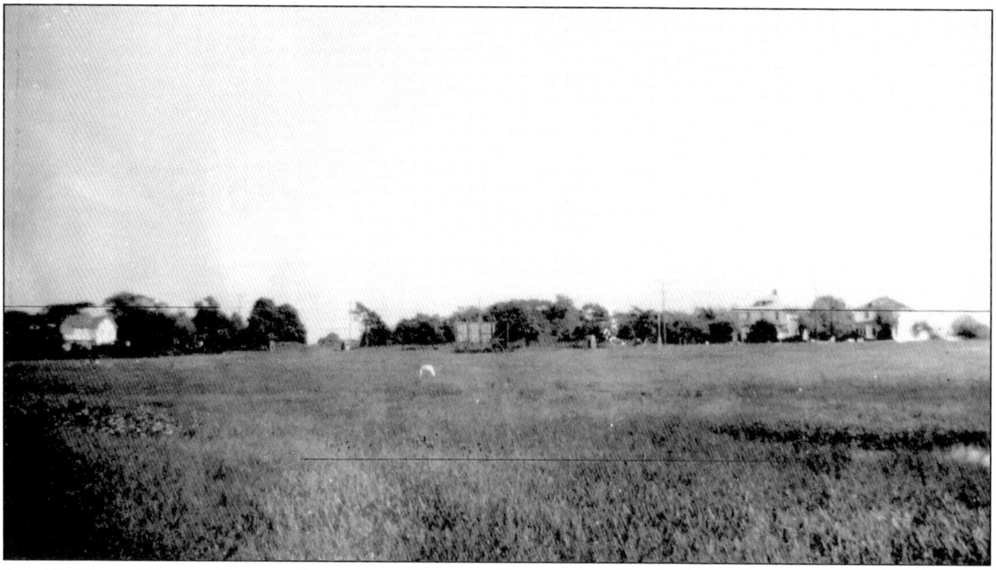

In 1947, residents discussed ways to honor those who had served and the creation of a recreation park was the popular choice. The All Wars Memorial Park is a living monument to their sacrifice and has been an everlasting contribution to the youth of the community. In 1953, the Linwood Women's Civic Club erected a monument at the field honoring men and women in all branches of the armed services.

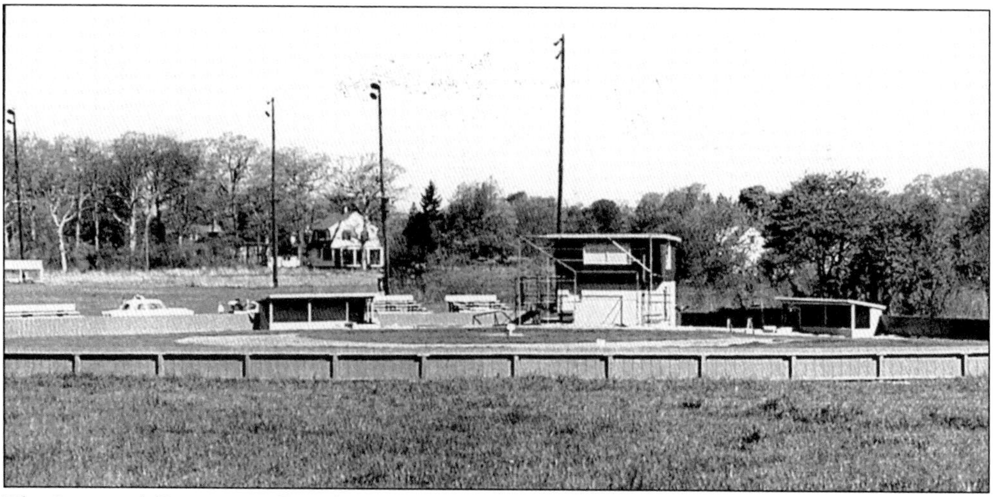

The Linwood Recreation Board was created in 1948 and Ken Frisbie, principal at Belhaven school, was the first president. The Linwood Little League was created in 1956, and the league's brand new field is pictured here.

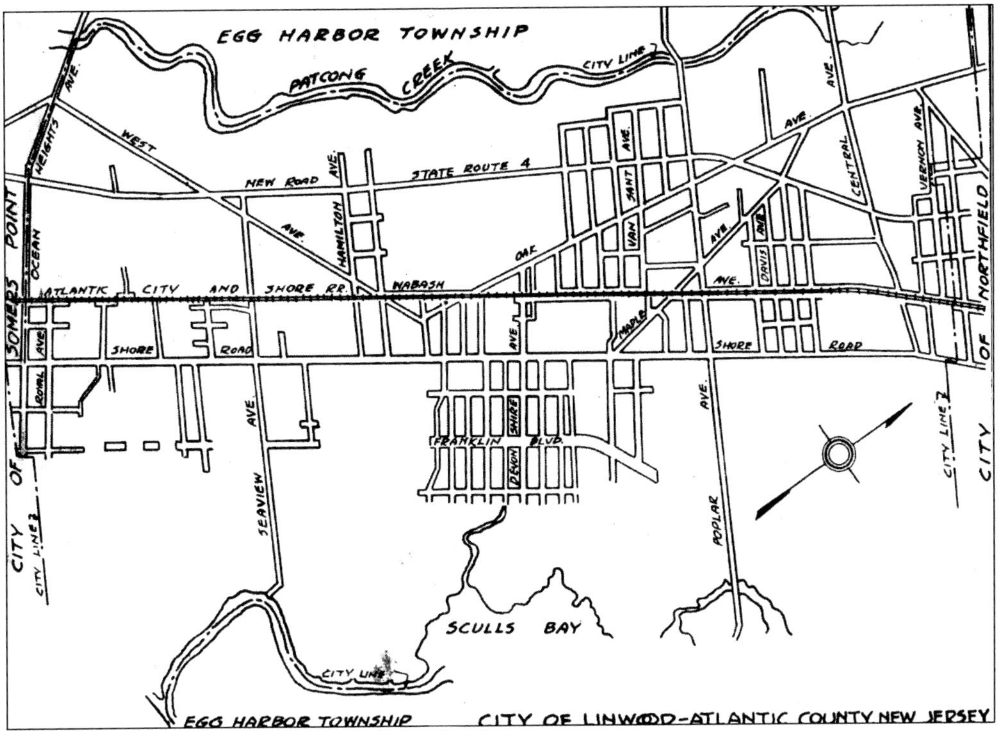

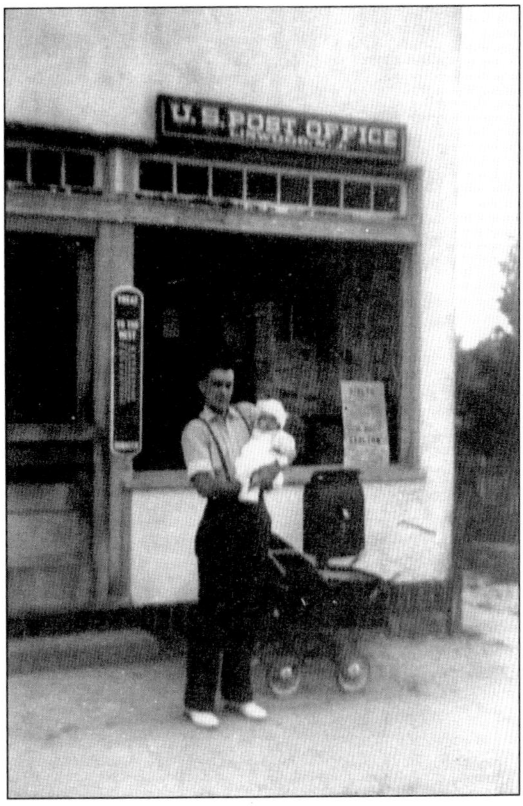

An old city map shows that Linwood had a traditional rural environment with lots of open space in 1947. Old-timers remembered that you could go up and down any street and know who lived in every house and of course, no one ever locked their doors at night. Even the post office was a simple structure. This back room was the 1940 post office, and it became the library when the mailroom moved into the front room of the building. In recent years it became a kitchen for pizza shops. Tom Dix, shown here with his newborn daughter, was the postmaster from 1936 to 1972, except for a brief stint in the navy in 1944–1945.

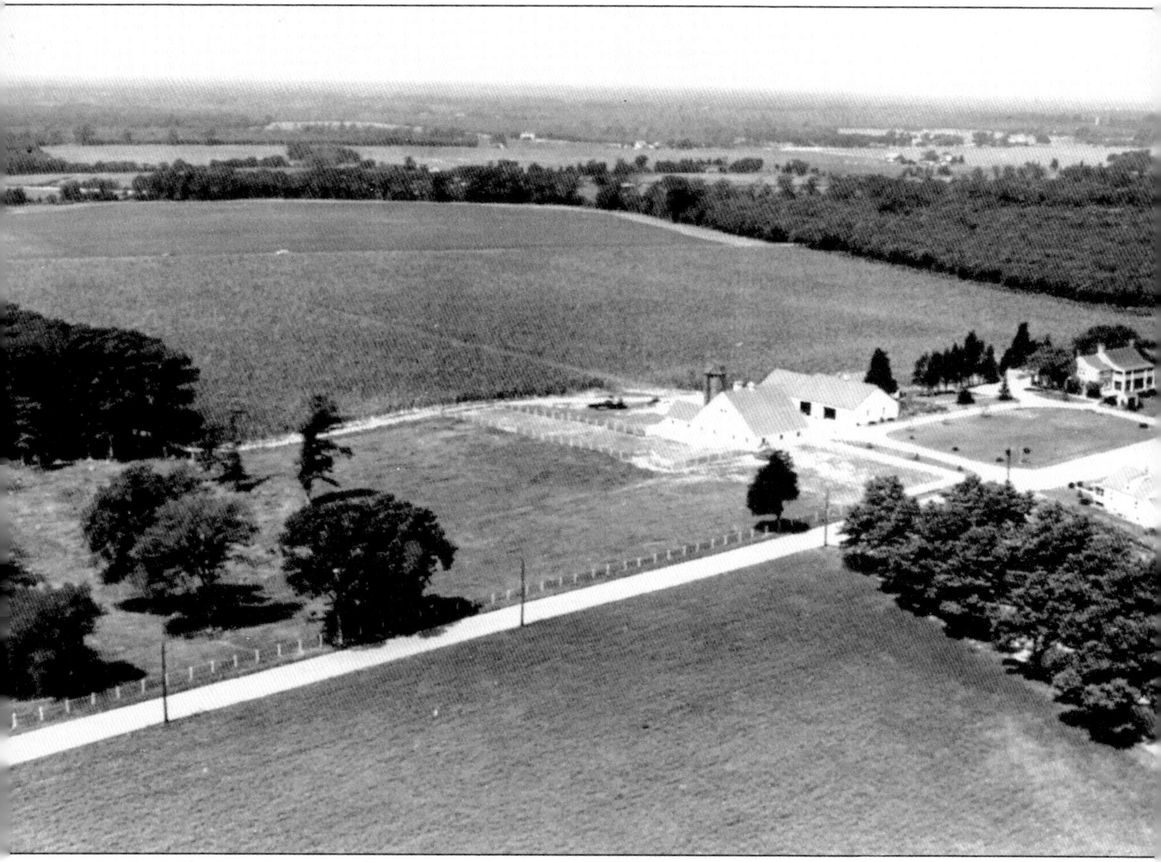

When this picture was taken in 1952, it had become obvious that farming would no longer be a way of life for Linwood families. The war had changed how people lived and worked. New jobs brought new people, and farmland was more valuable for housing. The Dennis Farm offered a huge tract of land for development. Divided by Route 9, the land could easily be split into two large tracts and the buyers were waiting. One of them was the new school district of Mainland Regional High School. The other was the Prudential Insurance Company looking for office space. The old 1906 picnic grounds among the walnut trees over by Off's Pond had disappeared, and most of the trees were piled high and burned. After some discussion about tearing down the old Somers home on the right, it was saved and it remains one of Linwood's historic treasures.

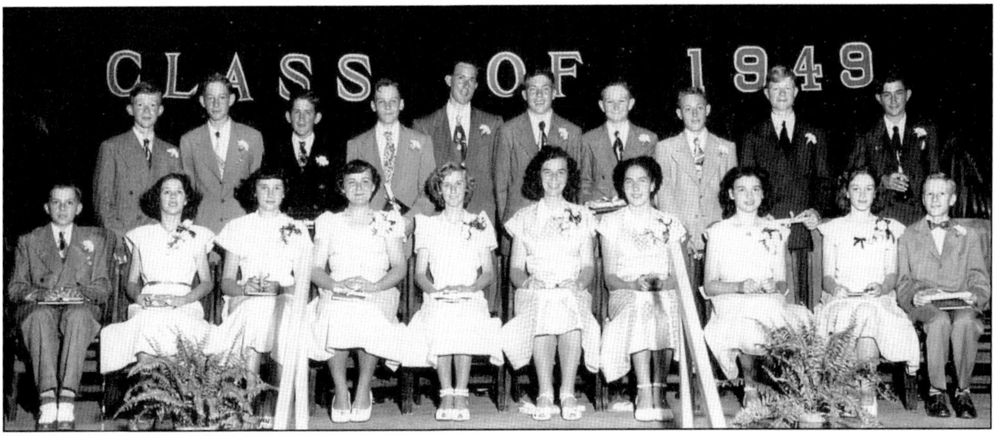

Pictures tell the story. The eighth-grade classes more than tripled between 1949 and 1960. Adams Hall at Central United Methodist Church was no longer big enough to handle the graduation ceremony. A 1959 addition at Belhaven School helped meet the needs of a growing population, but it was only temporary relief. Two other additions were in place by the end of the 20th century.

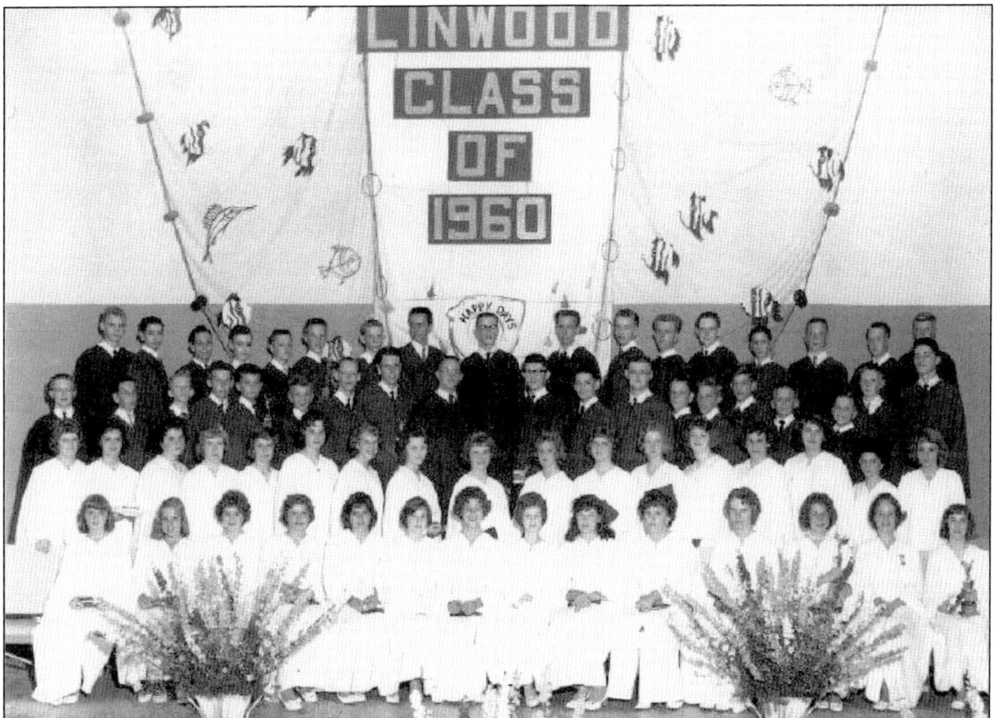

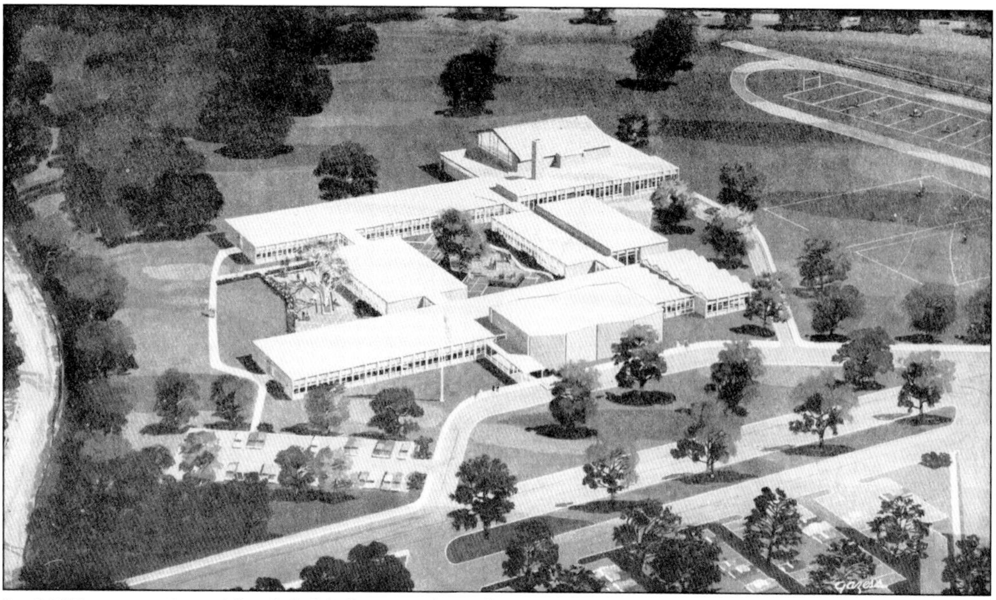

In 1958, voters from Northfield, Linwood, and Somers Point authorized the creation of a new regional high school district. A year later, they were asked to approve a building plan. Calling it "Not a monument, not a palace . . . Just a good building meant to serve its purpose," the board requested $1.9 million for construction. Voters approved it, and the school opened in 1961. Linwood students now went to high school in their own hometown.

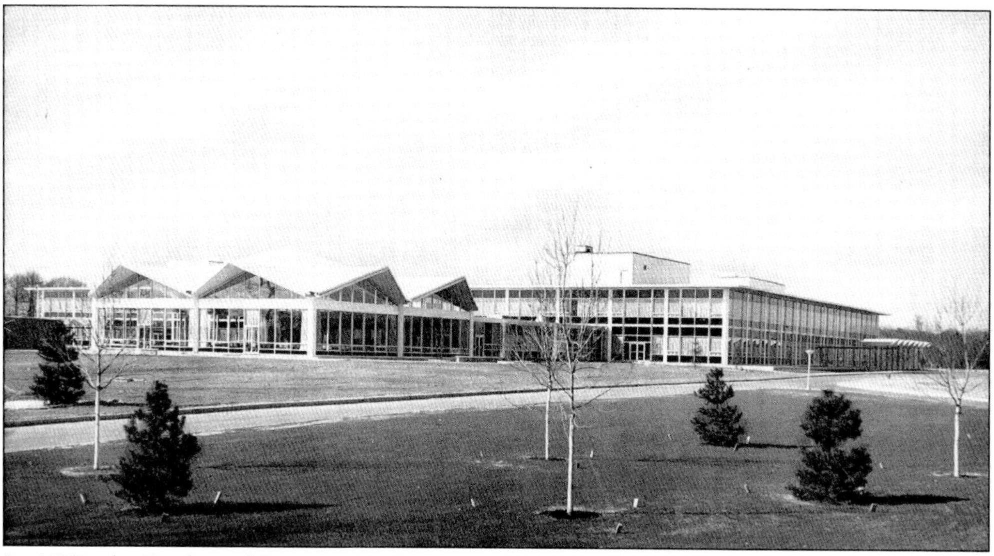

In 1957, the Prudential Insurance Company acquired 35 acres of the old Dennis Farm for a multimillion dollar office complex. When the building was dedicated in 1961, a time capsule was placed inside to be opened in 2037, the bicentennial of Atlantic County. Before the century ended, however, the office closed. Who will open the time capsule now?

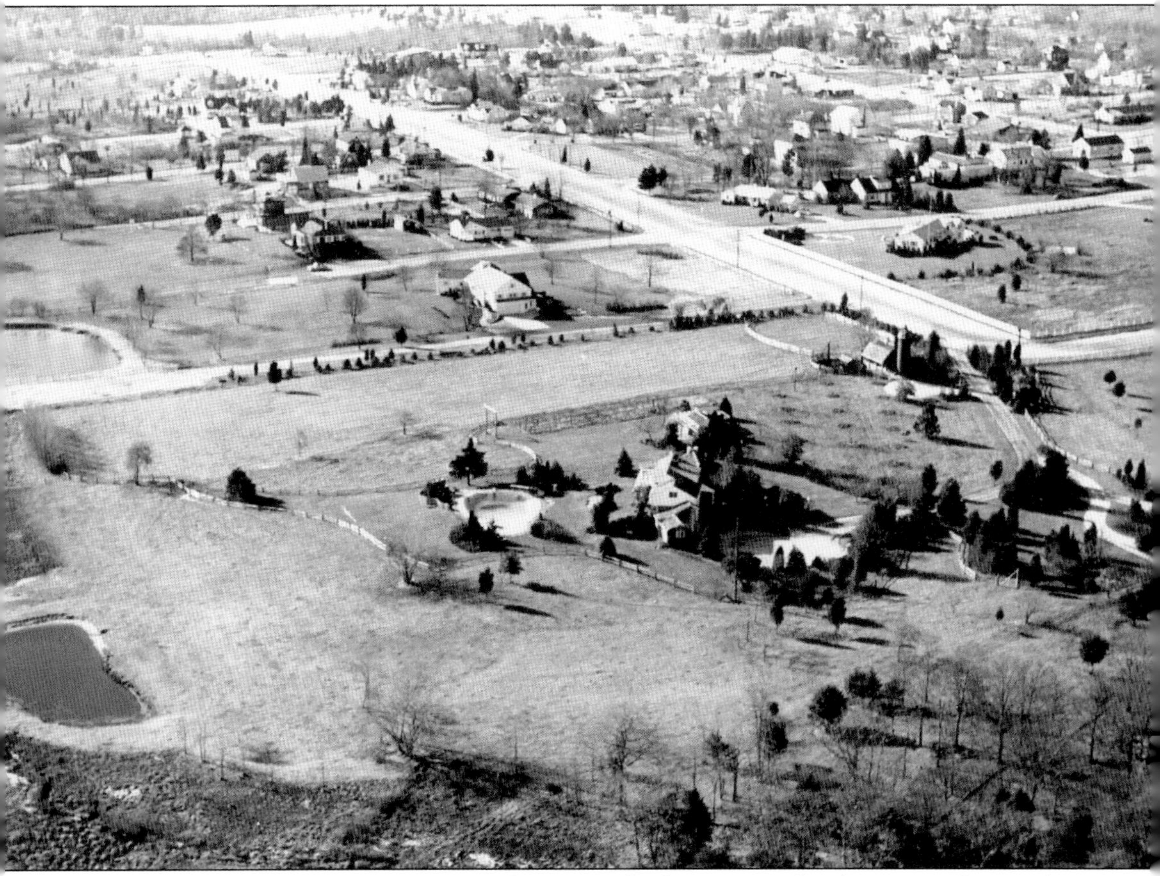

In 1955, the Gold Coast was on its way to becoming the first postwar development in Linwood. During the 1920s, a section of new homes called Woodlynne Manor was constructed along Woodlynne and Franklin Boulevards, and brick markers were built at the corners along Shore Road to set off the area. With the end of World War II, it was a logical place to begin building homes for people attracted to the area by new jobs that had opened up. Landfall Farms is featured in the foreground of this 1955 photograph.

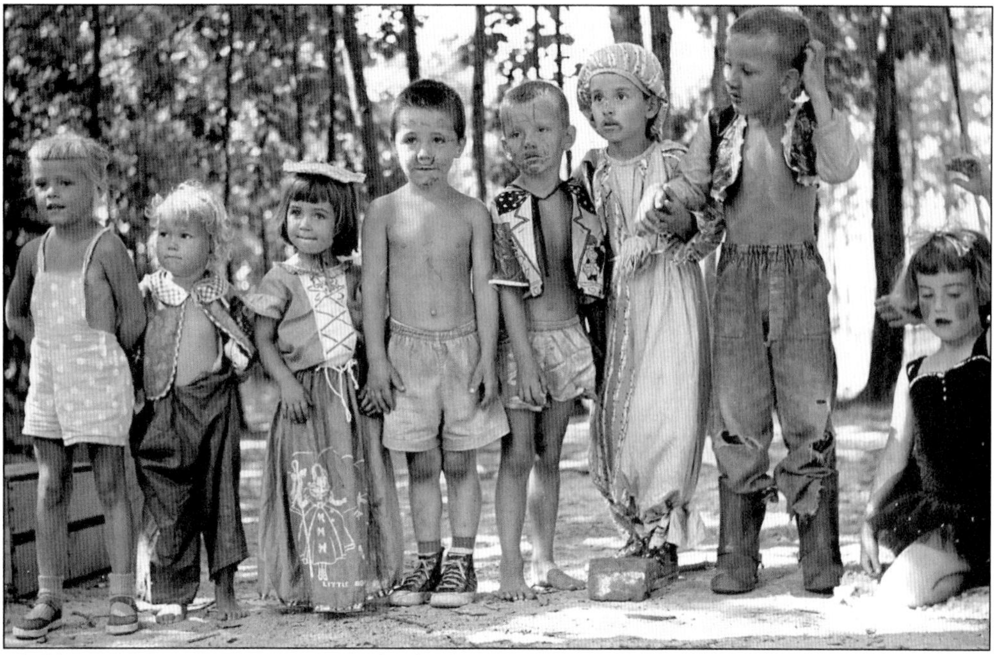

Children on Davis Avenue enjoyed a backyard circus in 1955. From left to right are Barbie Mulholland, Dolores Rinker, Margee Hannum, Philip Hannum, Ricky Bruce, Billy Rinker, Frankie Bruce, and Faith Jarvis.

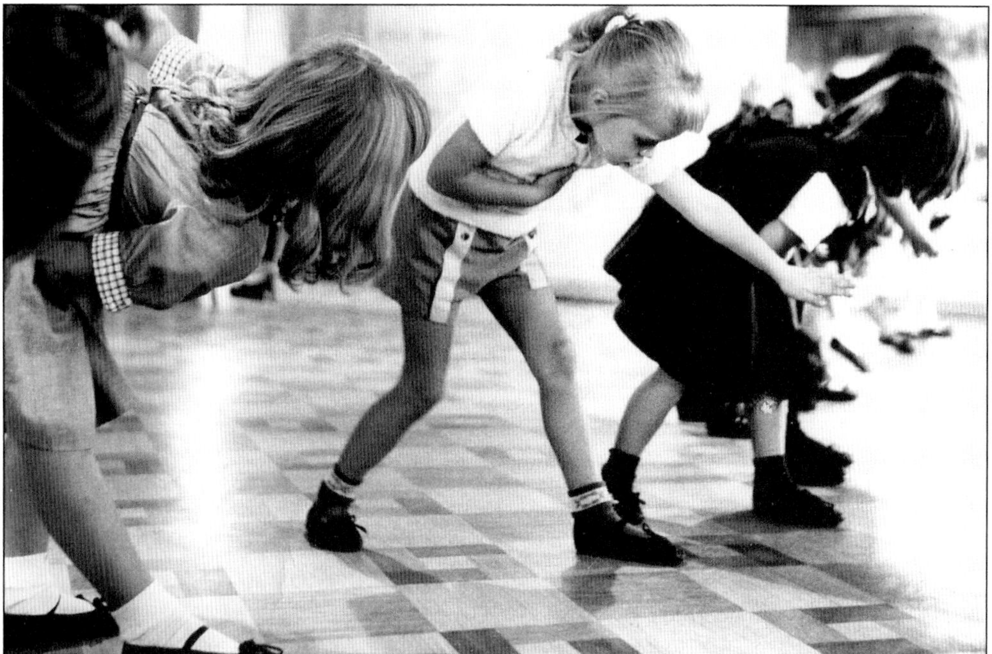

Life marches on. In the mid-1900s, Linwood was adapting to its new suburban landscape. New residents were settling in and children were participating in activities similar to those seen earlier in the photographs from 1906. Here, Barbie Mulholland (center) and her friends practice their dance lessons at the Sue Voss Studio in 1956.